CREATIVE RESEARCH ME
IN THE SOCIAL SCIEN
A practical guide

Helen Kara

First published in Great Britain in 2015 by

Policy Press
University of Bristol
1-9 Old Park Hill
Bristol BS2 8BB
UK
t: +44 (0)117 954 5940
e: pp-info@bristol.ac.uk
www.policypress.co.uk

North American office:
Policy Press
c/o The University of Chicago Press
1427 East 60th Street
Chicago, IL 60637, USA
t: +1 773 702 7700
f: +1 773-702-9756
e:sales@press.uchicago.edu
www.press.uchicago.edu

British Library Cataloguing in Publication Data
A catalogue record for this book is available from the British Library.

Library of Congress Cataloging-in-Publication Data
A catalog record for this book has been requested.

ISBN 978-1-4473-1627-5 paperback
ISBN 978-1-4473-1626-8 hardcover

Cover design by Qube Design Associates, Bristol
Front cover: image kindly supplied by istock
Printed and bound in Great Britain by CMP, Poole
The Policy Press uses environmentally responsible print partners

Contents

Contents

List of figures and tables

Figures

Tables

Debts of gratitude

So many people have helped with the creation of this book that I can't name them all. Inspiration and ideas have come from one-off conversations on buses and at conferences; ongoing discussions with members of the UK's Social Research Association, the British Library's social science department and the members of the Arts & Sciences Researchers Forum at Cambridge University; as well as innumerable exchanges on Twitter. I'm going to thank as many people as I can, but if you should be in here and I've left you out – well, that'll be the first of the mistakes in this book which are, of course, all my own responsibility.

For specific advice on quantitative methods, I'd like to thank Andrea Finney from the School of Geographical Sciences at Bristol University, and Patten Smith and Chris Perry from Ipsos MORI. I'm grateful to Elizabeth Rodriguez, aka @LibbyBlog, for pointing me to the crocheted model of hyperbolic geometry.

Special thanks for expert advice to Radhika Holmström, who helped with the section about working with the mainstream media, and to Caroline Beavon, who helped with the presentation chapter.

I am very grateful to three artist/researchers and endlessly patient sounding-boards: Carol Burns, Su Connan and Anne-Louise Denyer. Also to Nick Dixon, who pointed me to the work of David Edwards which I wouldn't otherwise have found, and who deserves extra special thanks for listening to me go on and on and ON about this book for months and months. Amanda Taylor kindly pointed me to Graham Gibbs' YouTube channel.

I'm really grateful to Leigh Forbes for moral and technical support. Also to Rob Macmillan of the Third Sector Research Centre, University of Birmingham, for ongoing support and for straightening out some of my tangled ideas about theory. And to Annette Markham of Aarhus University for taking an interest purely on the basis of a slightly cheeky email, and passing on some really helpful information.

My family are hugely supportive: Mark Miller, Julie Miller, Rosalind Hodge, Carl Hodge, Jamie Round, Dave Round, Pauline Ward, Clare Miller, David Miller, Vicki Miller, Bob Denyer, Lauren Denyer, Marie-Claire Denyer, John McCormack, Anne-Louise Denyer, Gavin Daubney, Lowell Black and Aaron Stevenson have all provided encouragement and love.

My friends, too, have been loving, supportive, and encouraging. In particular: Ian Bramley and Kevin Turner, Gilly and Dave Brownhill, Carol Burns, Zöe Clarke, Su Connan, Anne and Mike Cummins, Nick Dixon, Leigh Forbes, Sue Guiney, Radhika Holmström, Sarah-May Matthews, Lucy Pickering, Wayne Thexton and Katy Vigurs.

My partner, Nik Holmes, has helped far more than he realises, by making my life run smoothly and happily in a hundred different ways, such as fixing computer glitches, cooking delicious dinners and giving the best hugs.

This book is immeasurably better as a result of input from four proposal reviewers and especially two typescript reviewers, who did their job perfectly, praising the good bits and gently pointing out where and how improvements could be made.

Many of the staff at Policy Press have helped with this book, particularly Ali Shaw, Julia Mortimer, Emily Watt, Victoria Pittman, Laura Vickers, Dave Worth, Jo Morton, Kathryn King, Rebecca Megson and Helen Cook. I'd also like to thank the world's best copy-editor Judith Oppenheimer, who once again has saved me from several bloopers. And I'm grateful to Emma Wright, aka @editorialgirl, for designing my website and blog (helenkara.com and helenkara.com/blog) and helping a great deal with my promotional work.

These few words seem like utterly inadequate recompense for the time, care and expertise all these people have put into my work, but I hope the knowledge that I am really very grateful for their contributions will go some way towards rewarding their generosity. Also, I hope that when they see – and perhaps even read – the book, they will feel their input has been well used, and their effort was worthwhile.

Foreword

Kenneth J. Gergen and Mary M. Gergen

This is an important book. It is inevitably limited in length and selective in subject matter, but its implications resound across the social sciences and further. For almost a century the social sciences have allied themselves with a conception of knowledge as inhering in propositions supported or verified by empirical evidence. Whether it be knowledge of nature, of human behaviour, or psychological process, statements about 'what is the case' should be based on carefully and systematically controlled observation. Such a view presumes the fixed nature of the subject matter, independent of anyone's particular prejudices. Thus, sound and systematic methods of observation and assessment are required, methods that will prevent the contamination of knowledge by potential prejudices. Until recent years, virtually all books on research methods sustained this conception of knowledge. Or, one might say, books on methods functioned much like marching orders.

Times have changed, and most social scientists have now come to understand the way knowledgeable propositions are constructed within various scientific enclaves, carrying with them myriad assumptions and values that have no warrant save the negotiated realities of the groups themselves. It is this realisation that has led not only to wide-ranging critiques of the limitations of traditional empirical methods (e.g. experimentation, measurement, statistical analysis), but to an enormous flowering of qualitative methods. A new range of handbooks has emerged in the past decade, offering a wide and exciting range of qualitative methods of inquiry.

Yet, there remains within these cadres a silent legacy from the preceding decades of empiricist foundationalism. It is the attempt to set standards of excellence for the various methodological practices. There are the endless lists and rationales about what the researcher should and should not do if the work is to be creditable within the particular enclave. Helen Kara's present offering dares to question this legacy. As she properly sees, there are no necessary or essential rules of inquiry; the major question is what the researcher wishes to accomplish; what is worth doing, and for whom? When the goals are established, then the creative juices may begin to flow. 'How may I, as researcher, create the form of inquiry that will best suit my purposes and support my ethical concerns?' Here is a bold invitation for researchers to move beyond the available 'cookbooks', to mobilise their talents, insights and passions, and create the means to valued ends. We applaud the effort.

Kenneth J. Gergen and Mary M. Gergen
Pennsylvania, USA
March 2015

This book is dedicated to Nik Holmes in recognition of, and gratitude for, his dedication to me

How this book can help

This book is designed to provide you with an overview of, and insight into, the huge range of creative research methods available to researchers in the social sciences. Some of these may also be useful to researchers in the arts and humanities. The book will also help contemporary researchers who may be facing research questions that cannot be answered – or at least, not fully – using traditional research methods. However, this is not to suggest that the more 'creative' a research project is, the better the results will be! It is important to know and understand traditional methods in social science research, such as questionnaires, interviews and focus groups. It is also important to be familiar with good research practice, as the use of creative methods does not supersede the basic principles of good research. If you are new to research, you will find useful a number of well-written books and other resources covering traditional methods and good practice, several of which are referenced in this book such as Robson (2011) and Bryman (2012).

Doing research is an inherently creative activity at all stages of the process. The more methodological tools a researcher is able to use, the more effectively they are likely to be able to address the kinds of questions that arise today in social science research.

This book gives a broad overview of creative research methods, with lots of examples of their use in practice. Many of these examples are summarised in boxes throughout the text. I have chosen to cover as many methods as possible in brief, rather than a few in detail; therefore, if you are interested in using any of the methods outlined here, you are recommended to seek out the original reference(s) for more information.

For a relatively complete picture of creative research methods in practice you will want to read the whole book. However, it has been structured and indexed so as also to serve as a guide for readers who may be in need of ideas or inspiration for a particular stage or element of their research work. The following overview of the book's content explains what you will find in it, and where.

Overview of contents

Chapter One introduces and outlines the four key areas of creative research methods: arts–based research, research using technology, mixed-methods research and transformative research frameworks (for example, participatory, feminist and decolonising methodologies). It then considers what we know about 'creativity' and discusses how this operates in research. The chapter also gives a brief overview of informal and formal research and of evaluation research.

Chapter Two starts with a brief review of the history of creative research methods and then takes a look at good practice in creative research. It then gives a more in-depth introduction to arts–based research, mixed-methods research and research using technology, in practice. It also introduces autoethnography, which can include all three approaches.

Chapter Three begins with a quick review of research governance and theories of ethics. It outlines the transformative ethical frameworks of emancipatory, decolonised, participatory and feminist research, and also considers ways of managing ethical dilemmas in creative research. Then the chapter covers ethics in arts-based research, mixed-methods research and research using technology. Last but not least, the chapter considers the well-being of researchers.

Chapter Four covers creative thinking and creative reading. It explores some options for using literature and theory creatively and discusses creativity in cross-disciplinary work, and the role of the imagination in research. It also looks at ways of assessing the quality of quantitative and qualitative research, including the use of reflexivity.

Chapter Five looks at some creative methods of gathering data. These include the use of diaries and journals, drawing, using video, making maps, shadowing and vignettes.

Chapter Six reviews some creative methods of analysing data, including secondary data, documentary data, talk as data and video data. Arts-based analysis, mixed-methods analysis, analysis using technology and analysis within transformative frameworks are also covered.

Chapter Seven is about writing for research and begins with the importance of knowing, and writing for, your audience(s). The skills of receiving and giving feedback on your writing are briefly addressed, and there is a short discussion of the gaps and overlaps between fact and fiction. Then several methods of writing are reviewed, including journals, blogs, poetic writing, mixed-methods writing and collaborative writing. Ways of combining writing with other forms of representation are discussed, and some advice is offered on how to write better for research.

Chapter Eight covers the presentation of research data and findings. This chapter begins with the ethical aspects of presentation, and then looks at some dos and don'ts of data visualisation, before covering graphs, charts, diagrams, infographics and maps. The later sections address presentation at conferences and meetings, and mixed-methods, arts-based and participatory presentation of information.

Chapter Nine is about the dissemination and implementation of research, and knowledge exchange. It begins with the ethical aspects of creative dissemination and implementation, and then looks at dissemination through the online and mainstream media. Arts-based dissemination, mixed methods of dissemination and dissemination in transformative research are all covered. The final sections of the chapter look at implementation and knowledge exchange.

Further information and details of the examples referenced in this book have been collated on the companion website, which can be accessed at http://www. policypress.co.uk/resources/kara-creative/index.asp

 This icon indicates that a link to the resource(s) mentioned in the text may be found on the companion website.

ONE

Introducing creative research

Introduction

The early 21st century is a dynamic and exciting time for research methods. Methodological boundaries are expanding across all social science disciplines. Over the last 20 years, Denzin and Lincoln have been tracking developments in qualitative research methods through their edited collections, the most recent of which was published in 2011 (Denzin and Lincoln 2011). Even in the few years since then, the field has developed and expanded as researchers seek effective ways to address increasingly complex questions in social science.

This book re-conceptualises creative research methods into four key areas:

1. arts–based research
2. research using technology
3. mixed–methods research
4. transformative research frameworks (such as participatory, feminist and decolonising methodologies).

Of course these areas are not mutually exclusive. For example, it has been suggested that mixed-methods research has a key role to play in the development of decolonising methodologies (Botha 2011: 313). In this book you will find examples of research that draws on two, three or all four areas. In time, other creative methods may develop that don't fit into any of these areas. But for the time being this conceptualisation provides a useful way to think and talk about creative research methods that will help you give full consideration to the methods you might use to answer your research questions.

This book does not claim to provide a definitive account of creative research methods – the field is growing and changing so fast that no book could capture its entirety. You will find many excellent examples here, but many more have been omitted, due to lack of space. However, there should be enough here to excite and inspire researchers and to provide a snapshot of a stage in research methods evolution: a stage where multi-disciplinary research teams are using creative methods to help them vault out of silos and leap over boundaries. This will help readers who want to break out of traditional disciplinary confines, or who need to do so because their research questions are too complex to be restricted by the traditional methods and techniques of a single discipline.

One point that it is useful to clarify at the start is the relationship between 'methods' and 'methodology', particularly as the conceptualisation above includes both. These terms are often used synonymously, but they actually denote different aspects of research. Methodology is 'a contextual framework' (Grierson and Brearley 2009: 5) for research, a coherent and logical scheme based on views, beliefs and values, that guides the choices researchers make. Within this methodological framework, methods are the tools that researchers use to gather and analyse data, write and present their findings. Methodology and method are thus intimately linked both with each other and with the research questions (Mason 2002: 189). Researchers need to understand all three and how the relationships between them work, to help research audiences understand how and why researchers make decisions in the course of designing and conducting research. Further, while some creative research methods may be tremendously appealing in themselves, it is essential to choose methods for their ability to address the research question within the methodological context (Ellingson 2009: 176). Strictly speaking, this book should have been called *Creative Research Methods and Methodologies in the Social Sciences: A Practical Guide*, but that was much too wordy!

Like many books on research, this book is structured around different aspects of the research process: reading and thinking, gathering data, analysing data, writing and so on. While this could give the impression that these aspects can be separated from each other, in reality that is not the case. For example, writing is an essential part of the whole research process (Rapley 2011: 286). Reading is also likely to occur throughout the process (Hart 2001: 7).Notes from your reading may be coded and analysed in the same way as data. Documents can be categorised as data or as background reading (Kara 2012: 126). Treating different aspects of the research process as separate makes them easier to consider and discuss, but, like the conceptualisation above, this is an artifice; they are inextricably linked. Some research methods in themselves are designed to try to acknowledge this. For example, grounded theory, devised by Barney Glaser and Anselm Strauss in 1967, is a method in which theory is developed as data is gathered and analysed. Later scholars have built on this approach, for example by demonstrating that various types of diagrams can be co-constructed by researchers and participants as part of data gathering, data analysis, theory development and research presentation (Strauss and Corbin 1998: 153; Williams and Keady 2012: 218). For those who are particularly interested in grounded theory, there are a series of **useful videos** on the subject presented by UK researcher Graham Gibbs.

This book is written primarily for researchers working alone or in small teams in the social sciences, humanities and allied subjects, to help them give full consideration to the research methods they might use. In the Western world, there are many more examples of qualitative than of quantitative research (Alasuutari 2009: 140), and the balance in this book reflects that. However, that is not to say that qualitative research or the social sciences and humanities are inherently creative, while quantitative research or the physical sciences are uncreative. There is enormously creative work going on in quantitative methods and the physical sciences, such as in large-scale national surveys (for example Burton

2013) and science, technology, engineering and mathematics (STEM) research (for example Walsh, Anders and Hancock 2013: 20), but large-scale and STEM research methods are beyond the scope of this book. It is perhaps useful to note that, in social research, intangible subjects such as trust and intuition are being investigated through the creative use of quantitative methods (for example Priem and Weibel 2012; Burns and Conchie 2012; Hodgkinson and Sadler-Smith 2014) in addition to creative qualitative methods.

This book assumes a reasonable general knowledge of basic research methods terminology. If that is an incorrect assumption in your case, there is a useful **glossary of terms** online, or you could use a good general research textbook such as Robson (2011) or Bryman (2012). However, even if you do have a good research methods vocabulary, you need to know that the terminology of creative research methods is very fluid. For example, there are over 40 terms for the use of poetry and poetics in research, such as poetic narrative, found poems and field poetry (Prendergast 2009a: xx–xxi), and there are a similar number of terms for autoethnography (Chang 2008: 46–8). Some of these terms are intended to reflect nuances in emphasis. However, different terms may be used to mean the same thing. For example, interviews with two people who are married or partnered with each other have been called 'couple interviews' (as in Mellor et al 2013: 1399), 'relationship-based dyadic interviews' (as in Morgan et al 2013: 1277) and 'joint interviews' (as in Sakellariou et al 2013: 1565). There are a range of terms for dramatic presentations of research findings, including ethnodrama (see Sangha et al 2012: 286), research-based drama (see Mitchell et al 2011: 379) and research-based theatre (see Beck et al 2011: 687). While it uses terms consistently, this book does not attempt to provide definitive terminology for the field.

This chapter now continues by outlining creative research methods and their four key areas. It will then consider what we know about 'creativity' and discuss how this operates in research, before providing a brief overview of informal and formal research and of evaluation research.

Creative research methods

'Creative' is not directly synonymous with 'innovative'. There is growing pressure on researchers to innovate, leading to a situation where innovation is often overstated in an effort to get funding or to be published (Wiles, Crow and Pain 2011: 594). Of course some methods are innovative, and some that are both innovative and creative will be featured in this book, but some methods for which innovation is claimed are actually creative rather than innovative.

There is also scope for creativity in the use of traditional methods. For example, focus groups have been used in qualitative research since the 1960s (Green and Hart 1999: 21), so can hardly be described as 'innovative' today. But there is still scope for creativity within focus group methodology. For example, Belzile and Öberg (2012) draw on a wide body of literature to demonstrate that few researchers using focus groups pay attention to the interaction between participants, with most researchers treating focus group data in the same way as data from individual interviews. Belzile and Oberg use this insight to create a framework for researchers that is designed to support the inclusion of participant interaction within focus group design. There are many other examples of researchers taking a creative approach to a traditional method.

Even some of the STEM disciplines are finding inspiration from creative practices. For example, the problem of how to model hyperbolic geometry puzzled mathematicians for centuries until, in the 1990s, Daina Taimina realised that it could be done with knitting or, even better, crochet (Henderson and Taimina 2001). You can find a **demonstration** of crochet modelling hyperbolic geometry online.

It has been argued that social scientists are closer kin to creative artists and performers than to the physical scientists with whom we are traditionally allied (Smith 2009: 99). Most *arts-based research* methods draw on forms of creative writing and/or the visual arts: drawing, painting, collage, photography and so on. Other art forms used as the basis for research include music, drama, textile arts such as quilting and sculpture. Social science research and art are natural bedfellows in some ways, because the creative process works similarly for both (Edwards 2008: 96). But there are also tensions between them. For example, 'truth' in art is a link between a unique artwork and a recognisable aspect of the human condition, which is acknowledged by individual producers and consumers of art (for example, Edwards 2008: 111; Raingruber 2009: 261; Gabriel and Connell 2010: 517). The 'truth' in an artwork is not necessarily experienced in the same way by everyone, so this formulation presents 'truth' as multiple and contestable. Traditionally in research, 'truth' is a finding that can be replicated if the research is repeated. This depicts 'truth' as a single, shareable and indisputable viewpoint. More recently, some researchers have been considering that 'truth' may be as complex as artists suggest – multiple, partial, context-dependent and contingent – and so may be best explored by 'looking intensely from multiple perspectives' (Sameshima and Vandermause 2009: 277), such as through mixed-methods research.

Research using technology includes internet-mediated research, such as research through social media, as well as research supported by other kinds of technology such as mobile devices or apps. Some technology is devised specifically for researchers. This includes various types of data analysis software, such as SPSS (Statistical Package for Social Scientists) for quantitative data or NVivo for qualitative data; the online research management and sharing program Mendeley; or dedicated online survey providers such as SurveyMonkey. Researchers also use technology devised for non-research purposes, such as e-mail for communicating with a team of co-researchers, a spreadsheet program for managing questionnaire data or Twitter for gathering data from participants all over the world.

Technology itself has an influence on people's creativity, yet the role of technology in the creative process has not yet been fully understood or theorised

(Gangadharbatla 2010: 225). Also, technology is one topic in which students are often ahead of their teachers (Paulus et al 2013: 639). Research using technology is a very fast-moving field, adding many possible new dimensions to the research process. This book focuses primarily on creative uses of technology in research, rather than, for example, rehearsing the pros and cons of different software or hardware.

The rapid movement of technology can be daunting for researchers. While some people are fluent in web scraping, co-creation, APIs, mash-ups, blog-mining, apps and data visualisation, for others this is a foreign language. Unfamiliarity can be a deterrent; it can feel safer to stay in the land of surveys, interviews and focus groups, where we speak the language and understand the signs. In this situation it can be reassuring to know that nobody can keep up with all the advances in technology. Even if you consider yourself a complete Luddite, I recommend staying open to the possibilities that technology can offer to your research, even if only in one or two parts of the research process. And you can learn one step at a time. Almost all researchers are happy to use e-mail, word processing and text messaging these days, and it's only one more step from there to using Skype, creating graphs from your data or tweeting. The more of this kind of thing you do, the more confident, knowledgeable and skilled you will become. Also, the great thing about using technology is that if you get stuck on anything, at any level, you can almost always find a solution online. For those at the opposite end of the spectrum, and in danger of becoming over-dependent on technology, there is a **useful talk** online on ways to manage your tech-life balance.

Mixed-methods research involves combining different methods of data gathering and/or analysis, different types of recruitment or sampling, different theoretical and/or disciplinary perspectives and so on. It is often considered particularly useful for investigating complex social situations (Koro-Ljungberg et al 2012: 814; Gidron 2013: 306).

UK researchers Joanne Mayoh, Carol Bond and Les Todres studied the experiences of UK adults with chronic health conditions who looked for health information online. This is a complex phenomenon so the researchers decided to use mixed methods, with the aim of 'identifying and communicating both breadth and depth of information' (Mayoh, Bond and Todres 2012: 22). As there was not much previous research in this area, the first phase of data gathering involved two questionnaires, mainly quantitative, to gather broad data about patients' experiences of finding information and about the barriers perceived by non-users of the internet. The analysis of data from these questionnaires provided an appropriate focus for in-depth interviews, which could not have been achieved from the existing literature (Mayoh, Bond and Todres 2012: 27). Altogether, the findings gave a much clearer picture of the complex phenomenon of adults with chronic health conditions seeking health information online than could have

> been achieved by using any single qualitative or quantitative research method (Mayoh, Bond and Todres 2012: 29).

Traditional research methods have been around for so long, and are so pervasive, that they can seem to be 'right' and 'natural' (Dark 2009: 176–7). However, for some researchers, traditional methods may fix and limit meaning in a reductive way, while creative methods can more accurately reflect the multiplicity of meanings that exist in social contexts (for example, Inckle 2010). This can lead to methods being creatively layered alongside each other to build a richer picture. For example, interviews have been enhanced by various other methods of data gathering, such as photos in photo-elicitation (Smith, Gidlow and Steel 2012), diaries in diary interviews (Kenten 2010) and fixed-narrative and interactive developmental vignettes (Jenkins et al 2010). (See Chapter Five for more information about these techniques.) In each case, the researchers are confident that enhanced interviews produce richer and more insightful data than interviews, or the associated method(s), would do alone.

> UK researcher Dawn Mannay combined interviews with the use of photos, mapping and collage production in her insider study of the experiences of mothers and daughters on a social housing estate. Mannay had six participants. Two were asked to take a set of photographs showing places and activities that had meaning for them; two were asked to draw maps of their physical and social environments; and two were asked to produce collages, using images and words from a range of sources, to give a visual representation of their world. Each visual output was used as a basis for an interview with its creator. For Mannay, these visual methods provided a useful way of 'making the familiar strange', which enabled her to gain a 'more nuanced understanding of the mothers and daughters' worlds' (Mannay 2010: 100) than she could have done using interviews alone.

Dawn Mannay's own story, which is inspirational, is available online.

It could be argued that ethnographers are at the forefront of multi-layered methodologies. There are now many varieties of ethnography, including performative, institutional, collaborative, embodied, arts-based, participatory, virtual and narrative ethnography (Vannini 2013: 442). Ethnographers take the most eclectic approach to data gathering, using a very wide range of vehicles, from ecstatic dance (Pickering 2009) to mobile phones with GPS tracking technology (Christensen et al 2011: 233). Ethnographers also take a very varied approach to presentation and dissemination, using methods such as publicly exhibited arts installations (Degarrod 2013) and private film screenings (Franzen 2013: 422).

The same methods can sometimes be used creatively at different stages of the research process. For example, vignettes have been used as part of data gathering (see Jenkins et al 2010), data analysis (see Benozzo 2011), and writing (see Inckle 2010) (and see Chapter Five for more on vignette methodologies).

> Even failure can promote creativity in research. UK researchers Mark McCormack, Adrian Adams and Eric Anderson were interested in how the lives of bisexual men were influenced by decreasing levels of homophobia. They obtained ethical approval to conduct in-depth, face-to-face interviews with bisexual men in Los Angeles, New York and London, with participants being recruited online. However, this recruitment method proved both time consuming and ineffective; in two full days in Los Angeles, the researchers managed to secure only two interviews. With time running out, they decided to try a rather drastic recruitment method. They went to Venice Beach, a crowded bohemian area of the city, and shouted to people in the street that they were looking for bisexual men to interview. Using this method, they were able to secure 14 interviews in five hours. They treated this as a pilot, and repeated the experiment in several other crowded urban spaces in each of the three cities, wearing cowboy hats, carrying brightly coloured clipboards and shouting, 'Bisexual men, we're paying $40 for academic research,' at regular, 20-second intervals (McCormack, Adams and Anderson 2012: 233). Two of the three researchers did the shouting, while a third waited in a nearby location such as a cafe, ready to conduct interviews; they rotated roles throughout each day in the field. This proved a very successful recruitment strategy and they were able to secure an average of around three interviews per hour.

Traditional research aimed to be value free, apparently without realising that this is in itself a value. Traditional research methods are often presented as usable independent of their context, despite being products of specific cultural contexts (Gobo 2011: 433). Creative ethical research turns this on its head by using *transformative research frameworks* that are flexible enough to take account of relevant contextual factors. These frameworks are based on, and intended to promote, positive social values such as equality and justice. Examples of these creative ethical research frameworks include emancipatory or activist research, decolonised research, feminist research and participatory research, known collectively as transformative research frameworks (Mertens 2010: 473). These will be discussed more fully in Chapter Three.

The categories of 'arts-based', 'mixed methods', 'using technology' and 'transformative' are not mutually exclusive. For example, mixed-methods research may be conducted within a transformative framework (Sweetman, Badiee and Creswell 2010: 452). Transformative research may also be arts based (Blodgett et al 2013) and mixed-methods research may use technology (Hesse–Biber and Griffin 2013: 43).

Amy Blodgett and her colleagues in Ontario, Canada conducted participatory action research with a decolonising agenda in their investigation of the sport experiences of young Aboriginal athletes who were moving off reserves to take part in sport. Four academic researchers from Laurentian University in Ontario worked in partnership with three Aboriginal researchers from Wikwemikong Unceded Indian Reserve. The research team drew on the local and cultural knowledge and experience of the Aboriginal researchers and the methodological knowledge and experience of the academic researchers to ensure that the research was 'culturally appropriate and methodologically sound' (Blodgett et al 2013: 316). The research team decided it would be culturally appropriate to use an arts-based method of gathering data, and chose mandala drawings because the circle is highly significant in this Aboriginal culture and considered to be sacred. Participants were asked to begin by drawing a circle and then to 'reflect on their experiences relocating for sport and draw anything that comes to mind' (Blodgett et al 2013: 319). Each mandala was used to facilitate an individual conversational interview, which respects the Aboriginal cultural tradition of storytelling. Both the creation of the mandalas and the conversational interviews framed participants as the experts on their experiences, which, together with the methods being culturally appropriate, speaks to the decolonising agenda. At the suggestion of the Aboriginal researchers, some of the findings were disseminated by printing the mandalas on a community blanket and displaying them publicly at the Wikwemikong Youth Centre. This enabled sport and recreation staff to use the mandalas as educational tools for young athletes who were considering moving off the reserve to take up sport opportunities, partly to explain what that experience is like, and partly to encourage young people to pursue their dreams. Overall, the 'knowledge production process ... reflected circular links between individuals and their community, as well as research and action' (Blodgett et al 2013: 328). This is an example of transformative, mixed-methods, arts-based research.

Some transformative research uses mixed methods, including arts–based methods incorporating technology. For example, Ashlee Cunsolo Willox and her colleagues, conducting research with the Rigolet Inuit community in northern Labrador in Canada into the impact of climate change, gathered data through participatory digital storytelling, together with concept mapping and interviews (Cunsolo Willox et al 2013: 132–3). This research will be discussed in more detail in Chapters Five, Eight and Nine. *Lament for the Land*, a **film output from this research** about personal experience of climate change, told through the voices of people from northern Labrador, can be viewed online.

What do we know about 'creativity'?

Creativity is complex and notoriously hard to define (Carter 2004: 25, 39; Swann 2006: 9; Batey 2012: 55, Walsh, Anders and Hancock 2013: 21). Creativity is also difficult to measure (Villalba 2012: 1), so it is under-researched and poorly understood (Batey 2012: 55). Historically, creativity was viewed as a divine attribute (Sternberg 2006: 6, Hesmondhaugh and Baker 2011: 3), with only the gods being able to create something from nothing. A legacy of this is that some creative people still refer to the capricious 'muse' or 'inspiration' that may arrive – or not – at any time (Carter 2004: 25). Nowadays, creativity is more often viewed as a process of creating something from elements that already exist by putting them together in a new way (Carter 2004: 47; Munat 2007: xiv; Koestler 1969: 45, cited in Forceville 2012: 113). An interesting **TED talk** on creativity by the author Elizabeth Gilbert is available online.

Some scholars of creativity subscribe to a 'standard definition' including the criteria of originality and effectiveness (Runco and Jaeger 2012: 92), which stems from the work of Stein (1953) and Barron (1955) (Runco and Jaeger 2012: 95). Yet this definition says more about what creativity does and how it functions than about what it is. Also, creativity scholars now acknowledge that this definition may not be entirely adequate; there is no clear consensus that the criteria of originality and effectiveness are the best or only criteria to use in judging creativity (Runco and Jaeger 2012: 95). Some commentators take the view that originality is not a requirement for creativity (for example, Fryer 2012: 22).

Creativity is understood differently in different countries. Research in Hong Kong, China and America found that Chinese people tend to see creativity as an external social attribute, focusing on what creative people can contribute to society, while Westerners tend to see creativity more as an internal individual attribute (Niu 2006: 386–7; Paletz, Peng and Li 2011: 95). In Germany, creativity is seen as a process to help solve problems (Preiser 2006: 175), while in Scandinavian countries, creativity is seen as an individual attitude that helps people to cope with the challenges of life (Smith and Carlsson 2006: 202).

Some of this may be due to different linguistic approaches to creativity (Paletz, Peng and Li 2011: 95). For example, of 28 African languages surveyed by Mpofu et al, 27 had no word that directly translated to 'creativity'. The exception was Arabic, which has different words for creativity in secular and religious contexts (Mpofu et al 2006: 465). Polish also has two words for creativity: *twórczość* which refers to high-level creativity resulting in distinguished artistic or scientific achievements, and *kreatywność* for more everyday, personal creativity (Nęcka, Grohman and Słabosz 2006: 272–3). But there is no suggestion that fewer words for creativity means that the speakers of that language are any less creative. African countries where no word for creativity is spoken are as rich in humour and crafts, music and invention, arts and storytelling as any other countries. However, there is evidence that being bilingual promotes creativity, although the reasons for this are more complex than simply having access to more words (Kharkhurin 2011: 239; Swann, Pope and Carter 2011: 26).

Some scholars have theorised creativity by breaking it down into different categories. Two-category examples include 'small c creativity' for everyday

Table 1.1: Neçka's four levels of creativity

Type of creativity	Examples of use	Duration
Fluid	Creativity in speech; solving small problems using intelligence	Seconds to minutes
Crystallised	Solving larger problems using intelligence and knowledge	Minutes to years
Mature	Creating new texts or artefacts using intelligence, knowledge and skill	Hours to decades
Eminent	Creating new concepts or ground-breaking texts or artefacts	Days to decades

creativity and 'big C creativity' for notable creativity (Sternberg 2006: 6). Another two-category example suggests historical creativity for anything recognised as important over time and personal creativity for anything valued in its own context (Boden 1994, cited in Carter 2004: 66–7). Other commentators have proposed triple divisions, such as artistic creativity, the creativity of discovery and the creativity of humour (Clegg and Birch 1999: 7). The Polish theorist Edward Neçka has taken this approach one step further with his model of four levels of creativity (Neçka, Grohman and Słabosz 2006: 274–5) shown in Table 1.1.

These theories are useful in helping us to think about creativity in practice. Dictionary definitions can also help. The verb 'to create' in English simply means 'to bring something into existence'. It is synonymous with 'make' and 'produce'. So you could create an apple pie. You would be bringing it into existence; it would be *your* creation, not exactly like any other apple pie. But how 'creative' would that process be? You would not be bringing elements together in a new way, because countless apple pies have been made before. Unlike the verb at its root, the word 'creative' is synonymous with 'original' and 'ingenious'. To be truly creative, you'd need to create, say, a turnip and cockroach meringue. Which neatly illustrates the point that the results of creativity are not always positive (Carter 2004: 48).

Part of the difficulty in discussing creativity is that the word has become so ubiquitous in Western society that it can seem almost meaningless (Carter 2004: 140; Hesmondhaugh and Baker 2011: 2; Toolan 2012: 19). Also, there is a large body of literature on creativity, from many different disciplinary perspectives, that would take an entire book of its own to synthesise effectively. But we do know some things about the creative process. It's not about making something from nothing; it's about taking things that already exist and making new combinations. And while creativity is often viewed as a type of behaviour (Walsh, Anders and Hancock 2013: 26), it is not only about making things; creativity can also be applied to thinking, reading, playing and other activities. Creative thought involves lateral thinking, challenging accepted ways of seeing and doing things; defining problems as well as solving them (Carter 2004: 41). Reading is an interactive and embodied process: the reader is not merely a passive recipient of the text, but an active interpreter, bringing their own understandings and feelings to the process of creating meanings for themselves as they read (Pope 1999: 43, cited in Loffredo and Perteghella 2006: 10; Howard 2012: 214). Creativity in research (and no doubt elsewhere too) is not solely about thinking in the cerebral sense: it also involves elements of human 'knowing' such as intuition (Stierand and Dörfler 2014: 249), imagination (Lapum et al 2012: 103), 'reverie' (Duxbury 2009: 56) and 'wonder' (Hansen 2012: 3). Creativity is an essential element of play (Swann 2006: 45), and the combination of the two aids learning (Furlow 2001: 30, cited in Gillen 2006: 182). There is a good online **TED talk** about the relationship between play and creativity.

Education is key to developing creativity (Yamamoto 2010: 345). Yet, some education systems, such as those in countries like China and Singapore, focus on rote learning, which does not help children and young people to develop their critical and creative faculties (Teo and Waugh 2010: 206). Although creativity is hard to define or measure, it can and should be taught (Katz-Buonincontro 2012: 264). One way to teach creativity is to teach the creative methods of a given discipline (Teo and Waugh 2010: 212). This book is designed to enable and support the learning and teaching of creative research methods.

Creativity in research

Research is a complex human activity. Historically, research was viewed as a process in which experiments were conducted in conditions where all confounding variables had been eliminated and the researcher was a neutral agent who did not influence the findings. Now it is readily recognised that this is only one possible view of research, and there are many others. For example, some kinds of research are now seen as context-dependent, multifaceted endeavours in which a variety of people have influence over the process and its outcome. In particular, it is rare that social phenomena can be effectively investigated by following 'rigorous and pre-determined rules' for conducting research (Tenenbaum et al 2009: 118). Also, although some social science researchers still value the concept of objectivity, many recognise that, at least in some contexts, this is impossible to achieve. For example, people researching death and mortality cannot avoid having some kind of personal angle on the subject matter (Woodthorpe 2011: 99). This applies to other topic areas too, such as wealth and poverty, or health and sickness.

However it is viewed, any research project is the result of many decisions. The research topic, questions, method(s) of data gathering and analysis, presentation and dissemination all have to be decided. Within each of those areas lie numerous smaller decisions. How many questions should we put into the survey? This interviewee seems agitated; should I stop the interview and check what's going on with him? Which of three pertinent quotes should we use in the research report? Should I present the findings as bar graphs or pie charts? Which word can express what we're trying to say here? Is it ethical to include this outlier? Is it ethical to leave it out?

Research as an activity is suffused with uncertainty (Weiner-Levy and Popper-Giveon 2012). Uncertainty is closely linked with creativity (Grishin 2008: 115; Galvin and Todres 2012: 114; Romanyshyn 2013: 149). There is also a lot of overlap between creativity and problem solving (Selby, Shaw and Houtz 2005: 301). This renders research a fertile arena for creativity. In Nečka's terms, sometimes this will be fluid creativity, such as a joke shared in an interview or an effective formula chosen for use on a spreadsheet. Sometimes it will be crystallised creativity, such as an elegant research design, or buying a car to help with data gathering by increasing access to community members and experiences (Stack 1974: 17). Sometimes it will be mature creativity, such as research presented to homeless participants in the form of a graphic novel (Morris et al 2012). And sometimes it will be eminent creativity, such as the invention of action research by Professor Kurt Lewin in the 1940s. Researchers have recently demonstrated that creativity is relevant for both problem solving and analytical decisions, based on multiple criteria, aiming for new and useful outcomes (Čančer and Mulej 2013). This suggests that all research since the dawn of time has been a highly creative activity.

One of the defining features of creativity in research is that it tends to resist binary or categorical thinking. Mixed-methods research grew from people thinking 'Hang on a minute, why is it qualitative *or* quantitative? Why not both?' Also, putting people into separate categories, when scrutinised, often seems not to work as well as it might appear. For example, researchers in Asia and the Pacific found that 'The categories of "gatekeeper" and "vulnerable populations" are unstable, complex and often interchangeable' (Czymoniewicz-Klippel, Brijnath and Crockett 2010: 339). Some researchers are reluctant to divide people into mind and body (for example, Kershaw and Nicholson 2011: 2). For an increasing number of queer and other researchers, gender is non-binary. And Jones is confident that creativity is the basis for both arts and sciences, so in this dimension, at least, they need not be separate (Jones and Leavy 2014: 1).

All creative researchers stand astride boundaries, and this can be uncomfortable. For example, artists who are forced to squash their work into the unnatural shapes required by academia may find the process agonising (Durré 2008: 35). Alternatively, those who are required to keep their art separate from their scholarly work may feel 'the ache of false separation' (Leavy 2010: 240). People working within transformative frameworks are challenging power, and that can cause great discomfort, particularly when the powerful resist (Ostrer and Morris 2009: 74–5) or when researchers' peers in their own communities are as critical as those outside (Smith 2012: 14). Mixed-methods research can be uncomfortable when disciplinary norms and knowledge are challenged (Lunde et al 2013: 206). Yet, it is in exactly these boundary-spanning situations, where roles begin to become ambiguous, that creativity may thrive (Wang, Zhang and Martocchio 2011: 211).

Some research methods are reified in the literature as if they are indisputable and fail safe, yet any method involves decisions at every stage. We have seen that decisions are nodes for creativity. This may partly be due to the unconscious, intuitive aspect of decision making (Gauntlett 2007: 82–3; Smerek 2014: 10) that draws on the non-cerebral types of thinking mentioned above. Decisions also have implications that it is not always possible to foresee in full (Mason and Dale 2011:

1–2). For example, take the systematic review. This is intended to be a review of all the research already conducted to address a particular research question. The aim is to reduce bias (Petticrew and Roberts 2005: 10) by establishing selection criteria for the inclusion of research in the review, such as methodological soundness (Petticrew and Roberts 2005: 2). However, these criteria are defined by researchers and are therefore likely to carry biases of their own because different researchers will have different views of what constitutes 'methodologically sound'. For example, one researcher may think sample size is an important criterion, and they decide that any study with a sample of fewer than 60 participants is unsound. Another researcher may also think sample size is important, but they decide that studies can be considered methodologically sound with a sample size of 40 participants. The second researcher may further decide that the findings of studies with 40 to 80 participants will be considered as indicative rather than conclusive. This could mean that the first researcher leaves out several relevant studies with 59 participants or fewer, while the second researcher doesn't give enough weight to relevant studies with 80 participants or fewer.

This may not sound very creative, compared to apple pies and graphic novels. And indeed the place of creativity in research is still contested by some people. For example, it has been demonstrated that some researchers, particularly in traditional fields such as the physical sciences, can have negative attitudes towards creativity (Walsh, Anders and Hancock 2013: 27). In other fields, some research methods, particularly those used for studying social subjects, seem to encourage creativity (Rapport F 2004: 4–5; Mason and Dale 2011: 2). I would argue that, in any field, every research project is created by its researchers: we talk about 'doing' or 'conducting' research, but I would suggest that we 'make' research. Even where the method seems to be strictly prescribed, there is in fact a remarkable amount of scope for creativity, right from the setting of the research topic and questions (Robson 2011: 64). In the social sciences, humanities and allied subjects, taking a creative approach helps to expand the purpose of research: from simply finding answers to questions, to enabling us to see and understand problems and topics in new ways (Sullivan 2009: 62).

Creativity is sometimes conflated with art (Hesmondhaugh and Baker 2011: 1; Mewburn 2012: 126). We will see that the visual and performance arts have a lot to offer to research and researchers (Rapport F 2004: 8–9; Jones 2012: 2; Rose 2012: 10). And, indeed, this works both ways, as a wide variety of artists need to develop and use research skills to support their creations (Hoffman 2003: 1; Jones 2012: 2). The processes involved in making art can be surprisingly similar to the processes involved in doing research. 'Higher level thinking (as we like to call it) demands connections, associations, linkages of conscious and unconscious elements, memory and emotion, past, present and future merging in the processes of making meaning. These are the very processes which poets actively seek to cultivate' (Sullivan 2009: 121). I would argue that these are also the processes many social science researchers seek to cultivate. Smith and Dean speak of the 'mutual reciprocity' of creative arts practice and research (Smith and

Dean 2009: 12), and Gauntlett says that 'thinking and making are aspects of the same process' (Gauntlett 2011: 4). For the American education researcher and 'fiber artist' Judith Davidson, the relationship between research and art is cyclical: 'I think, analyze, dissect, and write, and this leads to an idea that becomes an art piece ... in the making of the art piece, I am also thinking, analyzing, dissecting, and creating a new interpretation. This process and its product then become fodder – experience, material, understanding – for yet another wave of work on the project in its more academic form' (Davidson 2012: 96). Artistic work seems to bring the 'making' into 'making sense'.

Beyond artistic practice, there are other aspects of creativity that are relevant to research. Rapport divides creative research methods into arts-based, narrative-based and redefined methods (Rapport F 2004: 8–12). For her, arts-based methods are primarily visual and performative; narrative-based methods focus on stories, often told verbally; and redefined methods take existing research methods and rearrange them into something new. Mason and Dale view all creative research methods primarily as redefined (Mason and Dale 2011: 22–3), which fits with our understanding of creativity as bringing together existing elements in a new way. In recent years, the move towards understanding and generating redefined research methods has gathered pace, such that we now have a growing body of literature covering creative methods. This includes creative methodologies, such as the transformative research frameworks mentioned above. It also includes some overarching methods, such as 'netnography', which is ethnography conducted in online environments (Kozinets 2010). And it includes creative methods for various parts of the research process, such as the use of diaries to corroborate, gather or construct data (Alaszewski 2006: 42–3), or the involvement of members of the public in publicly funded research with the aim of improving its quality and relevance (Barber et al 2012: 217).

Informal and formal research

Research has been defined as 'systematic enquiry whose goal is communicable knowledge' (Archer 1995: 6). Despite all those long words, research is also a normal human activity. We gather, analyse and use data constantly as we live our lives. Let's say you go to make some toast one day and find your toaster isn't working. That presents you with a problem to solve. You might check that the toaster is plugged in and switched on. If it is, and it still doesn't work, that's some data you've gathered and analysed to help you decide what your next step will be: checking the fuse box, perhaps. We also gather and analyse physical and emotional data. A dry sensation in the mouth and slight headache, once analysed, might lead you to drink a glass of water. Your phone ringing might make you feel excited (if you're waiting for important news) or happy (if you fancy a chat) or irritable (if you're hungry and someone has just handed you a plate of delicious hot food). You would analyse the combination of your physical and emotional sensations to help you decide whether to take the call.

Generally, we do this kind of informal 'research' without thinking of it as such – sometimes, without thinking at all. Yet it can be surprisingly creative. Traditional research doesn't recognise the potential of informal research, focusing instead on other tasks such as reading, thinking and writing. But informal and formal research are not mutually exclusive, and using informal research creatively can benefit more formal research (Markham 2013a: 65–6). For example, formal research questions often develop from informal research (Madsen 2000: 42).

When you think about this, it seems undeniable that informal research is inextricably linked with formal research, as physical and emotional data processing is a constant and inescapable part of our lives. This is beginning to be recognised, with more researchers privileging their informal research or 'embodied experience' and using their own sensory data as the starting point for creative investigation of a wide range of subjects, such as dance (Barbour 2012) and emotion (Stewart 2012).

Evaluation research

Most approaches to evaluation offer a high degree of flexibility about which methods to use and how to use them (Arvidson and Kara 2013: 13). This enables creativity in evaluation research. For example, Mertens (2010) conducted a transformative mixed-methods evaluation using technology.

> Donna Mertens, from Gallaudet University in Washington, DC, refers directly to her work as transformative and describes this as 'a framework of belief systems that directly engages members of culturally diverse groups with a focus on increased social justice' (Mertens 2010: 470). Gallaudet is the only university in the world specifically for deaf students, and staff are required to be fluent in American Sign Language (ASL). The university has a teacher-preparation programme to prepare teachers for working with deaf students who have an emotional or physical disability. Mertens led a transformative evaluation of this programme. Her first step was to gather a research team that reflected the diversity of the community of teachers in deaf education: two were 'culturally deaf' (born deaf and grew up using ASL), a third was also deaf but grew up using her voice and lip reading and had a cochlear implant that enabled her to function in the hearing world. The fourth team member was Mertens herself, a hearing researcher, fluent in ASL and with over 25 years of experience working in the deaf community. The team produced a mixed-methods design including an initial phase of participant observation, interviews and document reviews. Initial findings were used to develop an online survey to gather more quantitative and qualitative data. The survey findings were then used as a basis for more interviews. This proved an effective method for the evaluation, the findings of which led to the Dean of the University making a commitment to changing the programme (Mertens 2010: 473).

An **interview** with Donna Mertens in which she talks about her views on developments in the field of research methods is available online. Many of the methods in this book could be used in evaluation research.

CONCLUSION

All research is creative, at all stages of the process (Leavy 2009: ix). However, creative research methods, as discussed in this book, are particularly useful in addressing the kinds of complex contemporary research questions that traditional research methods are not able to answer (Taber 2010: 5). Also, creative research methods can be exciting and inspiring. One word of caution, though: the method(s) you use must flow from your research question, not the other way around.

This book offers a unique toolbox of ideas for today's researchers. The next two chapters look at some of those ideas in practice.

TWO

Creative research methods in practice

Introduction

This chapter gives a more in-depth introduction to arts-based research, mixed-methods research, and research using technology. It also introduces autoethnography, which can include all three approaches. The aim is to show some of the opportunities offered by these methods, as well as some of the challenges they present in practice. But first, to put the topic in context, we will briefly review the history of creative research methods and make some relevant points about good practice in creative research.

History of creative research methods

Throughout human history, people have turned to research to help them solve practical and intellectual problems. Some of the earliest researchers whose work we know include:

- Aristarchus of Samos, born around 310 BC, who was one of the first people to work out that the earth moved around the sun, rather than the sun around the earth;
- Eratosthenes of Cyrene, born around 275 BC, who was an early ethnologist and argued that the division between 'barbaric' and 'civilised' people was invalid; and
- Hippocrates of Kos, born around 460 BC, who argued that there was no merit in studying an illness without also studying the patient as a whole and pioneered lifestyle changes as a remedy for disease.

In China, Zhang Heng, born in 78 AD, used research to invent the seismometer for identifying earthquakes up to 500km away. Ma Jun, born around 200 AD, used research to improve the process of silk weaving, making it possible to weave more intricate patterns faster and more efficiently. He also used research to invent a mechanical compass.

Islamic researchers include Jābir ibn Hayyān, a Persian/Iranian from the 8th century, who was one of the founding fathers of practical chemistry, advocating experimentation and devising many research processes that are still in use today. Abbas ibn Firnas, who was born and lived in Andalucia in the 9th century, used research to develop a process for cutting rock crystal that enabled Spain to cut its own quartz, rather than having it cut in Egypt. And Muhammad ibn Zakariyā Rāzī, a Persian/Iranian whose life spanned the 9th and 10th centuries, was the first doctor to differentiate between smallpox and measles, based on observational research.

These are just a few examples of some of the earliest researchers we know about. There must have been thousands of others. Also, each of the above-named men was not a researcher in a single discipline, as the examples cited might suggest to today's readers. They were all polymaths, that is, people with expertise in a number of different areas, enabling them to draw on a range of knowledge to help solve problems. These polymaths didn't even see the need to stick to the subjects we would now regard as 'sciences'. For example, Muhammad ibn Zakariyā Rāzī also made significant contributions to the field of music; Zhang Heng was an artist; and Eratosthenes was a poet.

By the early 20th century, research had become a discipline of its own. In 1906, the editor of the journal *Science*, James McKeen Cattell, published a directory of 4,000 'men who have carried out research work' (Godin, Lane and SUNY 2011: 3). There have also been women researchers throughout history, from the earliest times, such as Merit Ptah, a doctor who lived in Egypt around 2700 BC, to contemporaries of Mr Cattell, such as Marie Curie, a Polish woman working in France in the early 20th century, whose research into radiation led her being the first woman to be awarded a Nobel prize. But, as Mr Cattell's words suggest, by the start of the 20th century, research had become part of the white, male, intellectual tradition of positivism, which was focused on mastering the world (Terre Blanche and Durrheim 2006: 14).

Because this tradition was so pervasive, social studies developing in the late 19th century, such as psychology, sociology and anthropology, tried to follow the methods of the physical sciences – and, indeed, renamed themselves 'social sciences' to indicate the link. Arguments about whether this was sensible raged throughout the 20th century and still cause dissent today. This book is not intended as a critique of scientific methods, which have revolutionised the lives of most of the world's inhabitants in fundamental areas such as food production, healthcare and transport (Broussine 2008: 14). But the reification of scientific methods makes it easy to forget that these methods were created to solve problems, and new problems sometimes require new methods if they are to be investigated fully. This is as much the case now as it was over 2,000 years ago, when Eratosthenes was using research to create the discipline of geography, or Zhang Heng to catalogue the stars.

One major problem with trying to apply the methods of the physical sciences to studying people in society is that it works only up to a point (Broussine 2008: 15). Most of the research methods in the physical sciences are quantitative: they employ techniques such as counting, weighing, measuring, heating, cooling, dividing and mixing to investigate physical aspects of the world. Of course quantitative methods can be useful in social research. But if you want to investigate questions like why some children have better exam results than others, or how to increase adults' participation in healthy lifestyle activities, or what is the nature of envy, you will need more than quantitative methods.

Researchers in a range of fields began to notice this in the early 20th century, and started to develop qualitative research methods. To begin with, the idea was that qualitative methods should be verifiable and rigorous in the same way as quantitative methods. But from the 1970s onwards researchers began to build arguments for qualitative research methods to have their own validity in particular contexts. These methods are now demonstrably able to make positive contributions to, for example, policy development (Donmoyer 2012: 672). In the 1990s social researchers began to consider the merits of mixed-methods research, combining quantitative and qualitative techniques to gain a fuller picture of the subject under investigation.

The development of research techniques, whether quantitative or qualitative, has involved enormous creativity (Gergen and Jones 2008: 1). The opportunities for expanding these techniques that are offered by technology, arts-based approaches, mixing methods and so on may be viewed by some as adding complexity. On the other hand, we may be coming full circle and returning to the view of the polymaths: that knowledge is worth having, no matter where it originates, and the more diverse a person's knowledge, the more likely they will be able to identify and implement creative solutions to problems. If we can overcome the idea of art and science being poles apart, the two approaches could inform and sustain each other, as evidently they used to do (Gergen and Gergen 2012: 15).

Some scholars are also questioning the compartmentalisation of different disciplines. Working across disciplinary boundaries is becoming more common (for example, Lyon, Möllering and Saunders 2012: 13), as is the conceptualisation of research as too broad an activity to fit into any single disciplinary category. Some argue that art and science need not be oppositional and can be complementary, with no hard line between the two (for example, Ellingson 2009: 5, 60). For example, phenomenologists tend to regard their research as both an art and a science, although different phenomenologists may disagree about the relative weighting of science and art in research (Finlay 2012: 27). **Two videos explaining phenomenology** – an unmissable one by the Muppets, and a more serious introduction – are available online.

Good practice in creative research

Creative solutions to research problems do not usually imply really wacky, left-field, off-the-wall ideas. Formal research is a complex undertaking with a great deal of history, and it helps to know about the workings and rationale for tried-and-tested methods. This will enable you to build on existing knowledge and experience, rather than, as the cliché has it, reinventing the wheel. Where creativity enters into the picture is in knowing about various methods but not being bound by that knowledge, such that, if the need arises, you can manipulate and develop theories and methods, within the constraints of good practice, to help you answer your research questions (Mumford et al 2010: 3).

Good research practice dictates that you start by framing your research question(s), then identify the method(s) which seem most likely to lead to a useful answer (Tenenbaum et al 2009: 117). Some of the methods in this book are beguiling in themselves, but it is not good practice to start a research project by deciding on a method before you have framed a question – unless you are making research simply to test the method.

Good research is also ethical, meticulous and links theory to practice. Creative methods can never be an excuse for unethical, sloppy or self-indulgent research. What this book will do is give you a wide choice of methods and, I hope, inspire you to take a creative approach to your own, good-quality research.

Arts-based research in practice

As we have seen, a large proportion of creative research methods are arts based. Equally, a large proportion of the arts are research based. Research is a fundamental part of arts such as theatre and the performance arts (Kershaw and Nicholson 2011), scenography (McKinney and Iball 2011), fiction writing (Spencer 2013), creative non-fiction writing (Brien 2013) and poetry (Lasky 2013). Research in the arts can be conducted in many ways and for many reasons. For example, research can be conducted into the history and background of a general aspect of the arts (Davis et al 2011; Gale and Featherstone 2011), or of specific works of art (Patten 2007), or in support of a work of art in progress (Hoffman 2003: 1; Atkinson 2010: 189; Coles 2013: 163), or to evaluate the audience's response to a work of art (Atkinson 2009, cited in Dixon 2011: 55–9). An **example of research in art practice** is provided online.

It is increasingly recognised that creative practice can be a form of research in itself (Sullivan 2009: 50; Hughes, Kidd and McNamara 2011). Inquiry through creative practice privileges such things as play, intuition, serendipity, imagination and the unexpected as resources for making sense. Those engaged in creative inquiry have asked, 'What are methods for, but to ruin our experiments?' (Kershaw et al 2011: 65). There is increasing acceptance of the idea that artists can conduct research in the process of producing art, and that the resulting artwork can be a valid research output in itself by embodying and communicating the knowledge produced in its creation (Biggs 2009: 67). Art can contribute to research by being documented and theorised, and research, in turn, can inspire and contribute to art, in an 'iterative cyclic web' (Smith and Dean 2009: 2). A good illustration of how art and science can work together in practice is shown in a **TEDx talk** given by the Swiss photographer Fabian Oefner, available online.

There is a vocal academic lobby suggesting that people who wish to use artistic techniques within their research should be as skilled in the arts they wish to practise as they are in research techniques. It may seem difficult to compare skill levels across different disciplines, but arts practitioners have their own informal version of peer review (Smith and Dean 2009: 26). For example, if a group of skilled musicians recognise someone else as a musician, then that person is a musician. 'In the poetry world, many would be poets, but it is the domain itself and its tacit yet established rules of quality that move a person into being considered a poet by others' (Piirto 2009: 96, citing Piirto 1998). Jane Piirto, an American professor and published and award-winning poet and fiction writer, will permit her postgraduate students to incorporate art into their research projects only if they are either a professional artist in the relevant field or have studied the art concerned at undergraduate level, because 'Then the art itself and its ways of knowing are respected' (Piirto 2009: 97). This can be seen as a laudable attempt to ensure quality and an understandable attempt to claim legitimacy for arts-based research, which is sometimes regarded as neither one thing nor another, rather than being viewed as a helpful inter-disciplinary step forward. However, Piirto's approach can also be seen as a rather exclusive and excluding position.

The counter-argument suggests that arts-based methods can be used by any researcher as long as the methods are appropriate to the research and its context. For example, a researcher wanting to gather data from children could use the 'draw and write' method (Wetton and McWhirter 1998) without being a skilled draughtsperson (see Chapter Five for more details of this method). Anyone can draw a picture, write a poem, make a collage. Creating a poor-quality artwork is not necessarily a failure, as there is scope for learning from the process; creativity involves taking risks, and it has been argued that it is in refusing to take those risks where failure lies (Douglas 2012: 531; Gergen and Gergen 2012: 162). Indeed, everyone has the right to artistic activity, which is usefully experimental and promotes creative thought. Arts-based methods 'have been used by a wide variety of researchers and professionals to assist people in expressing feelings and thoughts that ... are difficult to articulate in words' (Blodgett et al 2013: 313). And there is no reason why people cannot learn to make art in practice as they learn to make research in practice, thereby using more of their potential (Douglas 2012: 529; Gergen and Gergen 2012: 163). This is a more inclusive position, but, as with any research methods, it is important to ensure that all aspects of the research are conducted to a high level of quality (see Chapter Four for more on this).

If researchers think it would be helpful, they may choose to undertake some training in an arts-based technique (Blodgett et al 2013: 317), although whether this is appropriate will depend on the project and its context. Equally, for some researchers it may be appropriate to choose *not* to undergo training, because a researcher who is trained in an arts-based technique may be more likely, whether consciously or unconsciously, to influence the arts-based outputs of their participants (Cunsolo Willox et al 2013: 132).

Another option for researchers wishing to use arts-based methods, but themselves having little or no expertise or skill in the methods concerned, is to bring an arts professional onto the research team to provide advice and support. I have done this effectively and successfully in research projects with young people who wanted to present their work through drama. I have no background in theatre, so I brought in drama professionals who were experienced in working with young people and were willing to join the research team. I was responsible for ensuring the quality of the research; the drama professionals were responsible for ensuring the quality of the drama. This perhaps offers a middle way between the academics, who seek to ensure quality through artistic skill, and the researchers, who seek to use the methods most likely to help them answer their research questions.

Arts-based techniques are particularly useful for gathering and disseminating data. They also have applications in data analysis, writing and presentation. These will be discussed in more detail, with examples, in the following chapters. While the following is not an exhaustive list, arts-based techniques can be particularly helpful for:

- exploring sensitive topics
- working with participants whose native language is different from the language in which the research is being conducted
- working with people who speak different languages from each other
- working with people who have cognitive impairments such as mild dementia
- working with children
- honouring, eliciting and expressing cultural ways of knowing.

UK researcher Maggie O'Neill works with transnational refugees and asylum-seekers 'in the space between ethnography and art' (O'Neill 2008: 3). She collaborates with her participants, who come from countries such as Afghanistan and Bosnia, and with a variety of professional artists including writers, poets, photographers and performance artists. The aim is to enable refugees and asylum-seekers to tell their own stories, and to use these stories to inform theory, policy and practice. O'Neill's view is that life stories, art and collaboration are all transformative, that is they can challenge stereotypical perceptions and received wisdom. She writes: 'Art makes visible experiences, hopes, ideas; it is a reflective space and socially it brings something new into the world – it contributes to knowledge and understanding' (O'Neill 2008: 8).

Arts-based research is often particularly useful for investigating topics associated with high levels of emotion (Prendergast 2009: xxii–xxiii). Emotion is linked with creativity, and some specific emotions, such as happiness and sadness, have been found to promote creativity (Hutton and Sundar 2010: 301). Happiness encourages creativity in general, while sadness promotes analytical thought, which also supports creativity (Hutton and Sundar 2010: 301). This may go some way towards explaining why a lot of autoethnographic studies focus on sad subjects such as serious illness, grief, bereavement and trauma (for example Stone 2009; Sliep 2012).

Autoethnography in practice

Autoethnography is 'an approach to research and writing that seeks to describe and systematically analyze personal experience in order to understand cultural experience' (Ellis, Adams and Bochner 2011: 1). It was devised by American ethnographer Carolyn Ellis in the 1990s (Gergen and Gergen 2012: 44). 'Auto' comes from the Greek word for 'self', 'ethno' from the Greek for 'folk' or 'people', and 'graphy' from the Greek for 'write'. Autoethnography has huge potential for creativity, but it is not just a case of writing down your life experiences in a clever way. Autoethnographers tend to focus on specific and intense experiences such as crises and major life events, and link them with their cultural location and identity (Ellis, Adams and Bochner 2011: 4). Literary conventions of autoethnography link life experiences with wider concerns such as ethnicity, gender, social class and key reference points in time (Denzin 2014: 7–8), as well as relationships, the past, cultural themes, social constructs and theory (Chang 2008: 132–7). Autoethnography 'transcends mere narration of self to engage in cultural analysis and interpretation' (Chang 2008: 43). A **conference presentation on autoethnography** by Carolyn Ellis and Arthur Bochner is available online.

Like any research method, autoethnography needs to be linked with theory and practice or policy – although at times it can be hard to see how this is achieved, which has led to claims that autoethnography is self-indulgent and irrelevant (Denzin 2014: 69–70). However, these claims are usually based on critiques that compare autoethnography with traditional ethnography, wider social science or arts disciplines, and find it wanting (Ellis, Adams and Bochner 2011: 10–11). Those who assess autoethnography on its own terms are more likely to assert that it can be a truly scholarly practice, and some have demonstrated its impact on practice and policy (Chang 2008: 52–4; Lenza 2011).

Autoethnography has been used to focus on a diverse range of topics, such as: the emotional aspects of a teacher's return to learning (Benozzo 2011), anorexia and psychosis (Stone 2009), cross-cultural performance (Fournillier 2011) and outward-bound activities (Tolich 2012). Autoethnography can be used by a single researcher or collaboratively (Dumitrica and Gaden 2009: 2). Also, it can be used as a stand-alone method or as part of a mixed-methods study (Leavy 2009: 38). Autoethnographers often incorporate arts-based techniques such as poetry, photography and creative fiction to 'produce aesthetic and evocative thick descriptions of personal and interpersonal experience' (Ellis, Adams and Bochner 2011: 5). The aim is to produce 'accessible texts' that 'make personal experience meaningful and cultural experience engaging' (Ellis, Adams and Bochner 2011: 5). For example, one classic autoethnographic textbook is written as a 'methodological novel' (Ellis 2004).

Autoethnographic methods can also use technology.

Delia Dumitrica and Georgia Gaden, from the University of Calgary in Canada, spent six months collaborating on an autoethnographic project investigating ways in which gender is perceived and performed in Second Life (SL), a huge, online virtual world which has tens of thousands of users at any one time. The researchers became interested in SL at an academic conference, joined SL at the same time and spent a month exploring as individuals before joining up to explore the virtual world together. Both researchers are female, but one chose a male avatar (a symbol denoting the presence online of a human). They both experienced technical problems, particularly at the outset, which led to frustration and even despair at times, but they were able to overcome these sufficiently to complete their fieldwork. Dumitrica and Gaden gathered data in the form of field journals, which they re-read closely and discussed at length. 'The collaborative dimension furthered our critical self-reflexive process by allowing us to explore and compare each other's understanding and performance of gender in the virtual world' (Dumitrica and Gaden 2009: 8). This method enabled the researchers to take an analytic and critical approach to their research questions and to conclude that 'How gender is "done" in SL resides not only at the intersection between our own gendered perspectives and the platform, but also in the technical skills we have' (Dumitrica and Gaden 2009: 19).

Mixed-methods research in practice

Mixed-methods research has increased in popularity since the late 1980s (Alasuutari 2009: 139). The term 'mixed-methods research' covers a whole host of different approaches to the research process. It is most often used to refer to research that contains both qualitative and quantitative elements, but can also describe research which uses more than one qualitative method (Frost et al 2010; Lal, Suto and Ungar 2012) or more than one quantitative method. The most common 'mixed methods' research involves data gathered by using more than one technique, usually surveys and interviews (Fielding 2012: 131). An **introduction to mixed–methods research** by John Creswell can be viewed online.

Sabela Petros studied the support needs of older South African people who care for children or grandchildren affected by HIV/AIDS. He and his colleagues surveyed 305 urban and rural carers of people living with HIV/AIDS and/or vulnerable orphaned children. They then conducted interviews with 10 respondents, purposively selected because they fulfilled two conditions: (a) they had given responses to the survey that the researchers had not anticipated, and (b) they were caring for both adults with HIV/AIDS and vulnerable orphaned children. The data from these interviews was later used to construct case studies. Petros also interviewed nine purposively selected 'key informants' (Petros 2012: 279), that is, senior managers – six from the government and three from NGOs – to find out about legislation and policy on HIV/AIDS. The datasets were analysed separately before being compared so as to assess the level of corroborated or divergent findings, which helped to contextualise the carers' experiences (Petros 2012: 288). This was the first mixed-methods study of this topic in South Africa and enabled a number of new comparisons, including of the differences between urban and rural areas and the differences between carers' and officials' views of the situation, as well as the identification of gaps in public policy and ways in which these could be remedied (Petros 2012: 290–1).

It is also possible to mix methods in other ways, such as conducting research that draws on more than one theoretical perspective (Kaufman 2010), or uses a team of researchers from different disciplines (for example Sameshima and Vandermause 2009), or analyses data in more than one way (for example, Frost et al 2010). Presentation and dissemination of research almost always use more than one method.

Andrew Robinson and his colleagues in Australia conducted a complex piece of dementia research using mixed methods. They involved patients with dementia and their family carers; gathered qualitative and quantitative data in nine different ways; and worked to integrate the findings from their analysis. The research team included expertise from the fields of arts and humanities, science and neuroscience, psychology and neuropsychology, nursing, social work, counselling and education. 'These fields span both qualitative and quantitative research traditions – we found this essential for informed decision making and functioning in all stages of our mixed-methods research' (Robinson et al 2011: 335)

A **document** giving more information about the creative approach of Robinson and his colleagues to dementia research can be found online.

The point of combining qualitative and quantitative methods is that they offer us different ways to understand the world. Quantitative methods show us how much, which, when and where, based on a theory of normality and difference: is this within the curve, or outside it? Qualitative methods show us why and how, based on a theory of interactions, events and processes. But mixed-methods research is not inherently 'better' than single-method research. As always, it depends on the research question and its context. For some questions, in some contexts, only a single method will be necessary to find an adequate answer. Other questions, in other contexts, can be addressed fully only by using mixed methods.

One technique for combining qualitative methods is known as 'bricolage', from a French word meaning to make something using whatever materials are to hand. In research terms, this means drawing on theory from any discipline or disciplines, using a combination of data–gathering methods and analytic techniques and taking a similarly eclectic approach to the presentation and dissemination of research (Kincheloe 2005: 323–4). The researcher as 'bricoleur' can focus on the methods or techniques that they prefer or those that they feel are best suited to their research (Broussine 2008: 79). While some find this too haphazard, advocates of bricolage suggest that it provides more opportunities for sense making than do other methods (Warne and McAndrew 2009: 857), perhaps because the researcher is not fettered by a particular method or approach. This may also be because the technique of bricolage is closer to the approach an artist might use than to the approach a scientist might use, offering more scope for creativity, as well as the chance to 'make for making sense'. Indeed, scholars writing of bricolage often use arts-based metaphors like weaving, collage or patchwork (Wibberley 2012: 6).

American researcher Annette Markham built on the concept of bricolage to develop the technique of 'remix'. She uses this in cross-disciplinary workshops with scholars who work online and are new to qualitative research, to help them explore creative approaches to research. There are five elements to Markham's conceptualisation of remix.

- Generate – expand your perception of data beyond what you purposefully gather to include field notes, early drafts, doodles, photos, uncoded transcripts, coded transcripts and so on, any of which may trigger useful 'connections among ideas' in a 'wonderful chaos of inquiry' (Markham 2013a: 74).
- Play – either guided/rule-driven or free-form and open, but always using your curiosity and imagination to drive exploration and experimentation.
- Borrow – ideas, approaches, perspectives, techniques and so on from other researchers, disciplines and professions.
- Move – whether forward or backward, leading or following, move and allow yourself to be moved, maintaining awareness that research is 'always situated, but never motionless' (Markham 2013a: 77).
- Interrogate – constantly question data, literature, context, power, your own motivation and so on; all aspects of the research project and the subject under investigation.

Markham writes: 'The concept of remix highlights activities that are not often discussed as a part of method and may not be noticed, such as using serendipity, playing with different perspectives, generating partial renderings, moving through multiple variations, borrowing from disparate and perhaps disjunctive concepts, and so forth' (Markham 2013a: 65). Remix also implies creative reassembly of these disparate parts, although that may or may not lead to a cohesive final output; it may simply create a new connection between two hitherto unconnected elements. The process focuses on meaning, rather than method as such, so its marker of quality is the extent to which its results have resonance with their audiences.

   Annette Markham's **blog**, which contains more information about remix, can be read online.
   In combining quantitative and qualitative methods, some researchers embed qualitative methods within a quantitative framework, and some do the opposite

(Plano Clark et al 2013: 220). Even some of the most reified traditional methods, such as randomised controlled trials, are now being redesigned in some contexts to incorporate, or be incorporated into, mixed-methods designs (Hesse-Biber 2012: 876).

Sue Robinson and Andrew Mendelson, at the University of Wisconsin-Madison in America, studied the way photographs and text interacted for readers of a non-fiction magazine article. Their research embedded qualitative methods within a quantitative framework. For data gathering, they used pre and post-test surveys including open-ended questions, and a two-stage test involving a randomised experimental stage and then a focus-group stage. In the experimental stage, participants read one of three versions of the article: text only, photos only or text and photos. Each focus group contained participants who had all read the same version of the article. For data analysis, Robinson and Mendelson used inferential statistics, frequencies and textual analysis for the surveys; discourse analysis and inferential statistics for the experimental conditions; and narrative, discourse, textual or content analysis for the focus groups. This enabled them to elicit rich information about the meanings constructed by participants from their readings of the article, and also to compare the ways in which those meanings changed between the different types of media (Robinson and Mendelson 2012: 341).

Quantitative methods can be embedded within a qualitative framework using the technique of quantitisation, where aspects of qualitative data are converted into numbers for analysis. There are a variety of methods for this, including:

- counting, for example how many participants said X and how many said Y
- dichotomizing, that is, identifying whether a participant did, or did not, say anything within a particular theme
- frequencies, for example, which code was used most frequently, and which least often
- statistical analysis, which can 'highlight patterns and relationships between groups of participants, thus helping researchers identify meaningful comparisons between contrasting cases (for example participants, social contexts, and events)' (Collingridge 2013: 82).

It is possible to combine other aspects of research, such as theories or disciplinary perspectives. Some researchers are working towards 'integrated methods', where many different aspects and viewpoints are brought together.

Psychologists Anke Franz and Marcia Worrell, from the UK, and Claus Vögele, from Luxembourg, studied adolescent sexual behaviour in Germany and England. These multiple investigators drew on multiple theories to underpin their use of mixed methods of data gathering, which led to multiple datasets. They used Q methodology, questionnaires and measurement scales to investigate teenage sexual health, discourses about gender roles, sexual assertiveness and sexual self-efficacy. Data was at first analysed separately for each method of gathering data, then the findings were integrated 'to provide a holistic explanation of cultural and individual influences on adolescent behaviour' (Franz, Worrell and Vögele 2013: 383). This enabled more robust conclusions than the initial separate analyses because 'The quantitative part could not explain the influence of discourses on young people's behaviour, whereas the discourse research could not make inferences about the relationship of the discourses to individual characteristics' (Franz, Worrell and Vögele 2013: 383–4). Essentially, integrating their methods allowed Franz and her colleagues to gain a more complete picture of a very complex situation.

A **presentation** by Australian researcher Gabriele Bammer, who suggests that 'integrated methods' could become a new discipline in itself, can be viewed online.

Mixed-methods research can be challenging (Hemmings et al 2013: 261–2). Joseph Teye, from his doctoral analysis of the formulation and implementation of forest policy in Ghana, identified several challenges of mixed-methods research, including the following.

- Choice of sample size – quantitative researchers prefer large samples, while qualitative researchers are happy to work with a few participants in detail; this may be why the iterative approach of gathering and analysing quantitative data, then using the findings to inform qualitative investigation, is so popular.
- Mission creep – the scope of the research can end up being wider than originally planned, as new information is brought to light which is difficult or impossible to ignore; this can lead to more data being gathered than was at first envisaged, which then leads to the data analysis being more time consuming than expected.
- Resource constraints – using more than one method, for example for data gathering and/or data analysis, takes more time and expertise than using a single method.
- Difficulty prioritising research methods – prioritisation can be dictated by mission creep or resource constraints or both, rather than by the researcher's plans; it is hard to give equal priority to both or all methods used.
- Conflicts in data interpretation – particularly between qualitative and quantitative analyses.
- Difficulty integrating findings – this applies to analysis and reporting, and there are a range of views about the benefits or disadvantages of integrating findings at either stage or both, which means that no researcher's solution is likely to please all their readers.
- Managing power relations – gathering data from different groups of participants can mean the researcher has to adapt quickly to changing power relations (Teye 2012: 385–8).

Åshild Lunde and her colleagues in Norway set out to investigate an interdisciplinary research project on knee injuries in athletes. The original research team involved researchers from different academic disciplines, including physiology and phenomenology, and physiotherapy practitioners. They gathered quantitative data about the nature and extent of knee injuries in athletes, and qualitative data about athletes' experiences of knee injuries. The intention was to integrate these datasets, with the overall aim of predicting the outcome of rehabilitation. However, despite being highly skilled and motivated, making careful plans and trying hard, the original researchers found it impossible to integrate the datasets. The research funders decided to commission some more interpretive work from external researchers in order to investigate the barriers to integration. Lunde et al took on this investigation and identified a number of barriers, including different views about what constitutes good-quality research and lack of strong project leadership to help reconcile these views. Perhaps more importantly, the findings from the qualitative and quantitative datasets contradicted each other. These contradictions could have been used as a resource for the research, in the form of a springboard for further exploration, but instead they were seen as an obstacle. Lunde et al stress that this is not 'the typical narrative of expressed prejudice and hostility between quantitative and qualitative researchers' (Lunde et al 2013: 206) and that considerable collaborative efforts were made. However, the desired middle ground was not reached, perhaps because the process of reaching that middle ground would have compromised the professional identity of all researchers. There was not enough 'external force' or 'internal drive' to make this happen (Lunde et al 2013: 209), so the disciplinary status quo was maintained.

It does appear that most difficulties in mixed–methods research occur when disciplines collide (Hemmings et al 2013: 262). Some researchers advocate a 'qualitatively driven mixed methods approach', which is intended not to privilege qualitative over quantitative research, but to ensure a good level of interpretation (Hall and Ryan 2011: 106–7, citing Creswell 2006). Given the findings of Lunde et al reported above, combined with evidence that some quantitative researchers are not highly skilled in interpretation (for example, Laux and Pont 2012: 3), this would seem worthy of consideration. Either way, for good–quality and consistent mixed–methods research, it is important to plan from the start which methods to use, within an appropriate theoretical and methodological framework for clarity about why and how you will use those methods, rather than adding methods or devising a framework as you go along (Franz, Worrell and Vögele 2013: 386).

There are a huge number of examples of mixed–methods research in the literature, and only a tiny fraction can be represented here. There are at least two journals devoted to the subject – the *Journal of Mixed Methods Research* and the *International Journal of Multiple Research Approaches* – and some excellent books (for example, Teddlie and Tashakkori 2008; Creswell and Plano Clark 2010).

Research using technology in practice

Technology can be used to support and enhance all stages of the research process. It is most commonly invoked for data gathering, transcription and analysis. For example, data can be speedily and effectively gathered online using a dedicated program such as SurveyMonkey or by trawling social media platforms such as Twitter or Pinterest. Audio recorders can be used to record data from interviews and focus groups and to play it back for transcription, which can be done straight into a computer by typing on a keyboard. There are a number of software packages to help with data analysis, such as SPSS (Statistical Package for Social Scientists) for quantitative data and NVivo for qualitative data. However, technology can also support other parts of the research process, such as 'researcher reflexivity, literature review, representation of findings, ethics, and collaboration' (Paulus et al 2013: 639).

Dutch ethnographer Niels van Doorn decided to use a smartphone to support his ethnographic study of intimacy, spirituality and citizenship among lesbian, gay, bisexual and transgender (LGBT) collectives in Baltimore, America. Initially, he wanted the smartphone to help him navigate around a city designed for car users when he didn't have a car, but it soon became useful for other purposes: recording interview data, taking photos and videos and making notes in the field. It was also, of course, useful for communicating with people through calls and text messages. However, using this technology to support research was not problem free. On two occasions van Doorn had to end and reschedule interviews when his smartphone's battery ran down. He also lost some audio and video files and photographs before he could transfer them to his computer; this may have been due to user error, but that is not certain. The navigational information his smartphone provided was not always accurate, and at times he would accidentally 'pocket dial' participants at inappropriate hours. Overall, using a smartphone both helped van Doorn to do his research and changed the nature of that research (van Doorn 2013: 392).

Many ethnographers have embraced the possibilities offered by technology, both for use within conventional ethnographic studies and to shift the boundaries of ethnography itself.

Technology enabled New Zealand researcher Clive Pope to create a 'compressed ethnography' (2010: 134, citing Jeffrey and Troman 2004) of the Maadi Regatta. This is New Zealand's primary rowing competition, a seven-day regatta with hundreds of races. Due to the time-bounded nature of this event, Pope could not conduct a traditional ethnography using participant observation over an extended period of time. Instead, he 'spent 10 days and nights at the regatta site, living the everyday life of rower and rowing' (Pope 2010: 133). This was an intense experience that did not allow for full understanding at the time, so

Pope used digital photography and video to record parts of the regatta for later consideration. These enabled him to 'rewind, revisit and reframe the setting, repeatedly seeking new learnings and understandings' that 'replaced the inductive and emerging discoveries that often evolve in situ during prolonged conventional ethnographies' (Pope 2010: 135).

Doing research online can seem like a great idea in certain circumstances. For example, some geographically dispersed communities, such as distance learners and expatriates, come together in online environments. This can make it seem very appealing to study members of those communities in virtual locations (Lewis and McNaughton Nicholls 2014: 60), whether through observing them at the locations they choose to use or by consensual interaction at a dedicated location such as a chat room or forum set up specifically for research. There are logistical advantages for the researcher: for example, you don't have to go anywhere, and your data can simply be copied and pasted from the web. This is economical in time and cost, and can make the prospect of doing research online almost too tempting to resist.

However, it is also important to identify and address the limitations of doing research online, and the challenges it may present (Ignacio 2012: 239, Lewis and McNaughton Nicholls 2014: 58). The following are a few of those challenges and limitations.

- Technical skills – the researcher may need a certain level of technical skill, or help from someone who has that level of skill, for example to create a forum, or to make a web page of information about the research to use in seeking informed consent from potential participants.
- Sampling – research online throws up all sorts of problems with sampling, for various reasons; for example, not everyone has access to online environments, or the identity of online participants may be wholly or partly concealed, which can make it difficult to fill quotas. (This also, of course, applies to offline research, but in different ways; for example, people in some online environments routinely use pseudonyms and misleading avatars.)
- Quality of data – data gathered online may not be as rich, detailed or multi-dimensional as data gathered in other arenas.
- Text from web pages – researching online text can be challenging because it is subject to change or deletion. Also, it is necessary to decide what to do with links from the researched pages: should those links also be followed and researched? And what if there are further links from the resulting pages? Screenshots can be used to preserve text from web pages, but they don't allow the use of embedded links.
- Consent – just because information is in the public domain, for example on openly accessible blogs or Twitter, that doesn't mean the person who generated the information would be happy for it to be used in a research project. Yet obtaining consent can be difficult.

This is presented not as an exhaustive list, but as an illustration of the need to think carefully when considering the option of doing research online. It is not simply a case of transferring offline methods to an online environment (Markham 2013b: 435). Even with questionnaires, working online offers far more flexibility than hard copy. For example, there is no need for traditional formulations such as, 'If yes, please continue with the next question; if no, please go straight to question 8'. An online questionnaire can be designed to take respondents to the next question that is relevant to them, depending on their answer to the current question. Therefore, there can be various routes through an online questionnaire, which makes online questionnaire design even more complex than the offline equivalent. With qualitative methods, the complexity increases, such that any researcher will need to think very carefully through all the ramifications and implications of attempting to use these methods online. For some projects, a mix of online and offline methods may be best (Ignacio 2012: 244). The **blog** of the New Social Media, New Social Science? network contains useful information about online research.

CONCLUSION

The worldwide history of research methods is full of multi-skilled people working across disciplines. Yet, by the start of the 20th century the Western world had reached a point where most researchers did research in only one area and were not expected to know about anything else. White male positivists were in control, reasoning that research was a neutral activity, conducted in laboratories (and thereby somehow separate from society), and that researchers had no effect on the research process or its outcome.

In the second half of the 20th century the fallacies in that reasoning became apparent. Researchers began to view their work as value laden, symbiotically linked with society and inevitably affected by the researchers themselves. As they developed this new paradigm, researchers began to reach out beyond the bounds of conventional research to the arts, other research methods and technology, to find more useful ways to explore the world around us.

Chapter One of this book defined four main categories of creative methods for social research: arts-based research, mixed-methods research, research using technology and transformative ethical frameworks. This chapter has covered the first three of these categories. The next chapter will address research ethics in general in creative research methods, and transformative ethical frameworks in particular.

THREE

Creative research methods and ethics

Introduction

Ethical considerations need to permeate the whole of the research process. Ethical issues in research are most often thought of in terms of data gathering and risk of harm to participants, perhaps because historically that is where most harm has been done in notorious studies such as the Tuskegee syphilis experiments and Stanley Milgram's studies of obedience (Iphofen 2011: 53). However, ethics should underpin every single step of research, from the first germ of an idea to the last act after dissemination. And ethical problems require ethical decision making – which allows for creativity, even in places which may seem unlikely, such as research ethics governance committees (Stark 2012: 166). Also, perhaps surprisingly, there is a close link between working ethically and thinking creatively.

Michael Mumford and his colleagues, from the University of Oklahoma, in the US, studied the relationship between ethical decision making and creative thinking among scientists (Mumford et al 2010: 1). The ethics literature suggested four domains of ethical behaviour which between them could account for most instances of ethical misconduct. These domains were: study conduct, data management, professional practices and business practices (Mumford et al 2010: 2). Mumford and his colleagues studied 258 doctoral students from the physical and social sciences with 4–60 months of university experience. Participants were asked to complete a range of tests and measures assessing their cognitive abilities, personalities, creative-thinking skills and ethical decision making. Of course this study did not assess – could not have assessed – all types of creative thinking and ethical decision making. But it did find, conclusively, that among doctoral science students there are strong and consistent relationships between creative-thinking skills and ethical decision making (Mumford et al 2010: 13).

The work of Mumford et al (2010) suggests that taking a creative approach can help to make your research more ethical. It has also been suggested that being open about the creative aspects of your research, such as acknowledging that your research design is new or your writing is semi–fictionalised, is an ethical position (Piper and Sikes 2010: 572). This is because such a position recognises that research is constructed, with aesthetic aspects; something that was hidden by the traditional styles of social science writing and presentation (Rhodes and Brown 2005: 479).

Research governance

Research ethics, particularly in biomedical research, is governed by groups of people known as institutional review boards (IRBs) in the US, research ethics committees in the UK and by other names elsewhere (McAreavey and Muir 2011: 391). This system developed in reaction to notoriously unethical research such as the Tuskegee and Milgram studies noted above. Nowadays, most universities, health authorities and other bodies researching people in society have their own ethics committees, which scrutinise applications from researchers for ethical approval. These committees aim to ensure that research is conducted ethically and, in particular, to safeguard potentially vulnerable research participants. However, as we will see, researchers and committee members hold a variety of ethical perspectives and standpoints. This means that, in practice, the ethics of some committees can conflict with the ethics of some researchers.

Librett and Perrone found that the requirements of IRBs actually hindered the ability of ethnographers to conduct ethical research (Librett and Perrone 2010: 742). There were a number of reasons for this, such as that IRBs required informed consent to be obtained in the form of a contractual agreement between each individual participant and the researcher, while an ethnographer usually acts as a participant observer of a group, community or organization (Librett and Perrone 2010: 742). This makes it pretty much impossible to gain consent from every individual member or resident, let alone all the visitors the ethnographer might encounter. For example, Philippe Bourgois lived and worked in a ghetto neighbourhood of New York for five years while he conducted an ethnographic study of urban social marginalisation (Bourgois 2002). Also, Nigel Rapport worked as a porter in a Scottish hospital for a year, to study national identity (Rapport, N 2004). It would not have been possible for Bourgois to obtain informed consent from every adult, child, shopkeeper, drug dealer and so on, or for Rapport to obtain informed consent from every doctor, nurse, patient, visitor and others. Also, any ethnographer who tried to obtain informed consent in this way would disrupt the fundamental ethnographic method of participant observation, which aims to observe and experience natural behaviour rather than to influence the situation (Librett and Perrone 2010: 729).

Laura Stark (2012) turned the tables by conducting ethnographic research of IRBs at American universities. She found that, quite independently of each other, different IRBs used very similar techniques to reach their decisions. These were:

- looking for signs of good character in researchers' applications
- claiming justifications for expertise on which they were drawing, such as personal or professional experience
- relying on their previous decisions as precedents for making future decisions
- using meeting minutes as a tool for managing relationships, both with researchers and between board members themselves.

> This methodological commonality didn't lead to IRBs making the same decisions as each other: different IRBs reached different conclusions about similar studies, because they were made up of different people using their own discretion in different contexts. Stark argues that the methodological commonalities exist because the IRBs all have their roots in the same medical research scandals, such as the Tuskegee syphilis experiments. Stark's conclusion is that there are flaws and inequities in the way IRBs enable and restrict research, and that IRBs serve to protect institutional interests as much as – sometimes more than – the interests of potentially vulnerable research participants or even the overall quality of research.

A **YouTube playlist** is available with a range of videos on how to navigate research ethics committees.

Some scholars have concluded that IRBs, and their equivalents in other countries, are unable to address all the possible ethical difficulties that social researchers may face during the research process (Blee and Currier 2011: 401; Sieber and Tolich 2013: 46). In the UK, the Academy of Social Sciences, which is the umbrella body for the UK social science community, has called for a move away from the regulatory approach to research ethics and towards a more educative approach, so as to equip researchers more fully for managing the ethical difficulties they will face. **Information about this initiative** is available online.

Creative research can be highly ethical on the micro level, facilitating improvements in the lives of participants. For example, MacKenzie and Wolf's use of collage as inquiry with student teachers in America reduced the loneliness of participants and helped to create an inclusive community of learners who had deeper relationships with one another (MacKenzie and Wolf 2012: 17–18). Foster's use of drama with parents of pre-school children, in a Sure Start programme in a deprived area in the UK, empowered participants, reducing isolation and increasing their confidence (Foster 2013: 46). At follow-up, three years later, this positive impact had been maintained and also extended to some of the children, 'several of whom continued to attend dance and drama classes – which, [participants] admitted, would have been inconceivable prior to the drama group' (Foster 2013: 49). However, it can be more difficult for creative research to make an ethical impact on the macro level. For example, Foster found that national Sure Start evaluators weren't interested in seeing the parents' production, and that 'those in the position to make changes on a larger scale did not hear the stories that we intended them to' (Foster 2013: 50).

Theories of ethics

Ethics is a branch of philosophy that deals with the rights and wrongs of human behaviour. There are lots of books on ethics and research ethics that outline different types of ethical theory. Theories include deontology, which suggests that acts are good or bad of themselves, regardless of their consequences, so that telling a lie is bad even if it makes someone feel better. Then there is the opposite view, consequentialism, which argues that the outcome of acts is what matters, so if you make someone feel better, that's good, even if you had to tell a lie to achieve that outcome. These translate into research ethics such that those with a deontological perspective support a universal code of ethical practice that should guide research in any situation, while those with a consequential perspective believe ethical practice should be determined with respect to the particular research context (Kiragu and Warrington 2012: 176). A third position is virtue ethics, which tries to argue that if you're a good person you are likely to do good things, but doesn't really manage to convince anyone; there are too many instances of good people doing bad things, and vice versa. There is also value–based ethics, which suggests that people base ethical decisions on their personal values rather than on external principles such as those proposed by deontologists (Liegeois and Van Audenhove 2005: 453). In practice, most people draw on a combination of theoretical perspectives when they are faced with specific ethical difficulties, depending on the matter at hand (Sieber and Tolich 2013: 37).

The literature also covers different ethical standpoints, such as ethics of justice versus ethics of care. Ethics of justice is a deontological standpoint that emphasises the importance of obeying rules and sticking to principles, while ethics of care is a consequentialist standpoint that focuses on the context of a situation as paramount in resolving any ethical dilemma. Some people regard these as two opposing standpoints, while others see them as complementary (Edwards and Mauthner 2012: 21–2).

The most commonly cited ethical dictum is 'do no harm', which stems from the Hippocratic oath taken by doctors since the 5th century BC, and fitted well with the traditional view of research as a neutral, observational activity. However, more recently some social researchers have decided to include a social justice element within their research, seeing it as their responsibility to use research as a force for good.

UK-based researchers Susan Kiragu and Molly Warrington took a social justice approach in their study of girls' school attendance in Kenya. They were very aware of their privileged position as educated, comparatively wealthy women, and responded as positively as possible to requests for help from teachers and pupils. They gave food, water and pens to the schools and raised funds for a dormitory at one school to help protect girls from a very real threat of rape by local boys. The researchers shared their findings with people in power, successfully negotiating for practical support, such as sanitary towel provision, and mentoring by successful women. Some requests for help were particularly difficult to respond to, such as those from girls who feared, or had been traumatised by, forced genital mutilation, but the researchers did what they could to sympathise and support. 'All in all, we believe it is imperative for researchers to contribute in whatever way possible (material and/or non-material), not because they will benefit professionally from publishing participants' data, but because of the imperative of a social justice agenda' (Kiragu and Warrington 2012: 186).

It can be helpful for researchers to review ethical theories and standpoints if they want to deepen their understanding of the philosophical basis for their decisions. Researchers may also find it useful to review ethical codes and other resources that suggest ways of putting these theories and standpoints into action. Many professional groups and associations have codes of ethics, codes of conduct or similar documents. There are also a range of resources online to help with ethical decision making (for example RESPECT for research ethics, which synthesised a range of ethical codes of practice into a single **document**, and the **Association of Internet Researchers' Ethics Wiki**, which contains a wealth of resources for ethical decision making in online research).

Theories and resources are helpful only up to a point. It is not possible to plan for every eventuality (Bowtell et al 2013: 652), so doing research ethically means constantly making and reviewing decisions in a changing environment (Iphofen 2011: 7). As children, we're taught to make moral decisions in a binary framework: our behaviour is defined as good or naughty, we are expected to know right from wrong and the goodies always beat the baddies. Yet this won't serve us well as researchers, because the application of ethical principles to research practice is much more subtle and nuanced than simply favouring what is good or right and rejecting what is bad or wrong (Seal 2012: 698). Researchers are likely to find themselves facing situations where there is no perfect ethical solution. Nevertheless, they have to decide how to act – and, as we have seen, decision making involves creativity.

Creativity is morally neutral, being as applicable to crime as it is to good works (Schwebel 2009: 319). How people use their creative powers is their own choice. As we have seen, traditional research was viewed as value neutral and objective, existing purely for the pursuit of knowledge (Gergen and Gergen 2012: 30). However, traditional positivist research wasn't nearly as value neutral as it claimed to be, effectively privileging the privileged and contributing to a climate where terrible abuses such as the Tuskegee syphilis experiments could occur. By contrast, most researchers in the 21st century aim for some kind of social benefit to accrue from their work. Transformative methodological frameworks such as feminist, emancipatory, decolonised and participatory research are creatively designed to be more ethical by addressing and reducing power imbalances between researcher and researched. The 'transformation' aimed for is a move from oppressive to egalitarian practices, thereby supporting a wider shift from oppressive to egalitarian societies. These frameworks privilege researchers' insider knowledge, which has been shown to help in elucidating and contextualising the subjective experiences of research participants (Stierand and Dörfler 2014: 255).

There have also been claims for the ethical basis of arts-based research, in particular the use of expressionistic and performative methods of presenting and disseminating research. Gergen and Gergen (2012: 30–1) assert that 'If the social sciences are to play a significant role in society, it will not be through increased sophistication in their research methods, but rather through a multiplication in their skills of expression.' I wonder whether it might in fact be through both.

Feminist research

Feminist research has been described as using 'gender as a lens through which to focus on social issues' (Hesse-Biber 2014: 3). In the 1970s, UK researchers in the second wave of feminism, such as Liz Stanley, Sue Wise and Ann Oakley, began studying aspects of society relating to women, such as the family, housework, motherhood and lesbian experiences of homophobia. In the same decade US researcher Laurel Richardson was investigating the effect of gender on everyday customs such as opening doors for people – and regularly having academic papers rejected because her subject matter was seen as 'too strident' or only interesting to women (Richardson 2014: 65). These and other feminist researchers around the world were challenging the traditional research principles of objectivity and neutrality, and asserting that the identity and context of both researchers and participants was central to the research process (Ryan-Flood and Gill 2010: 4–5).

In the 1990s, third-wave feminists moved beyond using gender as a single lens, recognising that gender interacts with other sites of inequality such as ethnicity, sexual orientation and socioeconomic status (Ryan-Flood and Gill 2010: 4). This is known as 'intersectionality', a concept used to acknowledge identity as both multifaceted and closely linked with its social and geographical contexts (Naples and Gurr 2010: 24). After all, nobody is 'only' a woman, or a person of colour, or someone with a disability. An intersectional approach does not attempt to take into account every aspect of someone's identity, but aims to accept and reflect the complexity of identity and examine the relationships between different aspects of identity and their implications for power relations (Frost and Elichaoff 2010: 60).

The intricacies of intersectionality pose a considerable challenge to research methods (Hughes and Cohen 2010: 189, drawing on Denis 2008). For second-wave feminists, qualitative methods seemed most appropriate, and there is still a strong belief that this is the case (Hughes and Cohen 2010: 190). However, some feminist researchers, particularly in the US, recognise the value of quantitative and mixed-method approaches for answering some research questions (Hughes and Cohen 2010: 190–1).

Marianne Hester and her colleagues in the UK were involved in a mixed-method investigation of domestic violence within relationships, including focus groups, interviews and a questionnaire. Domestic violence is a complex phenomenon that occurs in same-sex as well as heterosexual relationships and may be perpetrated by women or men, although women and men have different experiences of abuse

(Hester et al 2010: 255–6). The researchers used a feminist approach to develop a questionnaire, informed by data from the focus groups, which was designed to be 'sensitive to the gender and power dynamics of domestic violence' in heterosexual and same-sex relationships (Hughes and Cohen 2010: 256). They received 746 usable responses that, when analysed, enabled them to 'differentiate between forms of abuse and their relative impacts' and 'provided reliable data on domestic violence in same-sex relationships' (Hughes and Cohen 2010: 261).

Emancipatory research

Emancipatory research, sometimes known as activist research, is a form of insider research where, for example, gay and lesbian researchers will investigate the effects of homophobia (Telford and Faulkner 2004: 549–50). This research framework grew from political activism and changing conceptions of human rights across Westernised nations in the second half of the 20th century (Morrow et al 2012: 8–10). Emancipatory research is intended to empower disadvantaged people.

A pivotal point in emancipatory research came from the disability movement. Paul Hunt used a wheelchair, as a result of muscular dystrophy, and lived in the first Leonard Cheshire home (Tankana 2007: 21). Hunt was a researcher and an activist (Tankana 2007: 38), so, in the 1960s, when the then Ministry of Health commissioned some research into the participation of residents in Leonard Cheshire homes, he and other residents expected the researchers to support their attempts to have some control of their lives (Barnes and Cotterell 2012b: 143). Sadly, the reverse was the case, as, on the whole, the researchers supported the status quo, in which people living with disabilities were regarded as unfit to participate fully in society. The residents were understandably upset and angry, and Hunt wrote a searing critique of the research, arguing that it was 'profoundly biased and committed *against* the residents' interests' (Hunt 1981, cited in Barnes and Cotterell 2012b: 144; emphasis in the original).

The creative work of Paul Hunt and of other disability researchers, such as Mike Oliver, laid the groundwork for the creation of the 'emancipatory research' model. Emancipatory research developed new ethical dimensions by questioning how social research is conducted and who controls its resources (Cotterell and Morris 2012: 61). This anti–oppressive research practice spread into the fields of mental health, feminist research, community research and numerous other areas.

Diana Rose and her colleagues in the UK carried out a piece of emancipatory/ activist research in the early 21st century, reviewing the effectiveness of electro-convulsive therapy (ECT), in which electric shocks are applied to a patient's brain to induce seizures (Rose et al 2002). Several of the researchers had experience of mental illness and mental health services, including ECT (Lloyd, Rose and Fenton 2006: 265). The research team gathered 26 reports of research into ECT by academic researchers, nine of which were produced in collaboration with or led by researchers who had experience of mental illness and mental health services.

They also gathered 139 individual accounts of receiving ECT that they found on the internet. They found that purely academic research identified much higher levels of satisfaction with ECT than either the research involving researchers with experience of mental illness and mental health services or the individual accounts. The highest levels of satisfaction were reported when data had been gathered by a clinician immediately after treatment. Combining this finding with their own experiences, Rose et al concluded that patients at this stage were likely to overstate their satisfaction, in the hope of avoiding further treatments and consequent negative side-effects, but would be more honest in discussion with other people who had experienced mental illness and mental health services, or when giving their own account online (Thornicroft and Tansella 2005: 2). This research was widely disseminated, and its findings and conclusions influenced both change to the UK's national guidelines on ECT and a review of training and information given on ECT by the Royal College of Psychiatrists (SCIE 2007: 9–11).

 Two videos about user-led research, presented by Diana Rose, are available online.

Decolonised research

Decolonised research is an approach that aims to detach research from imperialism and colonialism (Tuhiwai Smith 2012: 4–5). Colonised people do not want their story told for them by academics from other, more powerful cultures, however well-intentioned those academics might be. Nor do non-Western people necessarily accept Western views of situations or concepts (Smith, Fisher and Heath 2011: 499). Indigenous people the world over would prefer to tell their own stories and give their own views in their own ways. Traditional research methods, such as surveys, interviews and focus groups, are rooted in Western colonial cultural ways of knowing (Gobo 2011: 423–7). As with emancipatory research, indigenous academics and researchers are working to redress social injustice and increase self-determination (Tuhiwai Smith 2012: 4–6). This involves considerable creativity in approaching research projects. A **seminar** on decolonising methodologies with Linda Tuhiwai Smith, and a **conversation** on decolonising knowledge with Linda Tuhiwai Smith, Michelle Fine and Andrew Jolivette, can be viewed online.

Bekisizwe Ndimande investigated education in Gauteng province, a heavily populated and racially diverse region of South Africa. Although apartheid had been abolished, there were still many social inequities, with some townships remaining segregated, black areas lacking resources and black students experiencing racism in formerly white-only schools. Nevertheless, an increasing number of black students were moving into formerly white-only schools. Ndimande wanted to understand black parents' support for their children's attendance at discriminatory schools. He used a decolonising research framework 'in order to privilege those whose epistemologies have been marginalized and colonized, in this case the black parents who live in the impoverished townships' (Ndimande 2012: 220) (although not all those parents were impoverished themselves). This framework included:

- treating participants with respect
- being aware, and considerate, of indigenous cultures
- conducting the research in community languages
- being open and honest about his own life and beliefs
- identifying with participants' needs, experiences and concerns
- treating participants as partners in the research, rather than as data sources
- being aware of power imbalances between researcher and participants
- making an effort to connect the academic research world with the participants' world.

Ndimande concluded that while South Africa can legitimately be described as 'post-apartheid', it is not yet 'post-colonial', as the marketisation of education, in which parents and children are encouraged to choose between different schools, is in itself a colonial system (Ndimande 2012: 224). Using a decolonising methodology was intended to disrupt this system, but of course it usually takes more than one research project to make a significant change. However, Ndimande was able to identify this aspect of the colonial legacy and to make recommendations for ways to bring South Africa's indigenous communities back to the centre of its children's education.

In the research world, the English language is dominant (Perry 2011: 906–7). This is a colonialist situation that privileges English-speaking researchers and disadvantages those who do not speak English, no matter how clever or skilled they may be (Gobo 2011: 419–20). Within research projects, non-English speakers may be seen by researchers and research ethics committees as vulnerable or incompetent participants, when in fact they may be entirely able to participate in research if the research is conducted in their native language or a translator is provided (Perry 2011: 906–7).

Another colonialist aspect of research is that Western methods are often regarded as universal, when they may not be appropriate in other regions (Smith, Fisher and Heath 2011: 485–6). For example, Western researchers may take it for granted that consent should be given in writing, but this can prove problematic in cultures where oral communication is privileged and writing rarely used even by the few people who are able to write (Czymoniewicz-Klippel, Brijnath and Crockett 2010: 335–6). Ndimande conducted research in his native South Africa in indigenous languages including IsiZulu, Sesotho, IsiXhosa and IsiNdebele, which helped him to build rapport with his participants and enabled them to contribute more fully than if the research had been conducted in English (Ndimande 2012: 216–8).

However, Ndimande found that he had to be very careful in translating research questions, originally formulated in English, into indigenous languages that had no research discourse (Ndimande 2012: 219; see also Swartz 2011: 61). Similar problems arise with cross-national surveys and are complex to solve, requiring 'multiple skilled translators and survey specialists within each country working to arrive at an optimal translation' (Smith, Fisher and Heath 2011: 492).

As Ndimande's experience shows, these points are relevant not only to anthropologists and others who are likely to conduct social research beyond the boundaries of their home country. Many parts of the world are now multicultural, yet many research methods are monocultural (Gobo 2011: 418). It is important for any researcher to be sensitive to the potential for the cultural norms and experiences of participants and colleagues to affect the research process. For example, it is often taken for granted by Western researchers that participants should remain anonymous. However, working with young Sudanese refugee boys in America, Kristen Perry found some of her participants highly resistant to having their names changed, as her IRB required (Perry 2011: 899). On further investigation, she discovered that 'forced name-changing was a common tactic of repression by the Sudanese majority' (Perry 2011: 911). Perry's participants had – and, in at least one case, exercised – the choice of refusing to take part in her research. But surely it would have been more ethical for the IRB to work in a way that enabled researchers to respond flexibly to the needs of potential participants, rather than effectively excluding them as a result of its strictures. It has been argued that research governance organisations such as IRBs need to be 'decolonised' so as to enable researchers to be responsible to participants rather than institutions (Denzin and Giardina 2006: 35).

Although, as we have seen, there is some ethical decision making within IRBs (Stark 2012: 166), there is also considerable conflict between the values and priorities of research ethics committees and those of researchers (McAreavey and Muir 2011: 393). It can help if researchers are creative in presenting their plans to committees (Czymoniewicz-Klippel, Brijnath and Crockett 2010: 339).

Gloria González-López, from America, conducted research on incest in Mexico. Her IRB required participants to sign a formal document, including a detailed description of the study, and be given a copy to keep. This worried González-López: 'Would those who lived in extreme poverty have a private place to keep things like this document? What if someone in the family found the document, someone who had not known about the abuse? What if the person who committed the abuse found the document?' (González-López 2011: 447). Instead of trying to complete the ethics application form, González-López contacted the director of the IRB to discuss her concerns. The director was receptive, and presented her case to the IRB, which agreed that González-López could recruit participants on the basis of verbal consent (González-López 2011: 448).

A **video** giving more information about Gloria González-López' findings can be viewed online.

Participatory research

Participatory research, also known as participatory action research, is another transformative framework. Participatory research focuses on communities or groups and emphasises the full involvement of participants at every stage of the research process (Bhana 2006: 432). The research should benefit these communities or groups, as well as the researchers (Wassenaar 2006: 69). The aim is to empower disempowered groups, communities and individuals (Bhana 2006: 432). A **video introduction** to participatory action research can be viewed online, and a **website** with resources for participatory research is also available.

> Critical communicative methodology (CCM) is a particularly ethical type of participatory mixed-method research. Developed by the late Jesús Gómez in Barcelona, Spain around the turn of the century, CCM is based on the Habermasian principle that everyone has the right to participate in intellectual discussion, whether or not they are 'an intellectual' or can speak intellectual language. Gómez's view was that everyone has critical analytic abilities, and we can learn a great deal from people who have different backgrounds from our own. In CCM, every research project has a multicultural research team reflecting the diversity of the society being investigated, so as to ensure full involvement throughout the research process, from proposal development to dissemination of findings. The team is supported by an advisory committee made up of representatives from groups that are directly affected by the research. Thus, research participants play an active role throughout, although this changes rather than reduces the role of researchers, who are responsible for communicating academic knowledge to participants. Data is gathered using communicative methods, such as stories of daily life, focus groups and observations that are dialogic and involve the researcher sharing their knowledge and interpretations with participants. Quantitative data may also be gathered and analysed communicatively. Analysis is designed to identify what perpetuates, and what changes, inequalities, and to find solutions to society's problems. This method has already had a significant positive impact on some of Europe's most excluded groups, such as the Roma (Gómez, Puigvert and Flecha 2011: 239).

Outside a participatory framework, participants' views on the research process are rarely sought, though they may differ from researchers' views, even on key issues such as the value of anonymity (O'Reilly et al 2012: 220). However, even when using a participatory framework, there are limits to participation – ironically, most particularly in research governance, where participants' voices are largely silent (McAreavey and Muir 2011: 403). A short **video** about a participant's experience of taking part in dementia research can be viewed online.

Critiquing transformative research frameworks

It is not the case that using a transformative research framework will, in itself, iron out any potential ethical difficulties. For example, using a transformative research framework does not remove power imbalances between people of different races, genders, socioeconomic status and so on. Nor does it mean that all involved will have the same kinds of knowledge (Lomax 2012: 106) or the same understanding of what is, or is not, ethical (McAreavey and Muir 2011: 395). Researchers' experiences of oppression, as in the case, for example, of disability activist or feminist researchers, does not automatically mean that those researchers will understand how oppression is experienced by other people with disabilities or by other women (Mason 2002: 193). A transformative research framework may help all concerned to address power imbalances and differences within the research project, but doing so will still take time and effort above and beyond that needed for core research tasks. In some cases, such as when researching highly sensitive topics with vulnerable groups, it may be better to offer a flexible approach to participation, with options for participants to move through different levels of involvement at different times to suit their needs (McCarry 2012: 64). While this could bring accusations of misuse of researcher power, it is also true that researchers are trained and supported to make research, and are likely to have many more professional and personal resources than most vulnerable participants, and so have an ethical responsibility to know when and how to offer involvement or participation (McCarry 2012: 65). And practicalities can get in the way, because full participation involves a great deal of investment in support, training and inclusion, particularly with vulnerable participants (Gillard et al 2012: 252).

Also, transformative research frameworks can bring ethical difficulties of their own. For example, using a participatory approach may seem like a marvellous idea to a researcher, but considerably less marvellous to participants, who have much less to gain. This becomes even more of a challenge in longitudinal research, which has to compete with demands from participants' families and employers, among others (Weller 2012: 123). Conversely, little is written about the extent to which participants may expect researchers to continue their relationships with them after the end of a project, and the difficulty this can cause for all concerned.

UK researcher Carla Reeves carried out ethnographic research with sex offenders in a probation hostel. For many participants, the researcher was the only person they could speak to in confidence. Anticipating this, Reeves had planned when and how she would leave the research site, but unforeseen factors caused an earlier exit. Some participants asked if they could keep in touch with her, and she explained why this would not be possible – she would no longer have permission to enter the hostel, and consent for meetings outside was unlikely to be granted. However, as Reeves lived nearby, she did sometimes run into her former participants. This caused anxiety at times, such as when she was with a female friend and met a male high-risk sex offender with a history of raping adult women; Reeves couldn't warn her friend, for reasons of confidentiality. This made her wary of her former participant, which left her feeling ashamed, as if she had simply used her participants for the benefit of her research. This internal conflict was resolved only very gradually as her former participants were moved out of the area (Reeves 2010: 328).

A **video** with more information about Carla Reeves' research can be viewed online.

Participants are not often involved in the writing or presenting stages of research – although again there are notable exceptions, such as Ellis and Rawicki (2013) (discussed in more detail in Chapter Seven – also, relevant videos can be viewed online). And participants may be further marginalised, in a variety of ways, by the publication process. For example, in the long and thorough text on participatory action research by Chevalier and Buckles (2013), some participants are mentioned, such as Alberto (on pages 239–42) and the female forestry officer (300–3). However, these names do not appear in the otherwise comprehensive index; there are many names in the index, but only the names of research professionals.

Structural aspects of research, such as project design, timescale and budget, may need to be in place before a transformative research framework is implemented. This effectively sets up potential inequalities for any research encounter, with a framework being imposed on participants rather than agreed with them (McCarry 2012: 60–1). There is also 'the question of who participates and how' (Lomax 2012: 107). Factors that may exclude potential participants include logistics (meeting times and locations, access to technology and communication systems, languages spoken and so on) and the requirements of the research, for example level of commitment and abilities required. This raises questions about the extent to which participants are, or can be, representative of wider communities.

It is not always the case that more participation automatically leads to greater inclusion and empowerment of participants (McCarry 2012: 65), or that using decolonising methodologies actually 'decolonises' the research process. Transformative research frameworks are always worth considering but, if their use is appropriate, need to be used with thought and care, not 'bolted on' to put a tokenistic tick in the diversity box. Also, it is important to remember that not everyone views these approaches as ideal. For example, some researchers have called not for decolonisation, but for cultural integration in research through a 'geocentric' approach (Li 2014: 28).

Managing ethical dilemmas in creative research

Academics, particularly those in the field of education, are often encouraged by others to conduct activist research with the aim of reducing inequalities based on prejudice and so helping to create a more just social world (DeMeulenaere and Cann 2013: 552). A **video** that explores research justice through transformative research frameworks can be viewed online. While these transformative frameworks are designed to be more ethical than traditional top–down research frameworks, people working within them will still experience, and need to find ways to solve, ethical problems.

UK researchers Suzy Braye and Liz McDonnell conducted participatory research with young fathers acting as peer researchers to investigate the experiences of other young fathers. The researchers offered support in the form of training as needed and debriefing after interviews, and all participants were paid for their time. The team encountered several ethical difficulties. Peer researchers were unclear about whether they were 'peers' or 'researchers', which caused some difficulty for them in managing confidentiality, especially during the post-interview debriefing sessions. Also, the peer researchers found it difficult to be in a position where they were not supposed to give advice to research participants because, as peers, they wouldn't hesitate. They also didn't understand the rationale and need for the debriefing, thinking at first that they just had to pass on anything serious, rather than understanding post-interview debriefing to be a regular part of research practice, both for harm reduction for researchers and participants and for reflection on the interview in particular and the research process in general. As the researchers had taken the peer researchers' understanding for granted, this led to a few problems. The researchers concluded that becoming peer researchers changed people's experience of power in relationships, and that the reasoning behind some aspects of the research process needed to be more fully explained and discussed, including 'the political nature of the interview relationship' (Braye and McDonnell 2012: 278).

People who are new to ethics often expect a 'top down' approach, with a set of rules or guidelines that can be applied to different research situations. More experienced ethicists are likely to take a 'bottom up' approach, with each new research project being ethically assessed in its own, unique terms and context. Further, while there are some ethical absolutes – for example, causing harm in the name of research is never justifiable – experience also brings more recognition and understanding of the 'grey areas' in ethics, and acknowledgement that different ethical decisions may be equally defensible and legitimate (Lomborg 2012: 21).

Danish researcher Stine Lomborg studied the ways in which Danish people use personal blogs and Twitter, and how those social media were integrated into their users' everyday lives. Personal blogs and Twitter are publicly accessible and fall under the Data Protection Agency of Denmark's definition of 'non-sensitive information', so they could be regarded as freely available for researchers to use as data. However, they do contain a lot of personal and identifiable information, which some social media users might regard as comparatively private. For example, they might intend their blog posts and tweets to be read by people they know personally, for their own information and interest, rather than by an unknown researcher for career advancement. Considering this, Lomborg decided that she needed to ask permission from potential participants before using their words as data (Lomborg 2012: 25).

Using direct quotes from people's data, however that data was gathered, poses a range of ethical difficulties. How do you frame the quote? Do you introduce the person, give some of their key characteristics? Or would that lead your readers to respond in a particular way? Should you use a pseudonym? This is another of the many areas where the 'bottom up' approach to ethics is likely to be most useful, giving full and careful consideration of your unique research project in its own, individual context. When using direct quotes, it is helpful to clarify the reasons for the selection of each quote (Taylor 2012: 393). There are many possible reasons, such as: a single quote to illustrate a point in the narrative; a pair of quotes to show the widest range of a spectrum of viewpoints; a series of quotes to demonstrate a pattern in the data. Explaining the reasons for your decisions is good ethical research practice because it enables your readers to make well-informed judgements about the quality and rigour of your work.

Some ethical arguments have an equal and opposite argument. In her research mentioned above, for ethical reasons Stine Lomborg offered participants the opportunity to read her write-up in draft and gave them the option to ask for any of their direct quotes to be removed. As it happened, just one participant asked for one excerpt to be removed, and Lomborg granted the request. However, in Lomborg's view, this request was likely to have been made on account of personal feelings and wishes, rather than as a result of considered judgement about the extent to which the excerpt, in context, would add to the body of human knowledge (Lomborg 2012: 28). This was problematic for two reasons: first, it had the potential to undermine the quality of Lomborg's research, and second, it reduced the extent to which research decisions were the researcher's responsibility (Lomborg 2012: 28). The principle of 'interpretive authority' suggests that the researcher is a type of cultural interpreter, who is responsible for the rigorous analysis and interpretation of data (Markham 2012: 15). If this principle were applied to Lomborg's work, then granting her participant's request for an excerpt to be removed could be seen as unnecessary and inappropriate (Lomborg 2012: 29). Use of a participatory framework might have forestalled this problem – but it may be difficult to use participatory frameworks in conjunction with this kind of online data gathering.

Ethics in arts-based research

It can be argued that arts-based research requires a dual ethic: research ethics, of course, and also the ethics of authenticity (Parker 2004: 70–1; Leavy 2009: 151). Authenticity implies recognition. People may recognise authenticity by external factors: an artist's signature on a painting, or a certificate of origin from a trusted authority. Or people may recognise authenticity by internal factors, which are harder to describe: the experience of the artwork chimes with existing cognitive and emotional knowledge to create a resonance, a feeling of rightness. Of course, not everyone will experience an artwork in the same way, which is a potential problem for arts-based research. But if enough people can reach a similar understanding, through discussing and considering their individual responses in the process of creating research, then arts-based research may be deemed authentic (Clark, Holland and Ward 2012: 40). There are also micro and macro approaches to ethics in arts-based research. The micro approach focuses on ethics within the research project where, for example, it is particularly important to make 'full methodological disclosure' (Leavy 2009: 20) by explaining which methods you have used, why you chose them and how you have used them. This enables your audiences to understand your research more fully. The macro approach focuses on wider issues affecting the research project, such as political considerations and balances of power. Research is an inherently political activity, and many artists – writers, musicians, actors and so on – are socially and politically engaged. These artists may use research for 'the artful posing of questions regarding important social, political, and cultural issues by allowing them to be seen in a previously unavailable light' (Barone and Eisner 2012: 128). This is not in itself unethical, unless researchers also try to convince or coerce people to share their point of view.

Ethics in mixed-methods research

As we saw in Chapter Two, mixed-methods research can present some complex ethical dilemmas. Interestingly, some researchers have used qualitative methods to study quantitative techniques in practice, with results that highlight the ethical implications of the methods used.

Polish researchers Dariusz Galasiński and Olga Kozłowska made a qualitative study of a quantitative research technique: people's experiences of completing questionnaires. The research participants were unemployed Polish people, and the questionnaire was designed to examine feelings, behaviour and attitudes around unemployment. The researchers asked each participant to 'think aloud' while filling in the questionnaire. This was not their original plan, but the first participant did so spontaneously and the researchers found his comments so fascinating that they asked all the other participants to do the same. The aim was not to praise or criticise the particular questionnaire, or indeed to make a qualitative attack on a quantitative method, but to show how participants manage the tensions between their experiences and the answer categories in the questionnaire. Questionnaires effectively assume that people are, or can be, simply providers of information. Galasiński and Kozłowska found that participants would 'strategically navigate through the reality created by the instrument, attempting to satisfy their own "life story" and their strategic goals

> while, at the same time, completing the task of choosing the options provided by the questionnaire' (Galasiński and Kozłowska 2010: 280). This experience had a significant emotional dimension, often leading to outbursts of frustration. As a result, Galasiński and Kozłowska suggest that it may be unethical to use questionnaires to investigate difficult personal experiences such as mental ill-health, divorce or bereavement (Galasiński and Kozłowska 2010: 280). They also suggest that questionnaires may not be ideal for investigating 'highly contested, ideology-rich topics or events' (Galasiński and Kozłowska 2010: 281).

These kinds of ethical issues can also cause problems for research.

> Kariann Krohne and her colleagues, in Norway, studied the administration of standardised tests by healthcare professionals. They focused on several tests of cognitive and physical abilities administered by health professionals to hospital in-patients. The administration of such tests is supposed to follow a rigid procedure, right down to the health professional's script, to ensure reliability and validity (see Chapter Four for more on these quality criteria for quantitative research). However, Krohne et al found that health professionals regularly deviated from these procedures and scripts in response to patients' needs (Krohne et al 2013: 1172–3). The tension between the research requirement of standardisation and the care requirement of meeting individual patients' needs is always present for health professionals administering standardised tests (Krohne et al 2013: 1174). The health professionals who participated in the research prioritised the care requirement over the research requirement (Krohne et al 2013: 1176). This may have led to bias in the test results.

This is an interesting example of navigation between deontological ethics of justice – that is, the standardisation – and consequential ethics of care in a specific practice context.

Ethics in research using technology

Technology can be helpful in overcoming ethical difficulties. For example, audio or video 'podcasts' (short audio or video files published via the internet) can be used to help ensure that research participants are able to give fully informed consent (Haigh and Jones 2007: 81; Hammond and Cooper 2011: 267). A podcast can be made age appropriate when seeking consent from children. Podcasts are also useful for people who have memory or attention problems, as they can be played over and over again. Because they don't rely on the written word, podcasts are also useful for people with literacy problems or some forms of learning disability. Technology is also useful as a tool in teaching research methods. For example, a **video** example can be viewed online of a researcher working through a consent process with a research participant who has moderate aphasia (reading) and limited verbal output.

However, the use of technology for research purposes also raises a whole new set of ethical problems for researchers to solve. For example, mobile devices such as smartphones and tablets are increasingly used to communicate with research participants and record audio and video data for research purposes. However, these digital interactions can be traced by third parties, which may compromise participants' anonymity (van Doorn 2013: 393). Also, research using social media can compromise participants' safety if they are unaware of the extent to which social media sites such as Facebook, Twitter and Pinterest can be linked together. This means that someone giving their consent to participate in research via one such site may inadvertently provide the researcher with access to their content on other social media sites (Rooke 2013: 267).

The expansion of technology has created a lot of new opportunities for researchers, with associated new ethical difficulties. For example, online research can be passive, where people providing information online are not aware that it is being used for research, or active, where participants are aware of and have consented to be involved in the research. It would seem, at first sight, that active research is more ethical. However, it can be difficult to ensure that consent given online is fully informed. You can provide any amount of information about the research, the participant's opt-out options and so on, but it is impossible to be sure that the participant has understood and accepted this information. This is because a participant may give their consent through a single mouse click, without actually reading the information you provide. For example, in the summer of 2014, while this book was being written, researchers from Facebook published details of an experiment manipulating Facebook users' exposure to emotional content in their timelines (Kramer et al 2014: 8788). This research was in accordance with Facebook's data-use policy. However, many Facebook users felt that they had not given consent – certainly not informed consent – to participating in such research. The outcry on social media was so vehement that the researchers rapidly apologised and the editor of the journal that had published the research printed an 'expression of concern' about its ethical status.

The Facebook research may have caused only alarm to most of those affected, but research online that is not carefully carried out can put participants in actual danger. For example, whether the research is passive or active, if researchers do not maintain their participants' privacy, anonymity and confidentiality they can jeopardise those people's personal safety by leaving them vulnerable to crime through hacking or stalking (Rooke 2013: 267). It is essential for researchers to be fully aware of the potential implications of the use of technology within any research they conduct. For example, it is important to know that many participants are unaware of the size and nature of their personal digital footprint (and this probably applies to many researchers, too). Also, direct quotes from online research can be traced back to participants by using a search engine, so semi-fictionalisation can be particularly useful in reporting online research (Markham 2012: 5). If you are ever in doubt as to whether you might compromise the safety of an online research participant or cause any other unethical outcome, you should err on the side of caution (Rooke 2013: 268). It is essential that researchers should do as much as possible, proactively, to act ethically when working online (Markham 2013a: 69).

Well-being of researchers

A great deal of attention is paid to the need for researchers' duty of care to vulnerable research participants during data gathering – and rightly so. Historically, rather less attention has been paid to the potential vulnerability of researchers (Librett and Perrone 2010: 739; Bowtell et al 2013: 654), with many codes of research ethics failing even to mention that researchers need to protect themselves and take care, both when working in the field and elsewhere. Also, some research institutions fail to implement even the most basic health and safety regulations in managing the potential risks to the researchers they employ and send out to do fieldwork (Bahn and Weatherill 2013: 25).

> Australian researchers Susanne Bahn and Pamela Weatherill studied the lives of people with rapidly degenerating neurological diseases. In the process, they considered the potential emotional impact for researchers gathering sensitive data and the difficulties for researchers in recognising risk, and developed some strategies for increasing researchers' personal safety. They found that gathering data in people's homes can be risky, as the researcher is a stranger who does not know who will be in the house, their state of mental or physical health or what dangers may exist, such as aggressive dogs, or cables lying across the floor. There is also emotional risk from the experience of interviewing people in very distressing circumstances. Bahn and Weatherill offer a seven-point checklist to help with identifying and managing risk.
>
> 1 Has a mobile phone call-in system been established?
> 2 Is the researcher experienced in working with these types of participants?
> 3 Can researchers work in pairs?
> 4 Can researchers be given personal alarms?
> 5 If data is to be gathered in participants' homes, are other colleagues aware of researchers' whereabouts, and can researchers plan an exit strategy, for example parking in the street for an easy getaway?
> 6 Is debriefing support or counselling available?
> 7 What types of safety training are needed? (Bahn and Weatherill 2012: 33)
>
> Bahn and Weatherill's final recommendation is that safer data gathering practices should be included in research project plans, and budgeted for, and policies should be developed to support this (Bahn and Weatherill 2012: 33).

Even the more mechanical aspects of research, such as applying for ethical approval or using technological methods, can come with a heavy emotional cost

(Monaghan, O'Dwyer and Gabe 2013: 73; Moncur 2013: 1883). Suggestions for ways to manage this include: advance preparation, peer support, working reflexively and seeking counselling when necessary (Moncur 2013: 1885). A **video** offering a few thoughts on the emotional well-being of researchers can be viewed online.

It is important for each of us, as researchers, to take care of ourselves throughout the research process. Doing so will help in a range of ways, including promoting our creativity. Empirical research has shown that self-compassion, or being kind to yourself, is linked with higher levels of original creative thinking, while self-judgementalism, or being destructively self-critical, reduces original creative thought (Zabelina and Robinson 2010: 292). So taking good care of yourself will help you to think creatively, which in turn will enhance your research.

CONCLUSION

You cannot rely on rules to help you to act ethically in research. Principles such as 'use research to do good' and 'guard against bias' can be helpful. But ultimately, to be an ethical researcher, you need to think ethically before, during and after you make your research. Even this won't protect you against mistakes along the way and taking actions which, on later reflection, you will realise were not the most ethical option. But if you're making the best decisions you can, on the basis of the information available to you at any given time, then you're doing all that anyone can ask.

This chapter has given an overview of *what* an ethical researcher should do. The scope for creativity lies in *how* that is done. There are ethical dimensions to each aspect of the research process, so each of the remaining chapters in this book will include a short ethical section focusing on ethical issues of particular relevance to that stage of your research.

FOUR

Creative thinking

Introduction

Creative thinking is particularly useful at the start of a project, when all things are possible. At the outset it is helpful to think through your project as creatively as you can, including thinking creatively about methods (Mason 2002: 26) – which this book is designed to help you to do. But creative thinking is needed throughout your project, such as when ethical dilemmas arise or unforeseen difficulties occur. This chapter will show you why creative thinking is important and give you some ideas for ways to improve your abilities in this vital research skill. A good **TEDx talk** on creative thinking by Raphael DiLuzio and an interesting **blog post** on the same subject by Michael Michalko are available online.

Ethical thinking

Some novice researchers think ethical considerations are irrelevant until you get into data gathering. However, there are ethical questions to answer from the moment you have an idea for a research project. Why do you think that idea is a good one? What purposes would the research serve? These are ethical questions you should be asking yourself at the outset. Then, throughout the process, you need to identify and consider all the ethical issues that your research presents you with – or may present you with in the near future. Something that is often overlooked is a consideration of how your completed research might be used – or misused – by others with different agendas from your own. It's well worth trying to think this through and consider whether you can do anything to minimise the possibility of it happening. And, as we saw from Carla Reeves's work outlined in Chapter Three, there are even ethical considerations after your research is finished.

A short **video** outlining five ways to think ethically can be viewed online. Ethical thinking is closely linked to creative thinking, and this is discussed in more detail below.

Creative thinking

Thinking is essential to the research process. However, when you're thinking creatively about one aspect of a research project it can become very difficult to think creatively about other aspects – or, in some cases, even to think about them at all. For example, many early mixed-methods researchers were so focused on the effectiveness of their new research designs that they forgot that a theoretical framework could be valuable to guide their investigations (Evans, Coon and Ume 2011: 276). Creativity is a central ingredient of thinking, and the key to this is to allocate time for creative thinking (de Bono 1999: 115). The importance of taking time to think is often overlooked, perhaps because thinking is an invisible activity and therefore seems less valuable than visible activity with visible results.

 Thinking can be divided into fast and slow (Kahneman 2011: 12–13). Fast thinking is intuitive, easy, even spontaneous, particularly where someone has considerable expertise in a subject, and often is shallower and wider than slow thinking. Slow thinking is rational, deliberative and effortful, often narrower and deeper than fast thinking. Both kinds of thinking are involved in all stages of the creative process (Allen and Thomas 2011: 115), although if there are time constraints people are more likely to rely on their fast thinking abilities (Evans and Curtis-Holmes 2005: 386). A **video interview** with Daniel Kahneman in which he talks about 'thinking, fast and slow' can be viewed online.

Thinking can also be divided into convergent and divergent. Convergent thinking is useful for finding the correct solution to a problem, while divergent thinking enables you to generate lots of ideas. In this case, divergent thinking is more relevant to creativity (Hong and Milgram 2010: 272). The more ideas you generate, the more creative they are likely to be (Dippo 2013: 433). Divergent thinking involves not only generating ideas, but also evaluating them (Runco and Acar 2012: 70). Creative thinking and critical or analytical thinking are closely related (Prager 2012: 272).

All these types of thinking are active, but some scholars endorse a more receptive or reflective approach. For example, Galvin and Todres, drawing on the work of Heidegger and Gendlin, promote the idea of 'unspecialisation' as a way towards creativity through contemplative openness to new meanings (Galvin and Todres 2012: 114). They advocate using the 'empathic imagination' to integrate 'the head, hand and heart' and thereby avoid 'the excessive compartmentalisation of attention to specialized tasks' (Galvin and Todres 2012: 116–117). Romanyshyn agrees, using the poet Keats's concept of 'negative capability', or the ability to be comfortable with uncertainty, which Romanyshyn says will enable researchers to find new meanings (Romanyshyn 2013: 149). For Romanyshyn, as for Galvin and Todres, this supports integrative practice and avoids compartmentalisation, although Romanyshyn describes it differently as 'research with soul in mind' (Romanyshyn 2013: 149), that is, a more holistic and experiential discipline than traditional research. The concepts of unspecialisation and negative capability are akin to the concepts of wonder (Hansen 2012: 3) and reverie (Duxbury 2009: 56), and all speak of the necessity for researchers to be open to the unexpected.

Whichever way we approach it, thinking creatively helps us to look at the world in different ways. What everyone 'knows' to be true may seem explicit and clear, but in fact can make it difficult for us to examine our assumptions by preventing us from formulating questions we might otherwise ask (Shields 2002: 91). And it's impossible to detect our own cognitive biases, although we can sometimes identify those of others (Kahneman, Lovallo and Sibony 2011: 52). But we can spot some of the assumptions we make, and the things we take for granted, which can help us to think more creatively. One way to do this is to be alert for 'red flag' or normative words and statements, such as 'always' or 'never' or 'can't', or 'everyone knows that's just how it is' or 'it's not how we do things around here'. These kinds of words and statements can act as a helpful signal to look afresh at the subject or situation and ask some different questions (Strauss and Corbin 1998: 97–9).

Another useful way to identify assumptions and things we take for granted is to work with people from different disciplines. For example, political science is primarily interested in large, quantitative, national or international studies, while area studies mostly focuses on small, qualitative, regional studies. Historically, these disciplines have stood in opposition to one another. However, more recently some scholars have suggested that they might make a more useful contribution if they were treated as complementary, each with a worthwhile dimension to bring to the work of theory building (for example, Ahram 2011).

As we saw in the previous chapter, Mumford et al (2010) found a positive relationship between creative thinking skills and ethical decision making in doctoral science students. They also found that 'creative thinking seemed to promote ethical decisions in multiple areas' (Mumford et al 2010: 13). So it is likely that working on your creative thinking skills will also help you to improve your ethical decision making.

Mauthner and her colleagues, academics from the UK, consider ethical thinking to be an essential skill for everyone in the modern world. As the pace of change increases, researchers need to be able to think ethically on their feet if they are to manage new and developing situations ethically, rather than expect to depend on fixed, written guidelines. Mauthner et al (2012: 183–4) put forward seven headings for questions researchers need to consider as they conduct their research, from planning to dissemination. These are explicitly designed for qualitative researchers, but I suggest that they apply equally to quantitative researchers. The following is a brief summary.

1 Methods – is it OK just to *use* research methods, whether established or new, or should a researcher also understand how those methods work?
2 Sampling – what are the ethical problems that might arise as a result of the sampling strategy, and how might these be addressed?
3 Power – where are the balances of power between relevant individuals and organisations, and how might these affect the research?
4 Actions – how do the researcher's actions and choices affect the research, and how can this best be communicated to participants and users of the research?

> 5 Communication – what is the most ethical way to communicate about, and disseminate, the research?
> 6 Data – to what extent should the data be shared and/or archived?
> 7 Autonomy and values – what are a researcher's ethical and moral responsibilities, and what are the consequences of that researcher's ethical choices?

Perhaps the central aspect of a researcher's role is to interpret data, in the linked processes of analysing and writing about that data, for readers and users of research. If there were no need for analytic interpretation, there would be no research; no need for a qualified specialist to stand between the data and the readers or users of that data (Stenvoll and Svensson 2011: 574).

> Scandinavian researchers Dag Stenvoll, from Norway, and Peter Svensson, from Sweden, drew on conversation analysis techniques to identify three levels of 'contextualisation', or the way in which textual data can be interpretively linked with its context, both within and beyond the data. To demonstrate this, they analysed the English translation of a speech made by Belgian Prime Minister Guy Verhofstadt in the European Parliament. The first level they identify is 'literal contextualisation', or context explicitly described in the text. For example, Verhofstadt refers to specific and well-known historical markers such as the Prague Spring and the unification of Europe. These provide a clear historical context for the arguments put forward in his speech. Stenvoll and Svensson's second level is 'cued contextualisation', or context implicitly or indirectly described in the text. There are many ways in which this can be done, such as through choice of vocabulary, grammar, pronouns or rhetoric, the use of different 'voices' within the text and interactional elements such as laughter or applause that are recorded in the transcript. For example, Verhofstadt began his speech using the pronouns 'I' and 'you' ('you' being the European Parliament), then at a certain strategic point began to use the pronoun 'we', presumably to signify that, to some extent at least, 'we are all in this together'. Then he brought in the pronoun 'they', which set up a clear 'insider' and 'outsider' dynamic. The third level of contextualisation identified by Stenvoll and Svensson is contextualisation through absences 'that the analyst can justify as significant' (Stenvoll and Svensson 2011: 581). The comments of others, or a political/theoretical perspective, or both, can be used to help identify such absences. This three-level approach to contextualisation is highly creative. It does not claim to yield a complete and conclusive analysis, but to provide a set of transparent and well-justified interpretations that can form a useful basis for further discussion (Stenvoll and Svensson 2011: 572).

Creative thinking is essential in the process of interpretation: to help us question our own conclusions even as we draw them, remain open to others' ideas and keep searching for new connections to make and links to forge, both within our data and beyond (Freeman 2011: 549–50). The method or methods used should be made clear for the reader. For example, a feminist theoretical perspective might lead a researcher to interrogate a transcript for gender references. If none were found, this could be construed as a significant absence, which might lead to the question why the speaker has chosen to present his or her argument as if gender has no relevance. But, either way, the researcher should outline their theoretical perspective and any other factors relevant to the interpretation they make.

Creative use of literature

People often talk of 'a literature review' as if it is in itself a method or technique. In fact there are many ways to work with literature and documents to give context to your research. Some types of research, such as evaluation research, may use little or no formal academic literature, instead providing context from other sources. And some literature reviews combine formal academic literature with other types of literature and documents. Sources for context beyond the academic literature include:

- policy documents
- project documents
- web pages
- non-academic literature such as novels
- court transcripts
- documented testimonial evidence
- hard-copy ephemera such as leaflets or marginal notes
- digital ephemera such as tweets.

Reviewing literature is a creative endeavour involving the three pillars of research work: reading, thinking and writing. The aim is to outline what is already known about the topic (Bryman 2012: 98) and where your proposed research fits into that. Unless you're working in a very narrow field, you're unlikely to be able to read everything that is relevant to your subject. So, identify and read the key texts, and then make creative decisions about what else to read. You will need to explain how you searched for literature and/or documents, so make a note of the search terms you use online and the ways in which you find information offline. In reading, you have ethical responsibilities to the people whose work you read: to read carefully and thoughtfully, aiming to reach a full understanding of their meaning and purpose.

There are many types of literature review, and new ones are regularly invented. A **useful discussion about literature and decolonising methodologies** – one of the transformative research frameworks we discovered in Chapter Three – is available online. While there is no definitive typology of literature reviews, some types you may come across include:

- scoping review – to assess the amount and nature of existing literature, often as a preliminary stage to help decide what type of review to conduct (Grant and Booth 2009: 101)
- overview – a summary review, surveying the literature and describing its characteristics (Grant and Booth 2009: 99)
- rapid review (sometimes known as rapid evidence assessment) – to review what is already known about a policy or practice issue (Grant and Booth 2009: 100)
- historical review – a review that treats the literature chronologically and traces its development through time (Kaniki 2006: 21)
- critical review – in which the literature is not only reviewed but also critically evaluated (Grant and Booth 2009: 93)
- thematic review – structured around different perspectives, themes or debates in the literature (Kaniki 2006: 21)
- integrative review – including both experimental and non-experimental research (Whittemore and Knafl 2005: 547)
- theoretical review – a review of theoretical developments in a subject area, sometimes linking these with empirical evidence (Kaniki 2006: 21)
- methodological review – a review focusing on a particular research method
- empirical review – a review focusing on the empirical findings of research on a given topic (Kaniki 2006: 21)
- knowledge review – which includes other forms of evidence as well as academic literature, such as 'grey' literature and documented testimonial evidence (Fleischmann 2009: 87–8).

The important thing is to choose, or design, the type of literature review that is right for your research project.

Canadian researchers Janice Du Mont and Deborah White conducted a worldwide literature review to try to identify factors hindering the successful use of standardised rape kits in cases of sexual assault. Rape kits are usually used by health professionals or specially trained legal personnel to gather evidence, and that evidence is then handed over to other legal officials to be passed on to scientists for analysis. Therefore this needed to be a cross-disciplinary literature review. Du Mont and White searched academic sources of documents from the disciplines of psychology, sociology, medicine and law. They also searched for 'grey literature', that is, research reports and other documents that are not formally published and may be difficult to access. To find this grey literature, they searched the websites of international organisations, national governments, non-governmental organisations and research centres. Also, in 16 countries around the world they 'consulted academics, policy makers, and service providers with expertise in the area for leads on published and unpublished materials', some of whom went on to contact colleagues in a further nine countries (Du Mont and White 2013: 1230). And, as a third line of enquiry, they posted requests for

> information on two relevant online mailing lists. This creative search strategy yielded over 400 documents for analysis.

Creative reading for research will be careful, interpretive and supported by note taking. It also involves a fair amount of creative thinking. **Advice on creative reading** from some great writers can be accessed online. When you read a book chapter, journal article or other relevant text, to read creatively, you need to:

- read carefully to understand and digest the meaning of the piece
- evaluate the argument(s) put forward
- think about how the points made link with, or oppose, the arguments of other writers.

It may help you to:

- write a summary in your own words after you've read the piece
- note down your thoughts about the argument(s) being put forward, and about how those arguments relate to the arguments of others
- create a concept map, that is, a visual way of displaying major concepts from the literature and the connections between them.

Concept mapping is a structured way of diagramming complex data to show the relationships between ideas in a way that is easy to understand (Windsor 2013: 276). It was invented by Joseph Novak in the 1970s and can be used by researchers working alone, in teams or with participants. Concept maps are usually made up of concepts plotted hierarchically, for example from general to specific, with connections between concepts shown by lines or arrows (Dias 2010: 29). A few words can be written on each line or arrow to clarify the relationship. Concept maps are often used in education because mapping the same topic at different times is a good way of showing changes in understanding (Hay and Kinchin 2008: 171).

> Reinildes Dias, from Brazil, conducted participatory action research with Brazilian undergraduates who were learning how to read more effectively in English. Students used open source Cmap software to create concept maps. The use of software enables the concept map to include images, audio and video files, animations and so on, as well as hyperlinks to web pages. Dias found that the use of concept maps helped students to comprehend texts more fully and read more thoroughly. In particular, Dias observed that 'creating a visual representation of a text can enable students to follow how authors organize and bring together their arguments around a specific topic in the texts they write' (Dias 2010: 32). Also, concept maps can be shared, which enables discussion and collaboration.

Figure 4.1: A simple concept map

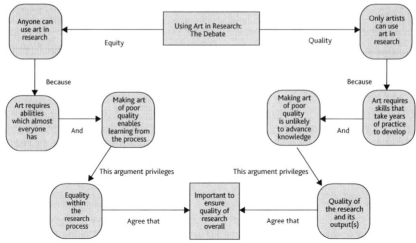

Figure 4.1 is an example of a simple concept map for my interpretation of the debate about using art in research, which was covered in Chapter Two.

Concept maps are also useful in thinking about research and can be used to map whole projects or aspects of a project, such as analytic themes and ideas. More information about the use of diagrams in research can be found in Chapter Eight. Another option for reading creatively is what Ellingson calls 'reading subversively' (Ellingson 2009: 58). This involves identifying as much as possible about influences on the text itself and on your reading of that text. To do this, as you read, ask yourself questions such as:

- When was this written? How might that time have affected it? How might the time in which I am reading affect my understanding?
- What was the context for this work? How might that have affected it? How might the context in which I am reading affect my understanding?
- What discipline(s) and/or profession(s) do the author(s) come from? How might that affect their work? What impact does my own disciplinary and/or professional identity have on my reading?
- Which institution(s) do the author(s) belong to? How might that affect their work? What impact does my own institutional affiliation have on my reading?
- Who funded the work? How might that have affected the way in which it is written? Does my own funding, or lack of funding, affect the way I'm reading?
- Who and what has been left out of this writing? Who and what has been given centre stage? Why?
- What is being claimed as 'truth' in this writing, who is making that claim and what political or ideological agenda does that serve? (Ellingson 2009: 58; Gergen and Gergen 2012: 38)

This approach to reading can lead to a deeper understanding of research, rather than simply taking it at face value.

Using theory creatively in research

The role of theory in research is something that novice researchers, and even at times the more experienced, can struggle to understand (Roulston 2010: 203). A theoretical perspective, drawn from available literature, acts as a lens through which you can focus your investigation; a theoretical framework can function as a navigational aid to help you steer a course from research questions to findings and dissemination (Evans, Coon and Ume 2011: 289). Theory can help you to think through most stages of the research process, particularly designing and planning a study, and gathering, analysing and interpreting data (Evans, Coon and Ume 2011: 276). 'Tightly tying all phases of the research process to a theoretical framework automatically provides a theory-based result, increases credibility, and fosters transferability to practice settings' (Evans, Coon and Ume 2011: 289). It has been argued that the use of theory within research is 'ethically necessary' (Childers 2012: 752). However, it is essential to use a theoretical framework that fits with the study, because otherwise the framework may distort your data and findings (Evans, Coon and Ume 2011: 289). A **video presentation** by UK-based researcher John Schulz about the role of theory in research can be viewed online.

Traditional research usually drew on one theory per project, and rarely strayed beyond disciplinary boundaries in search of theoretical inspiration. However, creative researchers today are combining theories from a range of disciplines to help them think about complex human situations. There are a 'myriad of useful theories' in subjects including sociology, anthropology, psychology, geography and economics (Kaufman 2010: 153). Integrating two or more theories in a single research project can enhance data analysis and increase the scope for dissemination (Kaufman 2010: 163). Combining concepts in this way has been shown to enhance creative problem solving (Kohn, Paulus and Korde 2011: 203).

Arts-based researchers may be resistant to theory, fearing that it could constrain their spontaneity and therefore reduce the value of their work (Smith and Dean 2009: 25). However, artists are well able to 'explore and explain complex theoretical issues' that can be significant across disciplinary boundaries (Sullivan 2009: 42). It is also true that theory is dynamic rather than static and, whether personal or widely held, is open to exploration and change (Tenebaum et al 2009: 118; Corvellec 2013: 23). This suggests that creative research can contribute to the building and development of theory as much as theory contributes to research: it is the combination of the two that is most valuable (Smith and Dean 2009: 25).

As we saw in Chapter Two, there is also a growing understanding that arts practice can help with the thinking process (Brearley and Hamm 2009: 40). This works both ways: theorists can learn from arts practice as much as arts practitioners can learn from theory. For example, American psychologist Ken Gergen has collaborated with several artists working with painting, drawing, etching and photography. Gergen drew on the artistic ideas of his collaborators to explore and develop theory, particularly relational theory and constructionism (Gergen and Gergen 2012: 167–85). He also practised sculpture as a way of developing relational theory (Gergen and Gergen 2012: 193–6). A **lecture** by Elliot Eisner, entitled 'What do the arts teach?', can be viewed online.

You will have your own theoretical perspectives and understandings, developed from your unique experience of the world. Many philosophers today hold the view that our individual experiences influence the way we perceive and comprehend the world around us, so that there can be no knowledge without a theoretical perspective (Smith 2009: 94). However, in order to use your own theoretical perspectives creatively as a researcher, you will need to identify and understand them and, as far as possible, to be able to analyse their influence on your perceptions and thoughts. Working reflexively offers a creative way to approach this, and is discussed in more detail later in this chapter.

It is arguable that every decision in a research project should be taken in accordance with that project's theoretical context, for the sake of consistency (Mason 2002: 178–9). However, in reality, some decisions will be taken for more pragmatic reasons, such as resource constraints. This is understandable, but, even when it is necessary, it is important to think through why each decision is being taken. Even in apparently mechanistic processes such as the transcription of data, there are a lot of decisions to be made, such as about whether – and, if so, how – to represent non-speech utterances or silences (see Chapter Six for more on this). A researcher who adheres to participatory and constructionist theories, that is, who considers that data is constructed by participants and researchers together, is likely to make different choices for transcription from a researcher with a more essentialist viewpoint, that is, that participants provide data for processing and analysis by researchers (Hammersley 2010: 553). As researchers, our decisions will be guided by our emotions and the beliefs we hold, unless we do the hard, but important, cognitive and emotional work to ensure that all our decisions are in accordance with the theoretical framework we have chosen for our research.

For example, some people may respond to this book by rejecting it without giving it full consideration because they believe that traditional styles of research are all we need, and so deem creative research methods to be irrelevant. Others may become so enthusiastic about novel methods that they forget one of the most basic principles of research: the method must flow from the research question. It can be hard to remember that the important thing is to use the methods that are most applicable for your research project, whether those methods are traditional, creative or a combination of the two.

Creativity and cross-disciplinary work

Tapping into literature from other disciplines can help you think more creatively about your own research, because researchers from different disciplines often have different ideas about what is important. For example, researchers from different disciplines will have different notions as to how the context for a research project might be theorised. Some writers on social research methods see place as neutral, irrelevant or to be anonymised (Anderson, Adey and Bevan 2010: 590). By contrast, geographers see place as a highly relevant part of the context for research. What's more, geographers view place as multi-dimensional, including, for example, both geographical and social location (Cresswell 1996, cited in Anderson, Adey and Bevan 2010: 591–2). Context may include a range of other elements, such as context in time, political context, theoretical context, regulatory and/or legal context, socioeconomic context, physical and/or material context and cultural context. It is easy to see how, in the same way that a geographer might privilege place within the context for research, a criminologist might privilege its regulatory/legal context, a health researcher might privilege its physical and socioeconomic contexts and so on. But for truly creative theorising, cross-disciplinary exploration can help you to consider all the possible elements of context and to ask: which elements are significant for my research? Which should I consider in more detail as I progress with my project?

At the time of writing, Google Scholar is a particularly useful tool for this kind of creative exploration. Generic search engines can also be helpful, particularly if you are interested in 'grey' as well as academic literatures. If you enter a general term such as 'research context' or 'context for research', you are likely to find publications from a range of disciplines. The British Library curates 'grey' electronic literature from the UK on social policy, social welfare and associated topics and makes it freely available through its **Social Welfare Portal**. Other countries may have generated equivalent websites. Don't restrict your reading to texts from your own discipline or closely related disciplines; work from other disciplines can open up new possibilities for your own work.

Danish researcher Svend Brinkmann used the novels of Michel Houellebecq as data. Houellebecq plays with the boundaries between fiction and non-fiction, particularly autobiography; he often gives leading characters one of his names and a similar appearance to his own, and includes some narrative details that are similar to those from his own life. He also plays with the boundaries between literary and scientific writing, making many references to the theory and practice of social science and conducting fictional experiments through his writing. For Brinkmann, 'Houellebecq's writings contain precise sociological descriptions of central aspects of human life in postmodern consumer society. In this sense, we can read his works as ... sociology' (Brinkmann 2009: 1386). Brinkmann's argument is that some literary works, at least, can be usefully included 'in the great social and human science conversation that is currently going on' (Brinkmann 2009: 1392).

Collaboration with people from different disciplines can also be useful in bringing extra creativity to your research. For example, in their study of methamphetamine addiction in the United States, Sameshima and Vandermause brought together a research team including specialists in education, nursing, photography, theatre, music and creative writing, as well as a participant who had experience of methamphetamine addiction (Sameshima and Vandermause 2009: 283). Each of these researchers brought individual expertise that, when combined with the expertise of others, enabled the development of 'new, greater, and deeper understandings', and the revealing of 'complex patterns ... which are not evident when researched separately' (Sameshima and Vandermause 2009: 278).

This kind of approach has been called 'crystallization' by American researcher Laura Ellingson. The concept of crystallisation was originally applied to research by the American sociologist Laurel Richardson, and Ellingson developed Richardson's concept into a methodological framework (Ellingson 2009: 4). Crystallisation involves multiple ways of analysing and presenting data. This includes at least one fairly standard form of analysis, such as thematic or narrative analysis, alongside at least one arts–based analytic technique (see Chapter Six for more on data analysis). It also includes more than one type of writing – poetry, report and so on – and/ or other presentation medium such as painting or video (Ellingson 2009: 10) (see Chapter Seven for more on writing and Chapter Eight for more on research presentation). The researcher will take a deeply reflexive approach (see below for a fuller discussion of reflexivity) and will embrace 'knowledge as situated, partial, constructed, multiple, embodied, and enmeshed in power relations' (Ellingson 2009: 10). Crystallisation provides a range of perspectives that offer a rich and complex analytic description that highlights subtleties in areas such as emotion, relationships and power that may remain obscure if fewer methods are used (Ellingson 2009: 11). However, crystallisation can be time consuming, challenging and frustrating, and may sacrifice breadth for depth (Ellingson 2009: 17–18). But even if you don't want to adopt it as a methodological framework, the ideas offered by crystallisation are useful for researchers to consider as they think through the process and presentation of their work (Ellingson 2009: 24).

Imagination

The imagination has been described as a 'primary tool' for research (Rapport, N 2004: 102). Imagination enables a researcher to examine the world in different ways and from different perspectives (Lapum et al 2012: 103). It certainly seems, from the history of research outlined in Chapter Two, that research would not exist without imagination. And this is not a new or recent idea. Charles Wright Mills, writing in the middle of the 20th century, was confident that imagination was a central plank of the craft of social science research (Wright Mills 1959) and he would not have been the first to hold such a view. Indeed, every idea for a research project must contain an element of imagination. The researcher has to be able to imagine what a research project might be able to achieve and how that might be done, and then work to make that happen. Within that process, specific types or sub-sets of imagination are needed, such as moral imagination for managing ethical dilemmas (Kiragu and Warrington 2013: 173) and analytic imagination for interpreting data (James 2012: 562). A **talk** on creativity and imagination by US creativity expert Gregg Fraley can be viewed online

> UK researcher Allison James (2012) suggests that imagination might be particularly useful when analysing secondary qualitative data. A researcher who gathers primary qualitative data forms a relationship with participants as they create meaning together, which inevitably will influence the researcher's analytic approach. A secondary analyst has a relationship only with words on a page. This is not 'better' or 'worse'; it is more freeing in some ways, more limiting in others. The secondary analyst has no memory of body language, facial expression, physical attributes, setting and so on to enrich her understanding of the data. But she comes to that data with fresh eyes, influenced only by her existing knowledge and worldview, which she can use, imaginatively, to help her build a picture of the participants, reflect on their situations and consider why they say the things they say. This approach may lead her to find some different meanings in the data from those found by the primary analyst, which can enrich the overall findings.

Using your imagination within the research context is a creative process (James 2012: 569). Yet 'imagination' appears very rarely in the indexes of books about how to conduct research.

> UK researcher Rob Macmillan applied imagination to theory within a qualitative longitudinal study of third sector organisations, with the aim of coming to understand how those organisations' activities operate, in practice, over time. Macmillan outlines and discusses three 'theoretical imaginings' which informed the research. These focus on time, space and action. The way time operates in third sector organisations was conceptualised in terms of ideas such as duration, sequences, cycles and speed, and considered in terms of 'objective' elements such as calendars, clocks and deadlines, as well as 'subjective' experiences of, or affected by, time, such as waiting and busyness. Space was conceptualised in terms of ideas such as: distance or closeness between partners; an organisation's position in its field – and, in particular, whether it is central or peripheral; the connections it has with others; and how the positions of organisations come to improve or deteriorate. Action was conceptualised in terms of 'agency', that is, who or what can act, and 'structure', that is, the context for that action. Each of these 'theoretical imaginings', used alone, could close down more avenues of exploration than it opens. Of course there are many other 'theoretical imaginings'

> that could be used – but using these three together as 'creative devices for raising questions and possibilities' helped the researchers to 'make sense of what we ... encounter empirically, rather than close down analysis' (Macmillan 2011: 28–9).

One way to use your imagination is to read creative writing such as poetry and fiction. Research suggests that this can lead to a better understanding of the social world (Djikic et al 2009: 28). As we will see in Chapter Seven, researchers are increasingly writing up their work using poems, stories, play scripts, screenplays and other creative techniques. These kinds of writing can produce fuller understanding of some aspects of a research project than traditional reporting methods. In particular, creatively written research enables more understanding of the emotional aspects of research than reports of research in traditional, non-fiction style (Kara 2013: 70).

Assessing research quality

It is important to think about, and be able to discuss, the quality of the research you are reading, using and conducting (Hammersley 2009: 26). Markers of quality in quantitative research are generally held to be reliability, replicability and validity (Bryman 2012: 46–7). Reliability refers to the stability of measures. A well-made ruler is very reliable: it will measure a perfect centimetre every time. A scale for measuring a human attribute or experience may be less reliable, and needs to be tested thoroughly before its reliability can be confirmed. Replicability is a form of reliability, and means that if an experiment is repeated – perhaps in a different place, or with different participants – the results will be the same. Validity asks whether the research findings are really what they appear to be. There are several kinds of validity, including:

- internal validity – whether there is a demonstrable relationship between cause and effect within the research context
- external validity – the extent to which the results of a study can be generalised beyond the research context
- measurement validity, also known as construct validity – whether a scale, test and so on really measures what it sets out to measure
- ecological validity – the extent to which research findings have relevance to real life.

Even the most creative quantitative researchers are likely to assess their work against these markers of quality. In qualitative research, however, the situation is different. Qualitative researchers began by using these quality markers, but soon realised that they needed different criteria. In the mid-1980s, Lincoln and Guba (1985, cited in Bryman 2012: 49) developed quality criteria for qualitative research. These were:

- confirmability, or the extent to which the researcher has allowed his or her own values to influence the research (akin to the overarching quantitative researcher's value of objectivity)
- dependability, or the extent to which the findings could apply at other times (akin to reliability)
- credibility, or how believable the findings were (akin to internal validity)
- transferability, or the extent to which the findings could apply to other contexts (akin to external validity).

Over the last 30 years, the debate about quality in qualitative research methods has continued, and new criteria have been suggested. Some academics have resisted the use of quality criteria, seeing them as too regulatory and inflexible for a developing field such as qualitative research methods, but others find them useful (Tracy 2010: 838).

American researcher Sarah Tracy, in a much-cited paper, suggests that quality criteria can help us to learn the principles and practice of our research craft (Tracy 2010: 838). Tracy analysed and considered the debates on quality in the research literature and proposes eight quality criteria for qualitative research, designed to be comprehensible, flexible, universal and supportive of dialogue and learning (Tracy 2010: 839). According to Tracy, good-quality qualitative research would be:

- on a worthy topic – relevant, timely, significant, interesting
- richly rigorous – suitable theoretical basis, appropriate methods, enough data
- sincere – good use of reflexivity and transparency
- credible – enough detail and explanation, inclusion of different perspectives, trustworthy findings
- resonant – aesthetic evocative presentation that has an impact on its audience(s), transferable findings
- significant – making a contribution on a range of levels, such as: theoretical, practical, ethical, methodological
- ethical – taking a holistic approach to research ethics
- coherent – doing what it claims, using suitable methods, making meaningful connections between literature, research topics, findings and interpretations. (Tracy 2010: 840)

Tracy suggests that adopting these criteria could have several benefits for researchers, including:

- provision of a common language for excellence
- promotion of dialogue among qualitative researchers from different disciplines
- a useful pedagogical compass
- support for dialogue with people in positions of power (Tracy 2010: 849).

Tracy points out that the criteria she suggests are not rules to be followed slavishly. In real research contexts, they may at times conflict. For example, full transparency might compromise participant anonymity, or a researcher may have to choose between making a theoretical or a practical contribution due to time or budget constraints. In such situations, Tracy's view is that researchers' primary obligation is to be truthful, both with themselves and with their audiences (Tracy 2010: 849).

So, given that quality markers for qualitative research have moved some distance from those used in quantitative research, where does that leave mixed-methods research? Of course, many of the quality markers will be the same for mixed-methods research as for any other research: ethically conducted, with sufficient data, transparently presented and so on. But there are some issues of quality that are specific to mixed-methods research. In the same year that Sarah Tracy's paper was published, the Office of Behavioral and Social Sciences Research of the National Institutes of Health in the US commissioned some work to begin defining quality in mixed-methods research (Klassen et al 2012: 378). The resulting guidelines suggest that good quality mixed-methods research will, among other things:

- be used when a quantitative or qualitative method, alone, cannot sufficiently address the research question
- intentionally combine or integrate qualitative and quantitative methods so as to maximise their strengths and minimise their weaknesses
- be underpinned by one or more theories
- be clear about where 'mixing' occurs – whether in data gathering, analysis, interpretation or elsewhere
- have sufficient allocation of time and resources to manage all the methodological and logistical issues that arise when multiple forms of data are gathered and analysed by a team of people from different disciplinary backgrounds
- be explained succinctly and clearly for funders, participants, readers and so on (Klassen et al 2012: 378–80).

 The **full guidelines** can be accessed online.

There have also been attempts to establish criteria for arts-based research. Canadian researchers Darquise Lafrenière and Susan Cox put forward four criteria for arts-based research methods (Lafrenière and Cox 2013: 325).

1. Appropriateness – is an arts-based method an appropriate way to address the research question?
2. Clarity – is it clear how the arts-based method has been used, and how it helps the research?
3. Reliability – are the researcher's interpretations verifiably rooted in the data?

4. Rigour – how effective and trustworthy were the data gathering and analysis processes? To what extent has the research question been answered?

Lafrenière and Cox also put forward six ethical criteria, covering access to data, anonymity, assessment (of arts-based works), authorship, potential harms and benefits to participants and creators of artistic work, and integrity (Lafrenière and Cox 2013: 329).

None of these criteria is presented in this book as final or definitive; there are other ways to think about research quality, and little or no consistency in researchers' approach to doing so (Roulston 2010: 201). Yet every researcher needs to be able to make sound judgements about the quality of research (Hammersley 2009: 15). The above criteria are included here for two reasons. First, they can be applied with some flexibility, which makes them more useful in assessing the quality of creative research than rigid criteria or standards (O'Reilly and Parker 2013: 195). Second, they have been produced by people who have studied and thought a lot about research quality, so they may help you in thinking about how to assess the quality of the research you read, use and conduct. The way you decide to think about and assess research quality will also, of course, be influenced by your own theoretical perspective (Roulston 2010: 224).

Some researchers assert that there can be no stand-alone quality criteria, because the quality of a piece of research will always depend on contextual factors such as when and where the research is conducted (for example, Smith 2009: 92). Yet 'the whole point of research is to make ... claims that apply across time and place' (Smith 2009: 98). One creative way to manage this paradox is through the application of reflexivity.

Reflexivity

Reflexivity locates you within your research (Mason 2002: 149). This stands in opposition to the traditional view of research as an activity in which the researcher is a neutral presence who simply manipulates variables, with no involvement or disclosure of any personal quality such as emotion (Jewkes 2012: 64). Yet all researchers have feelings connected with their research work, such as pride, anxiety, curiosity, fear and compassion (Jewkes 2012: 64). Perhaps the most fully reflexive type of research is autoethnography (Leavy 2009: 259–60), where reflexivity can be 'the primary vehicle for inquiry' (Broussine 2008: 36). Autoethnography is discussed in more detail in Chapter Two.

Reflexivity has been described as 'the me-search within re-search' (Pam Burnard, personal communication, 6 September 2014) and as 'critical self-awareness' (Broussine 2008: 36). The word 'reflexive' itself is a 'slippery concept' (Bryman 2012: 394) that has more than one meaning in research. It also has more than one meaning in language. In grammar, it refers to a sentence where subject and object are identical, as in 'I feed myself' or 'I wash myself' – or, of course, 'I research myself'. Used descriptively, it means 'able to reflect'. The grammatical meaning relates to the more autoethnographic approach to research, while the descriptive meaning is relevant to research more widely.

Reflexivity in social research is closely related to reflective practice in social care and health. This involves practitioners taking a step back to think about what they know about their work, and how they know that (Taylor and White 2000: 201), with 'a critical, learning perspective' (Barnes and Cotterell 2012a: 231). Researchers know things by drawing not only on their cognitive resources but also on their emotional (Jewkes 2012: 71) and sensory resources (Hurdley and Dicks 2011: 277), which are central planks of reflexivity. Reflexivity is also increasingly used by creative arts practitioners, for whom it 'validates their intuitive instincts within a framework of reflective enquiry' (Candy 2011: 44).

Methodological reflexivity in research requires the researcher to consider many interrelated questions, such as:

- How do I define my identity? How does that affect my research practice?
- What are my values and beliefs, and how are they operating in my research work?
- Which of my biases and assumptions are relevant here, and how are they affecting my research?
- What impact do my emotional responses have on my research?
- How does the time at which I am working affect my research?
- What effect has this research had on my relationships with others? What effect, in turn, has this had on the research? What about relationships between other relevant people?
- Which institutions are involved in my research? What effect have they had on the research? What effect has the research had on them?
- What are the political aspects of my research? How do they play out in practice?
- Where are the relevant power balances and imbalances? Are they changing during the research process? If so, in what way? What effect do they have on my research?
- How do these considerations affect the choices I make in my research?
- How can I use these considerations to inform, enrich and develop my research?
- Am I being as honest and transparent as possible about all these factors in presenting my research?

This is not intended as an exhaustive list, but as a starting point for creative reflexive research practice. Reflexivity in research is, in theory, something that can – some would say 'should' – permeate the whole research process. In practice, for that to happen, a researcher would need to stop and consider many questions at every stage of the research, which is clearly impractical. So another key question is when to focus on reflexivity. Some researchers keep a regular reflexive journal (see Chapter Five for more on journals), which is excellent practice. Others attend to reflexivity at more irregular intervals. If, like me, you tend toward being one of this latter group, I recommend that you make a 'reflexivity plan' for each research project and decide in advance when to focus on reflexive questions and how to record your findings (Candy 2011: 44).

Working reflexively can be beneficial for any research, as it adds new dimensions to the knowledge being gathered. It is most important to practice reflexively in research that has extra layers of complexity. This includes insider research (Smith 2012: 138), interdisciplinary research such as arts-based research (Haseman and Mafe 2009: 218–20) and research within transformative frameworks. Complexity and creativity are intimately linked (Burraston 2011: 117). Traditional research methods are 'designed to manage and contain complexity by seeking to control, limit and even deny ambiguity' (Haseman and Mafe 2009: 220). Conversely, creative reflexive research practice acknowledges and respects complexity. As a result, practising reflexively can be an uncomfortable, anxiety-provoking experience, requiring a high level of tolerance for uncertainty (Haseman and Mafe 2009: 220).

Atsushi Takeda is a researcher working in Australia, studying international marriage through the experiences of Japanese women married to Australian men. More Japanese women marry Australian men than vice versa, perhaps in part because of their cultural stereotypes, which label Australian men as sensitive and gentlemanly, while Japanese men are seen as chauvinistic (Takeda 2013: 294). Takeda reflects on the effects on his research of gender, ethnicity and marital status and of his own theoretical and cultural location, representing as it does the negative stereotypes held by his female Japanese participants of 'a chauvinist Asian man as opposed to the theoretically sensitive western man' (Takeda 2012: 294). Takeda is both insider and outsider. He is an insider as a Japanese person in Australia, fluent in both languages, who 'shared an ethnic and national identity' with his participants that 'perhaps enabled them to recount anecdotes about their experiences in relation to cultural and national differences' (Takeda 2012: 292). However, Takeda notes the importance of acknowledging that 'such similarities may block access to some information, since assumed understanding of a situation might mean that further commentary is deemed unnecessary' (Takeda 2012: 292). He is an outsider as an unmarried man 'whose life experience and gender meant that I could never entirely comprehend the women's experience of powerlessness or the horizons delimited by Japanese and western gender expectations' (Takeda 2012: 293). However, again, Takeda recognises that the outsider aspects of his identity and status offer opportunities that might not be available to a complete insider, such as a perspective involving the 'cultural and gendered ideologies' (Takeda 2012: 291) which inform the behaviour of women in international marriages. Takeda's reflexive work enables him to conclude that there is no clear dichotomy between the concepts of 'insider' and 'outsider', and that treating the concepts in this way 'overlooks interactive complexities in fieldwork that enrich the research relationships' (Takeda 2012: 293). 'Similarities and differences between researcher and research participants interact in my fieldwork in a way that creates a fluid state between insiderness and outsiderness' (Takeda 2012: 293). This reflexive approach demonstrates the high level of ambiguity within Takeda's research.

From the above discussion, it may seem that creative reflexive practice is relevant only to qualitative, and perhaps mixed-method, research. However, a few people are beginning to argue that this approach is also relevant to at least some areas of quantitative research.

Charles Shimp is a behaviour-analysis researcher from America. Behaviour analysis is a sub-discipline of psychology that developed from statistical learning theory in the mid-20th century and aims to produce analyses of human behaviour using traditional scientific methods. Shimp is attracted by 'radical behaviourism', which 'asserts that if we are to understand science, the behaviour of scientists has to be part of the subject matter of a science of behaviour' (Shimp 2007: 146). He says that, in his experience, quantitative research has 'involved implicit and unevaluated assumptions, incomplete descriptions of empirical and theoretical methods, self-interest and conflicts of interest, strongly held opinion accepted as fact, and political conflicts and angry disputes' (Shimp 2007: 146). As there has been no scientific analysis of the behaviour of behaviour analysts, Shimp concludes that, by their self-defined standards, behaviour analysts don't understand their own behaviour in studying the behaviour of others. He believes that this omission is due to the influence of traditional scientific methods and that rectifying it would help us to understand the similarities and differences between the behaviours of scientists and the wider population. For example, Shimp asserts that human values are irrevocably embedded within quantitative research, and its comprehension requires the understanding of the effects of those values on that research. He also argues that different forms of reflexivity may be relevant for other sub-disciplines of psychology, such as cultural reflexivity for cognitive psychology: 'There is no reflexive analysis of contemporary experimental cognitive psychology ... There are many studies showing how cognition differs across cultures, but cognitive psychologists generally appear to believe they can rise above these differences and avoid the potential implication that their own cognition, and therefore the science they construct, is itself culture dependent' (Shimp 2007: 152). For these and other, similar reasons, Shimp argues that the development of a reflexive quantitative behaviour analysis should be a high priority within the sub-discipline of behaviour analysis. '[F]rom the perspective of radical behaviourism, a reflexive analysis is not a luxury, it is a requirement: the behaviour of behavioural scientists, like the behaviour of everybody else, should be part of a science of behaviour' (Shimp 2007: 154).

Shimp's paper is creatively argued and convincing – at least, to this author. It may not be so convincing to his quantitative research colleagues: according to Google Scholar, in the seven years between its publication and the writing of this book, his paper was cited only three times. Yet perhaps, in years to come, quantitative researchers will begin to take up the challenge of creative reflexive practice, and so add new dimensions to the knowledge they generate.

CONCLUSION

Research is evidently a creative activity that requires creative thinking. Thinking creatively can help you to use literature and theory creatively, work across disciplinary boundaries, effectively assess the quality of others' research, use reflexive and ethical practice and make imaginative research. Yet, with the competing demands, deadlines and other pressures of everyday life, combined with the low social value placed on the apparently inactive process of thinking, time for creative thinking can be at a premium. It may be necessary to think creatively about how to think creatively.

FIVE

Gathering data

Introduction

The title of this chapter is something of a fence-sitting exercise. Traditional researchers speak of 'data collection'. Another term is 'data construction', which refers to the generation of data as a creative act, such as through writing a diary, taking part in an interview or working as a group to make a collage focused on a research topic. Which term you use depends on your standpoint. As this book is intended for people conducting research from a range of standpoints, I have chosen 'gathering' as a reasonably neutral term.

Traditional data collection involved research participants in effect being viewed as repositories of data that could be transferred to researchers – who themselves possessed no data until it was supplied by participants. Autoethnographers sit at the other end of the spectrum, gathering data primarily from themselves: their own memories, senses, emotions, thoughts, relationships, artefacts and documents. Many researchers occupy a loose middle ground, with varying levels of importance being placed on reflexivity, where the researcher's actions and reactions are examined as part of the investigation.

Ethics in data gathering

Gathering primary data is the most heavily scrutinised area of research ethics. As you begin to gather data, you have a direct responsibility to gatekeepers and participants, and an indirect responsibility to anyone else who has a stake in your research. Your responsibility is to ensure that your research does not cause harm to any of those people. It is always necessary to remember that while research is understandably important to researchers, for gatekeepers and participants it is just one of a myriad of competing priorities (Weller 2012: 123).

It is possible to be creative about the process of obtaining informed consent. In fact, sometimes it's essential.

> UK researchers Sue Adamson and Margaret Holloway conducted a study of spirituality in 46 UK funerals. There are considerable ethical difficulties in making research with newly bereaved people at such a sensitive and emotional time in their lives. Death and spirituality are often regarded as taboo subjects, and it was more difficult to get consent from funeral directors to support the research than to get consent from families to participate. The funeral directors who did support the research, perhaps as a result of their own ethical practice, did not present the

research as an option to most families suffering extra distress, such as through the death of a child or a violent death. While from a purely research point of view that could be seen as a limitation, from an ethical viewpoint it seems entirely defensible. The intense grief of a recently bereaved person may make it difficult for them to take in new information, which can reduce their capacity to give informed consent to participate in research. Adamson and Holloway counteracted this by using a staged and flexible process for consent (Adamson and Holloway 2012: 741). The funeral director usually made the first approach to the family, and then each stage was negotiated separately, with families able to consent to some stages but not others if they wished. For example, they could agree to taking part in interviews but not to the researchers observing the funeral. Families were also able to withdraw from the research at any point.

A UK **newspaper article** about the above research is available online.

Andrew Robinson and his colleagues, in Australia, studied people with dementia and their carers, with the aim of investigating the cognitive and functional abilities of people with dementia, the stress and well-being levels of their family carers and their experiences of dementia services. The researchers chose a mixed-methods approach, with quantitative and qualitative data being gathered in nine different ways over 12 weeks (see below for more details). They regarded the gaining of informed consent as a process rather than an event, offering discussion and explanations to participants over a period of several weeks where necessary. Telephone calls were made at participants' preferred times; face-to-face and telephone support was offered for participants' diary-keeping; and the number of researchers entering participants' homes was limited. Robinson et al refer to their approach as 'progressive engagement', which was intended to improve the quality of the data gathered, and also built strong relationships between researchers and participants (Robinson et al 2011: 331). The retention rate of participants was 100%, which is unusual for a study of this length, and participants said they enjoyed their involvement.

Of course, consent is not the only ethical issue in the data-gathering phase. It is essential to treat gatekeepers and participants with care, respect and courtesy throughout, and to look after your own well-being as a researcher. Also, because of the burden on gatekeepers and participants in assisting with primary data gathering, there is an argument that it is more ethical to use secondary data where possible. See Chapter Three for more information on these issues.

Reflexive data

Some researchers use their own sensory and emotional experiences as data. This is known as 'reflexive research' and includes a range of overlapping methods such as embodied research and autoethnography (see Chapter Two for more on autoethnography). Embodied methodologies can be used to study 'corporeal experience' such as body modification (piercing, branding, tattooing and so on) or self-harm (Inckle 2010), or to study emotional experience such as grief (Sliep 2012).

South African researcher Yvonne Sliep wrote through the first years of her grief for her son Thomas, who died suddenly in early adulthood. Sliep used the poems and prose she wrote in the first four years after Thomas's death as data for autoethnographic research. In accordance with good practice, she revisited her writings a number of times, which sometimes prompted amendments or new writings. Although she is an experienced poet, her creative writing had never been part of her professional life as a psychology researcher in applied human sciences. The autoethnographic process was challenging: 'I never thought that I would invite the professional to scrutinise the personal' (Sliep 2012:64). Yet she found that it offered 'unexpected gifts of insight' into grief and loss, above and beyond her own personal experience (Sliep 2012:65).

Staff from the Robert Wood Johnson Medical School in America have produced a useful **web page on reflexive research**.

Writing

Creative writing outputs, such as novels or poems, can be collected or created for use as data by social researchers (Watson 2011:398). There is an interesting contrast between the research aims of producing generalisations within a neatly wrapped-up narrative and the artistic aims of depicting and maintaining 'complexity, ambiguity and openness' (Watson 2011:399). This tension is, of course, present in all arts-based research, but is perhaps most apparent when creative writing is used as data in research that itself must be written up.

Some researchers are also skilled artists or writers, and bring those skills to bear on their research. For example, poets can engage themselves and others in 'poetic inquiry', often used to investigate slippery and complex topics such as identity (Guiney Yallop et al 2010) or emotion (Stewart 2012).

John Guiney Yallop is a Canadian researcher and poet who led a research project with three graduate students investigating identity using the method of poetic inquiry. They met for four sessions, each requiring preparatory reading and each with a focus on discussion and writing. The topic of the first session was 'Who am I?'; of the second, relationships; of the third, 'longing'; and of the fourth, 'possibilities'. For the fourth session, they were joined by Lorri Neilsen Glenn, at that time Poet Laureate for Halifax Regional Municipality. The participants wrote during and between the sessions, and they performed their writing at a public reading for the community of Acadia University in Nova Scotia. This research was evidently useful for the participants. 'Our writing was therapeutic; we make no apologies for research that is healing. We celebrate research that gives something to participants' (Guiney Yallop et al 2010: 28). Also, as the research was disseminated through a public performance and subsequent academic publication, it is potentially of wider use (see Chapter Nine for more on dissemination).

 A **TEDx talk** by Douglas Hoston Jr about poetic inquiry that examines culture can be viewed online.

Sheila Stewart is a Canadian educator and poet based in Toronto. She used poetic inquiry to investigate shame, through reflecting on her own poems and other work and writing. 'My poetry might be called a kind of "data" though that word sits uneasily with me ... I use poetry to inquire into the shifting space of memory because poetry works with fragments, images, the symbolic and unconscious – supporting transformative holistic learning and a knowing, embodied self' (Stewart 2012: 116–17). For Stewart, this enables work at 'the edge of knowing', because poetry has more chance of conveying complexity than does prose, and comes closer to expressing the inexpressible.

Other researchers use creative techniques to help their participants produce creative texts.

Gillian Fletcher is an English-born Australian resident who used metaphor elicitation to study the differences and similarities between rhetoric and practice in people's experience of HIV prevention work in Myanmar. She found that managers' rhetoric included concepts like 'mutual learning', 'participation' and 'two-way communication' (Fletcher 2013: 1553). She then undertook metaphor elicitation with field workers from HIV prevention projects. Metaphor elicitation began with a question asking participants to describe an aspect of their work, such as an HIV prevention session, using a metaphor of their choice. Once the participant's initial metaphor was established, Fletcher used the imagery therein to interrogate and to help the participant to expand their metaphor. Metaphors used were very varied, including traffic lights, making pots and a hen looking after baby ducklings, but all represented the giving of instruction and/or information as a way of caring for people (Fletcher 2013: 1556). This method showed a disjuncture between the rhetoric of equality and the practice experience of unequal power relationships between those with information and those who need that information. Fletcher concludes that metaphor elicitation could be used wherever there is a 'commonly held rhetoric' and a wish to discover whether or not that rhetoric aligns with practice (Fletcher 2013: 1560).

Metaphor elicitation is a technique taken from market research, where it was devised by Gerald Zaltman in the mid-1990s. A description of Zaltman's metaphor elicitation technique (ZMET) can be viewed online.

Diaries and journals

Researchers from several disciplines, from psychology to anthropology, have asked participants to record data in the form of individual diaries (Harvey 2011). These are known as 'solicited diaries', to set them apart from pre-existing or 'unsolicited' diaries, which are most commonly used by historians (Alaszewski 2006: 43). Solicited diaries can be used to record quantitative and/or qualitative data and can be used alone or to complement other methods of data gathering. They can also be tightly or loosely structured by the researcher to meet the needs of the project in hand. This method requires a good level of willingness and commitment from participants, but if that is in place, diaries can be a valuable resource for capturing all kinds of data, including quite personal, sensitive information (Kenten 2010).

> UK researcher Charlotte Kenten, building on the work of Zimmerman and Wieder (1977), combined diaries and interviews to investigate 'the everyday ways in which self-identified lesbians and gay men are made aware of their sexuality' (Kenten 2010:1). She asked participants to keep records, every day for two weeks, of when they became aware of their sexuality. These records were kept in a diary structured by the researcher, with one page of A4 per day, including several prompts for the participants. The researcher also conducted semi-structured interviews with participants at the start and end of the two weeks. The interviews added value by providing context for the diaries, reducing the likelihood of misunderstandings and offering greater depth of insight than the diaries would have done alone.

Researchers' own diaries, also known as field notes or field journals, can also be used as data (Friedemann, Mayorga and Jimenez 2010: 462).

> American researcher Judith Davidson made an autoethnographic study of her post-tenure period using her own diaries, a few years after they were written. She had not written her diaries with the intention of making them public or of re-using them in any way. This meant that they documented her authentic experiences, responses and emotions. There were 303 diary entries from a 21-month period, which took her three years to transcribe, code, analyse and write into research. As Davidson was studying herself, albeit from a short distance of a few years in time, she found that 'Notions of subjectivity and objectivity were convoluted, intertwined, and downright hard to disentangle' (Davidson 2011: 88). She made artworks to help with this process and ultimately exhibited them at an academic conference (see Chapter Eight for more details).

A **journal article** on the use of diaries and field notes in research can be accessed online. If permission is granted, the personal diaries of others can also offer valuable data for social research.

Diaries are helpful in circumventing a classic form of bias in research: inaccurate recall (Alaszewski 2006: 26). A related development of the diary method is experience sampling, in which participants are asked to report their experience through a short questionnaire at scheduled intervals. This was originally done with paper diaries, but is now more commonly done with digital devices such as tablets or mobile phones (Burgin et al 2012).

UK researchers George MacKerron and Susana Mourato studied the relationship between the well-being of UK residents and their immediate environment. They developed an app called Mappiness for the Apple iPhone, which was free to download and would prompt participants, at random moments, to answer a brief questionnaire about their well-being and their immediate circumstances, such as who they were with and what they were doing. Participants could choose the start and finish hours each day, and the frequency of prompts – the default was two prompts a day between 8am and 10pm. Over one million responses were gathered from almost 22,000 participants. GPS satellites were able to find the exact location for each respondent and to define it using geographical coordinates. The researchers used secondary data and existing categories to identify the habitat type of participants' locations and the prevailing weather. They found that participants' happiness was greater in natural environments. The researchers conclude that the 'geo-located experience sampling methodology' they devised has many potential applications in psychology, health and social research (MacKerron and Mourato 2013: 992).

A **TEDx talk** about the research by George MacKerron can be viewed online.

Interviews

Interviews are a common and worthwhile technique for gathering data, useful in many research projects. They can range from highly structured, where all the questions are predetermined, to unstructured, and even combinations of the two, such as in the 'Biographic Narrative Interpretive Method' (Bolton, Vorajee and Jones, 2005). In this method, the interviews are structured by the interviewer asking just one basic question of all participants, such as, 'Please would you tell me your life story?', with the aim of eliciting a full narration requiring no further questions or interventions of any kind.

Conducting interviews is always a creative process, because interviewer and interviewee work together to create meaning (Hollway and Jefferson 2000: 11). A **talk on creative interviewing** by Jennifer Mason can be viewed online.

However, in terms of research methods, the standard interview, with one interviewer, one interviewee and at least one question, has been well rehearsed in the literature. Here we are interested in enhanced interviews, where the interview is supported with other methods, such as visual methods or artefacts.

As we saw in Chapter One, researchers have creatively enhanced the interviewing process by basing interviews around other methods of data gathering, such as diaries or photographs created by participants. Interviews can also be enhanced by basing them around other objects such as images or artefacts (for example, Sutton 2011: 193).

> In their ethnographic study of religion, Catrien Notermans and Heleen Kommers, from the Netherlands, found that interviews based on verbal stimuli were hampered by participants' emotions, which could make it hard for them to communicate with researchers. Notermans and Kommers were working with pilgrims travelling from the Netherlands to Lourdes in France, a sacred site focusing on Mary, the mother of Jesus. The researchers collected approximately 30 cards with different visual representations of Mary and used them as a basis for in-depth follow-up interviews two years after the pilgrimage. 'The icons helped ... to elicit the stories that otherwise would probably not have been told' (Notermans and Kommers 2012: 615).

Artefacts are objects created by people, and were originally of interest to archaeologists for what they could reveal about life in times gone by. Social researchers have become interested in artefacts for what they can reveal about life today, and this is often investigated through interviews enhanced by artefacts.

> Jennifer Rowsell, working in Princeton, US, used interviews centred on artefacts to develop a good understanding of school students aged 11–14 from African-American and Caribbean-American backgrounds. Rowsell asked her participants to bring artefacts they valued, and used the interviews to explore why they valued those things. The artefacts 'brought family narratives and attachments to life' (Rowsell 2011: 341) in ways the researcher was certain she could not have achieved through verbal interviews alone.

There is more scope for enhancing interviews by conducting them online with hyperlinked multimedia materials to stimulate responses. Electronic interviews take more time and effort to set up than do face-to-face or telephone interviews, and it is essential to pilot the interview thoroughly, as there is no scope for adjustment during the interviewing process. However, once the system is set up, electronic interviews take much less time to administer than face-to-face interviews and remove the need for travel or transcription, which significantly reduces costs.

> Kaye Stacey and Jill Vincent (2011) studied the quality of mathematics teaching in Australia by interviewing 21 mathematics curriculum leaders from around the

country. They created a structured interview format, with hyperlinked multimedia resources such as lesson videos and textbook pages, and sent this to participants on a CD. Participants typed their interview responses, with no prescribed minimum or maximum length, and e-mailed them back to the researchers. The researchers suggested that the whole process would take around five hours to complete; some participants found it took much longer than this, but the quality and quantity of responses was generally good. Fifteen participants took part in a brief evaluation of the technique, with 12 (80%) reporting that they thought more considered and higher-quality responses would be obtained from electronic than from face-to-face interviews. The majority of interviewees found their electronic interview to be a convenient and satisfying experience. The researchers concluded that the method is quite inflexible, although support for interviewees by e-mail and telephone was available. However, the disadvantages were far outweighed by the advantages of obtaining higher-quality interview data from a lower-cost method, particularly given the large distances between researchers and participants (Stacey and Vincent 2011: 621).

The use of online video telephony systems such as Skype can help to fill the gap between face-to-face and online interviews.

In his research into sustainable tourism, UK researcher Paul Hanna offered his participants the choice of being interviewed face to face, by telephone or via Skype. This was partly an ethical decision, as he recruited participants online, so some were a considerable distance away, yet he expected participants who were likely to be interested in sustainable tourism to choose to minimise travel for ecological reasons. Indeed, all the participants who lived far away chose to be interviewed by telephone or Skype, with both methods being equally popular. Despite a few technical hitches, Hanna found that conducting interviews via Skype was more useful than by telephone, as it enabled visual contact and non-verbal communication in a similar way to face-to-face interviewing (Hanna 2012: 241). Also, it was easy to record both the visual and audio elements of the interview (Hanna 2012: 241). And both interviewer and interviewee were able to be in a comfortable, safe, personal location, without one imposing on the other's personal space (Hanna 2012: 241) or the need to find a (possibly expensive) venue for the interview.

The use of visual methods, such as photos, may make it easier in interviews to discuss sensitive or uncomfortable subjects that 'can be difficult to articulate and uncover through written or talk-based methods' (Allen 2011: 488).

New Zealand researcher Louisa Allen obtained ethical approval to use photo-elicitation for researching sexuality with young people aged 17 and 18 within school settings. She asked participants to create a photo-diary of 'how they learned about sexuality at school', using a 24-exposure disposable camera, over a period of seven days. Participants gathered data in ways the researcher would not have considered, such as by structuring photos with the help of fellow students posing in an embrace. Participants also gathered data in places the researcher could not have gone, such as the boys' locker room. Each participant then took part in an individual semi-structured photo-elicitation interview. This process enabled the discovery of 'unknown unknowns' about the ways in which young people learn about sexuality in school: from adults, from the physical environment and from each other (Allen 2011).

Photo-elicitation can be used alone, or as part of a range of methods to create a richer overall dataset (Allen 2012: 446). A **video** about photo-elicitation can be viewed online.

Video

Observational data can be gathered using video. This can be particularly useful for a full picture of the matter under investigation because the resulting data is richer and can be analysed much more thoroughly than observational data gathered by hand. However, such a thorough analysis is very time consuming. Video data is also useful for studying the lives of people who communicate on a different level from the researcher, such as people with dementia (Jost, Neumann and Himmelmann 2010) or children (Aarsand and Forsberg 2010). It is also possible to collect and analyse pre-existing video data, for example from YouTube (Kousha, Thelwall and Abdoli 2012) or from smartphone users (Willett 2009, cited in Rose 2012: 93–4).

Mary Ann Kluge and her colleagues in America and New Zealand used video in their case study of Linda, a 65-year-old woman who had minimal experience of sport and didn't like exercise, yet decided to aim for master's level as a senior athlete. The researchers chose video because of its potential for capturing real-time thought and action and the wider context of sporting events. The researchers tracked the physical, emotional and social aspects of Linda's experience from her very first training session to her winning a race at the Rocky Mountain Senior Games. They gathered many hours of video footage that, as well as providing a comprehensive record, offered a view of changes in Linda's physique as her training progressed (Kluge et al 2010: 286).

The collection of research data using video has become increasingly common in recent years (Knoblauch 2012). However, the process is fraught with problems, requiring decisions at every level, including what and when to film, where to point the camera and how to analyse the material (Luff and Heath 2012). This presents considerable scope for creativity. One way to deal with this is to hand over the responsibility to participants, as with Louisa Allen's research outlined above.

A **short video** about observational research can be viewed online.

Online and other secondary data

Technology has enabled researchers to gather all sorts of data online, both qualitative and quantitative, at all levels, from a single individual tweet to 'big data'. Much of this is 'secondary' data, that is, data that has been created for a purpose other than research. For example, researchers from the UK and US gathered approximately 600,000 tweets from 9 to 11 August 2011 to study riots that took place in London and other British cities (Tonkin, Pfeiffer and Tourte 2012).

Some research questions lead to secondary and primary data being gathered both online and offline.

> Spanish ethnographer Roser Beneito-Montagut argues that interpersonal communication is the same online as offline, and that online social interactions are often inextricably linked with offline social interactions (Beneito-Montagut 2011: 717). For example, two people in a room together may communicate with a third somewhere else via Skype, and during the conversation a fourth may join in via text messages exchanged with one of the other three. Beneito-Montagut began her online ethnography by observing interactions over six months on several social networks such as MySpace, Twitter and Facebook. She also gathered and analysed quantitative data, for context and to help her design a theoretical sample. She then recruited six participants who were frequent internet users, and interviewed them face to face before following them online for five weeks. During this time she copied data they put on the web, captured screenshots and saved hyperlinks, to create a record of participants' actions and interactions online. She then interviewed each participant again, this time online. This process of gathering secondary and primary data, both online and offline, was designed to capture the complexity of social interactions and interpersonal relationships online, and thereby provide us with a better understanding of how these relationships take place (Beneito-Montagut 2011: 732).

The internet offers enormous possibilities for the gathering of secondary data: documents, images, videos, dialogues, statistics, social media interactions and so on, from all over the world. Secondary data can also be collected offline, such as books, photographs and ephemera (that is, documents not intended to be kept, such as leaflets or tickets). There is huge scope for creativity in the use of secondary data in research.

Transformative data gathering

The transformative research frameworks discussed in Chapter Three require research methods that are integrated with their philosophical and ethical perspectives. For example, decolonising methods require 'methods that not only work to deconstruct power dynamics between researcher and researched and indigenous and nonindigenous but also are respectful of and resonant with the rich oral histories and cultural practices of indigenous communities' (Cunsolo Willox et al 2013: 129). Participatory research requires researchers and participants together to 'effectively mix, sequence and integrate appropriate tools to support genuine dialogue and the exercise of reason in real settings, including complex situations marked by uncertainty and the unknown' (Chevalier and Buckles 2013: 7).

> As we saw in Chapter Three, critical communicative methodology (CCM) is a particularly ethical type of participatory mixed-methods research. In the early 21st century, CCM was conducted with Roma communities across several European countries. Having no territory of their own, the Romani people have long been excluded from social decision-making processes and are subject to high levels of individual and structural discrimination. One research project, the WORKALÓ project, aimed to find out why the Roma are excluded from the labour market, to identify ways to create job opportunities and to help individuals become more employable (Munté, Serradell and Sordé 2011: 262). As with all CCM research, participants – in this case Romani people – were involved from the start on the project's advisory committee, and were involved in planning and designing as well as carrying out the research. Instead of focusing on what the Roma lack, the project focused on what and how they could contribute to European society (Munté, Serradell and Sordé 2011). The project team chose communicative methods of data collection: stories of daily life, discussion groups and observations in different workplaces (Munté, Serradell and Sordé 2011: 265). Their research was presented at the European Parliament, jointly by academic and Romani researchers. This led (among other things) to more formal recognition of the Roma communities in Europe and to the development of a European strategy to ensure that Romani people can 'participate effectively in making the decisions that affect the lives and well-being of Roma communities' (Munté, Serradell and Sordé 2011: 263).

The WORKALÓ project has its own **website**.

There are a wide range of data collection methods that will fit within transformative research frameworks. These include:

- mapping (see below for more on this)
- culturally appropriate methods – storytelling, quilting and so on
- spidergram – on a very large sheet of paper, with the topic at the centre; again for anyone to write or draw whatever they wish about the topic
- timeline – marked on a very long sheet of paper (even a whole wall long, for participatory work) and extending into the past or the future or both, where anyone can write or draw whatever they wish about the topic

- ranking options – writing each option on a card or Post-It note, then putting them in order
- ranking options against criteria – using a matrix with options down the side and criteria for selection across the top, then ranking or weighting each combination
- overlays – using small stickers or symbols to prioritise items on maps or spidergrams.

Open Space Technology (OST) is a highly egalitarian method of managing diverse groups of people that can also be useful for gathering data within transformative research frameworks. It is ideal for use when the research question carries some urgency. It is a good way of managing complexity and is also helpful when there is the potential for conflict among participants (Owen 2008: 16). Despite its name, it doesn't require any technology at all. You need a 'bulletin board' where people can pin, stick or arrange cards or Post-It notes – this could be a wall, a table, a floor; whatever is most appropriate. You also need a space where participants can stand or sit in a circle or circles. I have used OST, slightly adapted, for data gathering as follows. To begin with, anyone who wishes can write something relevant to the research question on a card or note and put it on the 'bulletin board' for all to read. When these are done, the cards or notes are grouped by participants into sub-topics or themes, and each sub-topic or theme is placed in a different part of the room, together with flip-chart paper and several pens. Participants move around the room freely, discussing the sub-topics or themes and writing key points on the flip-chart paper. New cards or notes, sub-topics or themes can be produced at any stage. When everyone has said and written everything they want to say or write, the data gathering process is complete. A short **video** showing the process of OST in action can be viewed online.

Some research uses technology for mixed-methods, arts-based research, within a transformative ethical framework.

Ashlee Cunsolo Willox and her colleagues in Canada used digital methods in their participatory decolonising study of the impact of climate change on the people of Rigolet, a remote community in northern Labrador. The researchers and their participants constructed data in week-long digital storytelling workshops. Each workshop began with idea generation and discussion around the local effects of climate change, and concept maps were used as a visual representation of these discussions (see Chapter Four for more on concept maps). Then participants learned how to use computer software, design stories and edit and produce videos. They brought in their own photographs, artwork and music to enrich their stories. As the stories were being created, participants shared their ideas and gave each other feedback on their plans. At the end of each workshop, that week's participants came together for a group screening of all the stories they had produced (Cunsolo Willox et al 2012: 132).

A **participatory video project** in which young people tell their stories of life in Rigolet can be viewed online.

Drawing

In research involving children, data is often gathered by drawing (for example White et al 2010; Sorin et al 2012). For example, 'draw and write' is a tried-and-tested technique of gathering data that enables children to express their views and opinions in their own terms. It was devised in Nottingham in the 1970s by UK educational researcher Noreen Wetton, and used in the 1980s for a large national piece of research into children's perceptions of health issues. Yet, it is not a widely known technique, even though it is easy to administer and has a broad range of potential applications.

To begin with, children are given a stimulus for ideas, which may be a drama performance, video recording or simply a discussion. Then they are asked to draw images that show what they think and feel about a specific issue. For example, they could be asked to draw a picture showing how a character feels at a particular point in a performance, or showing healthy and unhealthy foods, or showing what helps them to learn their lessons. When they have finished their drawing, they are asked to write a few words (or, if they are not able to do this themselves, to tell an adult what to write) to describe the picture. The resulting data can be analysed using qualitative and quantitative techniques (Wetton and McWhirter 1998: 273).

The 'draw and write' technique is particularly useful for gathering data in the classroom. I have worked successfully with teachers to devise ways of aligning research with the curriculum, such that the exercise can serve useful educational purposes for children as well as useful data-gathering purposes for research.

The 'draw and write' technique has been expanded in the 'concentric circles of closeness' technique, which has been used by several researchers investigating the relationships of children and adults (Eldén 2012: 71).

Swedish researcher Sara Eldén (2013) used concentric circles of closeness to research children's relationships with their carers. She gave each child a sheet of paper with several concentric circles, and asked them to draw a self-portrait in the central circle. Then she asked them to draw pictures of people who took care of them, people they took care of and people who were important to them, in the surrounding circles, with the most important or closest people placed nearest to the child and those least important placed furthest away. This enabled young participants to produce a complex map of connections, demonstrating practical and emotional care given and received.

Drawing can also be used as a method of investigation in its own right by researchers who have some artistic skill.

UK researcher Hannah Gravestock drew figure skaters in performance as the basis of an interdisciplinary research method. Gravestock is herself a figure skater, and an artist and theatrical designer of costumes and scenery. This range of experience and expertise enabled her to 'examine the role of the figure skater through the eyes of the designer/drawer and the designer/drawer through the eyes of the figure skater' (Gravestock 2010: 201). This process increased her understanding of each role and of the relationships between the roles (Gravestock 2010: 203). Drawings of performance helped her to understand it more fully, and so to develop her skating practice. Similarly, by reflecting on performance through her drawings, she was able to develop her skills in costume design. As a result of the research conducted through her drawings and performances, Gravestock developed a new costume design and a new skating performance (Gravestock 2010: 201).

Hannah Gravestock has her own **website**, which shows more about her work and the links she makes between figure skating performance, design and research.

Mapping

Some researchers use actual maps, drawn and/or annotated by participants, to support and enhance the collection of verbal data through interviews or focus groups. Maps can be drawn by hand, using a computer, or both. 'Mental maps', that is, a map showing what someone thinks about a place, have been used for decades in research investigating 'the roles and meanings of space and place in everyday lives' (Gieseking 2013: 713). Map annotation can be useful in community development, where participants can write, draw or place stickers or Post-It notes on a map of the area to indicate desired facilities and/or areas in need of improvement.

Mapping is useful for revealing complex relationships between thought, emotion, places, objects and concepts (Newman 2013: 228). Using mapping for data gathering can enable researchers to gain insight into the ways participants see their world: 'what is important to them, what their lived social relations are, and where they spend their time' (Powell 2010: 553). Most research participants are likely to be familiar with one or more of the common varieties of map, such as static road maps or hiking maps, or interactive maps such as Google maps and car satellite navigation systems. However, it is important for researchers to remember that maps are not used in all cultures, and so may need more explanation in some contexts (Powell 2010: 543).

UK researcher Jacqui Gabb devised the technique of emotion maps in her mixed-methods qualitative study of family life in northern England. She created a floor plan of each family's home and made coloured emoticon stickers showing love/affection, anger, sadness and happiness. Then each member of the family, in some cases including intimate friends and/or pets, was designated by another sticker of a specific colour. Each participant was then given a copy of the floor plan and a set of stickers, and asked to put the stickers on the floor plan to show where an emotional experience or interaction had taken place. The emotion maps were appealing and easy for adults and children to use, and they also made it easy for the researchers to compare participants' data, even adults' and children's data, which is quite unusual. Also, the emotion maps revealed very private acts such as moments of shared intimacy, or children moving into parents' beds at night, which were not shown by any other method used (Gabb 2010: 463–4)

A **video** of Jacqui Gabb and her colleague Reenee Singh discussing emotion maps can be viewed online.

Maps can include quantitative or qualitative data, or both. Geographic maps, of countryside, city or ocean, are the most common type of map. But there are many different types of map. Some kinds that may be useful for researchers include:

- thematic maps – often based on a geographic map, showing variations on a theme between geographic areas, for example levels of unemployment
- topological maps – showing links between places but without accurate distances (for example, the London Underground map)
- pictorial maps – drawn more for aesthetic purposes than for accuracy
- choreographic maps – to show people how and where to move during a performance or event
- social maps – to show relationships between people and networks
- concept maps – to trace links between ideas
- cognitive maps – representing people's perceptions of place
- transect maps – showing the location and distribution of resources and land/ space uses.

To use maps for data gathering, you need to make some initial decisions. What is the frame of the map (Newman 2013: 230), that is, what will you include and exclude? Is it a map of a workplace, school, street, community? Or do you want your participants to decide on their own frames? At a practical level, what size of paper and how many coloured pens do you need? Or, if working digitally, do you have the necessary software, hardware and technical support?

Shadowing

Organisational ethnographers have gathered data through a range of non-research workplace activities. For example, Nigel Rapport spent a year employed as a hospital porter at a large teaching hospital in Scotland while researching the topic of national identity (Rapport, N 2004: 100). Sophie Gilliat-Ray (2011) shadowed a British Muslim hospital chaplain. Both ethnographers found that the methods they used enabled them to gain wider and deeper insights into the working mores and practices of their participants than traditional research methods would have done.

Shadowing involves following a single person conducting an activity, over a period of time, to find out what they do, think and feel, and as far as possible to discover the reasons why. It is an intensive, tiring process, often involving hours of data collection each day, with several more hours of data cleansing and processing each evening. However, it enables the gathering of rich data within a reasonably natural context, which can lead to more significant insights than data gathered using traditional methods such as observation (Bartkowiak–Theron and Sappey 2012: 8).

Shadowing can be used alone, or in combination with other methods, and can also be used in a range of contexts. For example, researchers carrying out a qualitative longitudinal study of motherhood shadowed mothers and young children for a day, with the aim of emphasising and including as much as possible of the complexity of a family environment in their study (Thomson et al 2012: 188). Thomson and her colleagues were developing a data archive to be used for secondary analysis, so they used only a digital camera for recording while they were shadowing, to take pictures of things rather than people. They also wrote detailed ethnographic field notes at the end of each day. This method provided 'a way of enriching existing understanding through a developing relationship' (Thomson et al 2012: 190).

Vignettes

While vignettes can be used at several stages of the research process, they are most commonly used for data gathering. They can be purposefully constructed (for example, O'Dell et al 2012), or gathered from qualitative data or field notes (for example, Trigger et al 2012).

Lindsay O'Dell and her colleagues researched 'atypical' roles for young people in the UK. They used individual structured interviews based on four vignettes, two depicting young people in typical roles (babysitter, part-time weekend employee) and two in atypical roles (language broker, carer). The characters in the vignettes were aged 14, a little younger than the 16- to 17-year-old participants, to enable participants to identify with and relate to the characters. The researchers found the analysis challenging because, in discussing the vignettes, participants moved quite fluidly between their own perspective, that of the character and a moral perspective of what 'should' happen. This led the researchers to advise any future researchers planning to use this method to 'design the materials with appropriately structured questions that enable and facilitate the exploration of participants' voices and I-positions' (O'Dell et al 2012: 712). The researchers used dialogical theory to overcome their analytic problems, as it enabled them to show that multiple voices could enrich rather than hinder the results of the research.

Vignettes can be particularly useful in researching sensitive issues, where they enable the exploration of participants' views without requiring personal disclosure

(Bradbury-Jones, Taylor and Herber 2014: 427). A good example of **vignettes** created to show some of the everyday challenges presented by early onset dementia can be viewed online.

> David Trigger and his colleagues are Australian anthropologists who used vignettes from their fieldwork to demonstrate that dramatic events in the field, albeit uncomfortable and awkward at times, can be very productive for researchers. David Trigger was conducting research with an Aboriginal population in north Australia when he unexpectedly had sorcery performed against him by a senior man whom he had offended and who was trying to harm him in return. Martin Forsey was reaching the end of his research into how students negotiate social and cultural differences when he became an accomplice in vote-rigging for awards at a student ball. Carla Meurk investigated feral pig management in the tropics of Far North Queensland, which included shadowing marksmen on a pig hunt and coming within metres of dangerous feral pigs running at high speed from the dogs that were hunting them. These vignettes were held by their authors to 'highlight robust interpersonal dynamics between the researcher and the social fields that form settings for our studies' in a way that couldn't be achieved through more traditional techniques such as interviews (Trigger et al 2012: 525).

Other researchers have also used this technique, but – as so often in the emerging field of creative research methods – use different terminology. For example, Theresa Petray, another Australian anthropologist, experienced a dramatic event when she found she had unwittingly become a witness in a murder investigation (Petray 2012: 555). This event was every bit as uncomfortable, awkward and productive as the vignettes explored by Trigger et al (2012). Lucy Pickering, a British anthropologist who studied hippies and drop-outs in Hawai'i, had a less dramatic but equally fruitful incident when one of her research participants and her visiting mother gave opposing analyses of her experience of an ecstatic dance in Hawai'i (Pickering 2009: 1). But neither Petray nor Pickering use the word 'vignette'. Some anthropologists refer to these incidents as 'revelatory moments' (for example, Trigger et al 2012; Tonnaer 2012), but Petray and Pickering don't use this terminology either.

Time

Personal history and time are potentially useful resources for researchers studying human experience.

> UK researcher Joan Smith used life-history interviews to study the factors affecting career decisions made by female secondary school teachers. This research was prompted by the fact that women are under-represented as head teachers of secondary schools in England and Wales. She asked participants to tell her about their professional experience and what had influenced their

career decisions. This method of interviewing enabled participants to define for themselves the factors that had affected their careers, rather than responding to a researcher's preconceived ideas. Smith found that her method 'allows for profound understandings of the complex reasons that lie beneath people's decisions and actions' (Smith 2012: 496).

 A short **video** outlining rationale for and method of conducting life-history interviews can be viewed online.

In New Zealand, psychologist Joanna Sheridan and her colleagues Kerry Chamberlain and Ann Dupuis used timelines to research fatness and weight loss. Their participants were nine women who were obesely overweight, had lost weight representing 27–44% of their body mass and had sustained that weight loss for at least five years. Each participant worked with a researcher to construct a timeline on A3-sized graph paper. The vertical axis represented weight, the horizontal axis represented time. Participants were asked to focus on the part of their lives when weight was of concern; the durations varied from 10 years to life. Participants were also asked to depict significant life events, activities and experiences, and to produce material objects to illustrate these that could be laid on the graph and form part of discussions with the researchers. 'The timeline creation process and the subsequent talk it provoked ensured a deeper, richer and more nuanced (re)presentation of experience' (Sheridan, Chamberlain and Dupuis 2011: 557).

Mixed methods

Mixed–methods data gathering can be very helpful in the right circumstances.

As we saw earlier in this chapter, Andrew Robinson and his colleagues conducted a complex piece of dementia research in Australia. They focused on the cognitive and functional abilities of people living with dementia, the stress levels of their family carers and their experiences of dementia services. To do this, they gathered nine different kinds of data:

1 demographic data
2 scales and questionnaires assessing cognitive function and stress levels
3 participants' self-assessments of whether they were happy or unhappy with services (by telephone)
4 researchers' notes of telephone calls
5 participants' weekly diary of services received within and beyond the home
6 participants' diary note of 'the most significant event of the week regarding services'
7 researchers' notes of monthly interviews on pro formas

8 researchers' other interview notes
9 audio recordings of interviews.

This approach had some challenges: it was 'complex, time consuming and potentially prone to fragmentation' (Robinson et al 2011: 342). However, it also proved successful and rewarding for both participants and researchers.

Mixed methods don't have to involve quantitative and qualitative research; they can be entirely quantitative, with a range of different measurements, or entirely qualitative.

Katrina Rodriguez and Maria Lahman, in America, investigated the ways in which 'Latina college students make meaning of their intersecting ethnicity, class and gender' (Rodriguez and Lahman 2011: 603). They gathered data through individual interviews and a culturally responsive focus group in the form of a traditional Mexican dinner hosted in the home of one of the researchers. They also used participants' photographs and scrapbooks. This mixed-methods study was entirely qualitative.

Canadian researcher William James Harvey and his colleagues (2012) devised and tested a hybrid qualitative method of gathering data from children with attention–deficit hyperactivity disorder (ADHD) in a study of their physical activity experiences. This method is based on photography and collage.

William James Harvey and his colleagues in Quebec, Canada gave each of their participants a disposable camera so that other people (teachers, friends, parents and so on) could take pictures of participants engaging in physical exercise, whether at home, in school or elsewhere. Then the participants chose which pictures to use to create a scrapbook, with the help of a research assistant, documenting their physical activity experiences. They also took part in semi-structured interviews to 'describe and discuss their experiences' (Harvey et al 2012: 65). Half of the participants were interviewed while they made the scrapbook (concurrent technique) and half were interviewed after making the scrapbook (consecutive technique). Each scrapbook-making session and interview was recorded on videotape. Harvey et al found that the concurrent technique led to longer interviews yielding more and richer data (Harvey et al 2012: 73–4), with an average of 94 transcribed pages for the concurrent technique and 32 for the consecutive technique (Harvey et al 2012: 69). The researchers concluded that the concurrent technique was much more effective in enabling the voices of children with ADHD to be heard (Harvey et al 2012: 74).

Another hybrid qualitative method was devised by designers and has since been adopted by social scientists.

Designers Kirsten Boehner, William Gaver and Andy Boucher worked with groups of volunteers in Norway, the Netherlands and Italy to develop their method of 'probes'. Their work was funded by the European Union and aimed to design new technology for supporting older people in communities. The designers didn't want to take the conventional focus on problems and needs, instead choosing to find out about participants' 'hopes and fears, curiosities and dreams' (Boehner, Gaver and Boucher 2014: 186). The 'probes' were carefully designed items that set tasks for participants, such as specially made postcards with questions to answer, maps of participants' communities with suggestions and tools for annotating them and customised disposable cameras for taking photos from particular locations or in relation to particular topics. Participants were asked to use the probes that appealed to them, over a time period of some weeks, and then to return them to the designers. The process 'disregards traditional utilitarian values in favour of playfulness, exploration and enjoyment' (Boehner, Gaver and Boucher 2014: 194) and is designed to privilege partial, multiple, contingent findings rather than the more usual certain and generalisable findings. The designers were comfortable with uncertainty, error and surprises, and found participants' responses to the probes to be useful for exploration and inspiration about possible new products. The first attempt at using probes was described as 'inspiring and engaging' (Boehner, Gaver and Boucher 2014: 186) and the method was developed thereafter by designers and by social scientists.

A short **video** about probes and how to use them can be viewed online.

French researcher Jean-François Coget, now based in America, developed an iterative mixed-methods qualitative approach for studying professional intuition, which he called 'dialogical inquiry'. This has four phases:

1 a one-to-one life-interview, to help the researcher understand the participant's relevant experiences and perspectives
2 shadowing and videoing the participant at work
3 using theoretical sampling to select relevant episodes from the video data
4 dialogue with the participant about the selected episodes to understand, in particular, the unconscious causes of the participant's actions.

Coget has used this approach to study the use of intuition in the work of movie directors, emergency room doctors and winemakers (Coget 2014: 176). It has proved to be 'an interesting alternative method' for studying unconscious aspects of intuition in real-life settings (Coget 2014: 185).

Coget's approach draws on participatory research in its first and fourth phases, uses technology in the form of filming and editing equipment and relies on video, which is an artistic medium. So dialogical inquiry is a data-gathering technique that incorporates elements from all four areas of creative research methods.

A useful **article** about Coget's method of dialogical inquiry can be accessed online.

CONCLUSION

As this chapter has amply demonstrated, there are many highly creative ways of gathering data. In fact, there are many more than I have had the space to include here. I hope that those I have included, to illustrate the breadth and inventiveness of data-gathering techniques, will perhaps inspire you to develop one or more of your own. As you will have seen from the examples in this chapter, skills that would not usually be thought of as relevant for research – from writing poetry to figure skating – can be put to use in data gathering. In my own PhD research I developed and tested a method of gathering data based on storytelling that was both enjoyable and effective. If I can do it, so can you.

SIX

Analysing data

Introduction

In general, the analysis of data may be both the most specialised and the least well understood aspect of making research. A common failing of research reports and journal articles is not to explain the process of analysing data clearly enough for readers to gauge their level of confidence in the findings or for researchers to replicate the analytic method (Odena 2013: 364).

There are many ways to analyse any given set of data. Suppose that you hold a focus group with eight first-generation immigrants from different countries of origin. You begin by having each person share some basic demographic data by way of introduction: where they have lived, how old they are, their occupation(s) before and after immigration, who and where their family members are. Then you facilitate a discussion of their experiences of emigration and immigration around themes drawn from the academic literature, including wealth and poverty, coercion and freedom, belonging, emotion, status, togetherness and separation. The resulting data would be amenable to quantitative and qualitative analysis. In quantitative terms, you could do only descriptive statistical analysis, as the size and nature of your sample would not support inferential statistics. But it might be interesting to calculate such things as the length of people's journeys; the similarity or difference of participants to the national picture of immigrants; the variance in distances between family members. In qualitative terms you could of course focus your analysis on the themes from the academic literature that you used to facilitate the discussion in the first place. But you could also:

- use a recognised analytic technique, such as interpretive phenomenological analysis (Finlay 2011: 140)
- look at the metaphors people used, to see what they might tell you (Fletcher 2013: 1555–6)
- analyse interactions between people in the focus group to find out what those add to the analysis of data content (Farnsworth and Boon 2010; Halkier 2010; Belzile and Öberg 2012)
- consider any silences, pauses or omissions in order to try to uncover what might have been left unsaid and why (Frost and Elichaoff 2010: 56)
- ask someone else to analyse the data independently to see whether or not they reach the same conclusions as you (Odena 2013: 365)

- involve your participants in the analysis, for confirmation and reciprocal learning (Nind 2011)

and so on.

It is not possible, in a single book chapter, to explain the many different approaches to analysing data in sufficient detail for readers to use them all effectively. The aim of this chapter is to give you an overview of some of the more creative approaches to data analysis, together with an understanding of where rules must be applied. This will help you to identify areas of data analysis that you would like to investigate further, and provide some signposts to enable you to do so.

Ethics in data analysis

As you analyse your data, you're responsible to a lot of people: participants, funders, commissioners, supervisors, examiners and so on. This applies whether you're analysing primary or secondary data, or both. Even analysis of historical or archival data can involve responsibilities to the descendants of participants (Seal 2012: 689–90) and can be emotionally demanding for the researcher (Einwohner 2011: 423; Seal 2012: 689).

Data analysis is difficult and the process can seem impenetrable. It is essential that you do not invent or distort your data, or misuse statistical techniques (Poon and Ainuddin 2011: 307). For example, some people who are new to the quantitative analysis software SPSS decide to run all the tests it can do. In this way you are likely to find one or more which give a statistically significant result – if you're using a 5% level of probability, then five from 100 will do so by chance. This kind of 'fishing' is highly unethical. The key is to know which statistical test or tests are appropriate to use for your data-set (Davis 2013: 17).

An interesting **panel discussion** with American academics and practitioners about data, analysis and ethics can be viewed online.

Data preparation and coding

Meticulous data preparation is essential; there is not much scope for creativity in accurate transcription or data entry. Coding data can also feel quite tedious and may be very time consuming. When it has been prepared and coded, data usually needs to be sorted into categories and sub-categories, a process that can become very complex (Mason 2002: 151).

However, even these apparently repetitive and laborious processes require some creativity. For example, take the transcription of data recorded by audio or video. There are a large variety of decisions to be made about transcription, and there is no 'best way' or 'right answer' (Hammersley 2010: 556). These decisions include such things as: should you record non-speech sounds that people make, such as laughter, coughs, sighs and so on? If so, how? Do you record pauses? If so, do you measure their length, or just note each occurrence? When transcribing video data, should you include body movements, gestures, information about the surrounding environment? How do you lay out your transcription on the page, and how do you identify the different speakers/actors in the transcript? (Hammersley 2010: 556–7). Similar decisions are required for quantitative data: is it in a spreadsheet already? If so, is the spreadsheet fit for your purposes? If not, what do you need to do to make it so? If the data is not in a spreadsheet, how can you construct one to facilitate your analysis? How do you code missing data? And so on. Gathering data online can often avoid the need for much, if any, data preparation (Stacey and Vincent 2011: 621), but, in these cases, care must be taken to set up your data gathering in such a way that the format of the data gathered will enable the necessary analysis.

Quantitative versus qualitative data analysis

Quantitative and qualitative data need to be analysed separately, using different techniques, and in research where both quantitative and qualitative data have been gathered, the datasets will be analysed separately before the analyses are integrated to produce the research findings.

Quantitative data analysis involves the use of statistical techniques to describe data, compare different groups of data and make inferences about populations from random samples. There is no room for creativity in the actual calculations, unless you are a skilled statistician with enough knowledge and experience to move the field forward by, for instance, creating a new algorithm (for example, Mulder 2011: 15). There is also scope for creativity in taking an analytic technique developed outside social science and using it within social science. For example, sequence analysis was first developed in biological research to compare DNA sequences and is now used in social research for analysing sequences that have 'a specific order of crucial importance that cannot be changed' (Brzinsky-Fay and Kohler 2010: 360), such as life histories and career trajectories. But again, considerable expertise is required to identify analytic techniques from one field that can be usefully applied in another.

Chapter Five mentioned the research of UK and US researchers Emma Tonkin, Heather Pfeiffer and Greg Tourte (2012), who gathered 600,000 tweets about the London riots of August 2011. Their approach to analysis was interesting. They began by identifying duplicate tweets (including retweets). Then they identified references to other participants in the social network, which enabled them to create a graph of participation. They also identified recognisable individuals and locations, repeated phrases or hashtags and URLs. The researchers then used natural language processing (that is, computerised analysis of language as it is used) to identify interesting terms and index tweets containing those terms. That enabled them to create frequency tables of those interesting terms, which meant

> that they could identify popular topics and show how those topics changed over time (Tonkin, Pfeiffer and Tourte 2012: 52).

What is important in quantitative data analysis is to understand the rationale behind any statistical technique that you might consider using, and so be sure that you select the right technique(s) for the question you are aiming to answer. For most people, creativity in quantitative data analysis lies in deciding which techniques to use, and how, in the context of each unique research project – and, of course, in interpreting the results (Bryman 2012: 592). However, it has to be said that even professionals such as quantitative sociologists don't always understand the purposes of the statistical tests they use (Engman 2013: 257). Also, research has shown that quantitative analysts are not always skilled in interpretation (Laux and Pont 2012: 3).

There is more scope for creativity in qualitative data analysis. There are several kinds of qualitative data analysis, including:

- content analysis – a semi-quantitative technique for counting the number of instances of each category or code (Robson 2011: 349)
- thematic analysis – identifying themes from coded data (Robson 2011: 475)
- narrative analysis – analysing stories from primary or secondary data (Bryman 2012: 582)
- conversation analysis – detailed analysis of the verbal and non-verbal content of everyday interactions (Bryman 2012: 527)
- discourse analysis – analysing patterns of speech and interaction in a detailed and sometimes semi-quantitative way, for example by measuring the length of pauses (Bryman 2012: 529)
- metaphor analysis – analysing metaphors from primary or secondary data (Fletcher 2013: 1555–6)
- phenomenological analysis – analysing participants' stories from, and descriptions of, their 'life-worlds', or individual experiences and perceptions, with a focus on meaning (Papathomas and Lavallee 2010: 357; Mayoh, Bond and Todres 2012: 28)
- life course analysis – analysis of the 'interaction between individual lives and social change' (Brittain and Green 2012: 253).

This is by no means an exhaustive list, but is intended to illustrate the range and diversity of approaches to data analysis.

> UK researchers Ian Brittain and Sarah Green used life course analysis to study the rehabilitation of former soldiers after disabilities sustained in combat. The 'life course' is the sequence of different roles and situations an individual finds themselves in over time. The life course exists in a wider historical and socioeconomic context, containing systems of opportunities and constraints within which individuals can make choices and create their own life journeys

(Brittain and Green 2012: 253). The researchers collected relevant newspaper and internet articles from around the world, quoting former soldiers speaking about their rehabilitation. They read each article several times, to familiarise themselves with its content, and then carried out a more detailed analysis, noting preliminary comments, associations and summaries. These notes were used as guidance in identifying themes, which were clustered into subordinate and overarching superordinate themes before being collated and discussed individually to deepen the analysis (Brittain and Green 2012: 255–6).

Secondary data

Because there is so much that can be done with any dataset, and because data gathering can be onerous for participants, researchers' attention has turned more and more to the opportunities offered by secondary data – that is, data previously gathered for some other purpose (sometimes research, sometimes not) and that can be used again.

Greek researcher Helen Briassoulis researched tourism and development by analysing an **online petition** to stop the creation of a golf course at Cavo Sidero in Crete. The petition website contained informative text and video, plus the details of over 10,000 signatories from around 25 countries, and around 4,000 comments from signatories ranging from a single word to several hundred words. Where possible, signatories' identities (academic, tourist, golfer and so on) were deduced from their comments or from wider web searches (this was not possible in all cases because signatories could choose to remain anonymous). Also, comments were placed into categories, which were initially defined from the theoretical framework for the research and then refined during the process of analysis. This approach to analysis helped the researcher to understand 'the patterns and determinants of opposition to golf development' in local and global, specific and general terms, over time and from diverse socio-cultural contexts (Briassoulis 2010: 724).

For researchers used to gathering their own data, or for those who find the prospect appealing, the idea of working with secondary data may seem less attractive. Some may fear that it would feel too clinical or distant if they didn't have intimate personal knowledge of the context in which the data was gathered. Indeed, for some research disciplines, such as ethnography, it is essential for researchers to gather their own data (James 2013: 564). Being present for data gathering may add layers of sensory experience that wouldn't otherwise be available, but that still doesn't mean the researcher knows everything (James 2013: 567). Analysis of secondary data can be just as creative as analysis of primary data, requiring judicious use of the researcher's analytic imagination (James 2013: 570). Careful and rigorous analysis of the same dataset as secondary and primary data may lead to different insights, but that doesn't mean either set of findings is 'wrong' (James 2013: 574).

Some of the other pros and cons of secondary data are conveniently listed on a **web page**, while another web page provides access to some **online sources of secondary data** – these are UK-generated, but other countries will have close equivalents for most cases, which should be relatively easy to find online.

Analysing documentary data

Documents are not only containers of data, they can also be tools for people to use as they act in the world (Kara 2012: 126), as the following examples show.

- Legal judgements are used by lawyers as benchmarks to assess new cases.
- An individual may use their 'last will and testament' to benefit a charity.
- An organisation's statement of customer service standards may be used by customers in negotiations with that organisation.

The analysis of documents will benefit from taking this into account. There are three steps to analysing documents: superficial examination, or 'skimming'; thorough examination by careful reading and re-reading; and interpretation (Bowen 2009: 32). During this process, 'meaningful and relevant passages of text or other data are identified' (Bowen 2009: 32) and patterns, categories and themes can be found within the data. In a mixed-methods study it is also possible to apply pre-existing codes, for example those used with other datasets in the study such as interview transcripts, to documentary data (Bowen 2009: 32). This can be a useful technique for data integration.

John Vincent, from the US, and Jane Crossman, from Canada, used textual analysis to examine gendered narratives and nationalistic discourses in Australian newspapers' narratives about Australian tennis players Lleyton Hewitt and Alicia Molik during the centennial Australian Open Championships. The researchers collected three national daily papers with extensive sports coverage, chosen to appeal to three different types of readership, from the day before the championships began to the day after they ended. They found 108 articles focusing on Hewitt and 79 focusing on Molik. Each was read twice and narratives relating to gender and nationality were highlighted, and the articles were then transcribed as MS Word documents. Then the researchers used open and axial coding to generate 'multiple and layered elements' of analysis (Vincent and Crossman 2009: 264). Open coding was used to organise the raw data into themes and categories by searching and re-searching the transcripts for dominant narratives, contradictions and inconsistencies. Axial coding was used to link these themes and categories with each other and with individual codes. When the coding was done, the researchers used a multi-theoretical framework focusing on gender, power and nationality to focus and amplify the findings of the research, to 'uncover the textual constructions of gender and national identity permeating the dominant discourses' (Vincent and Crossman 2009: 265). Vincent and Crossman found that multiple levels of coding, combined with a well-developed theoretical framework, offered a rigorous and systematic approach to analysis that resulted in a 'dynamic and layered analytical framework that led to theoretical and data-driven insights' (Vincent and Crossman 2009: 265).

Analysis of talk

There are two central methods of analysing talk: discourse analysis and conversation analysis. While neither method is new, both are highly creative, with scope for further creativity in finding new ways to use and develop each method.

Conversation analysis (CA) is an evolving analytic method based on the idea that any verbal interaction is worth studying to find out how it was produced by the speakers (Liddicoat 2011: 69). CA requires a detailed form of transcription, capturing not only the words that are spoken but also aspects of talk such as intonation, volume of speech, pauses, non-word utterances such as 'um' and 'er', overlapping talk, interruptions and non-verbal sounds such as laughter or coughs (Groom, Cushion and Nelson 2012: 445). The aim is to facilitate a thorough analysis of people's conversation in normal everyday interactions, perhaps focusing on specific types of interaction such as greetings or leave-takings. CA has also been used to study people's talk in more artificial situations such as research interviews (Groom, Cushion and Nelson 2012: 440). Unlike discourse analysis, which focuses on talk within context and structure, CA focuses on what people actually do as they talk (Liddicoat 2011: 8). When it was first devised in the 1960s–70s, CA was used in isolation from theory, but more recently it has been situated within theoretical frameworks around topics such as power and identity (Groom, Cushion and Nelson 2012: 446). CA is a demanding and time-consuming analytic technique (Mercer 2010: 8), although it doesn't require the gathering of much data (Bryman 2012: 525). There is considerable scope for creativity in using CA with different theoretical frameworks and as part of mixed-methods investigations.

Discourse analysis (DA) is based on the concept that the way we talk about something affects the way we think about that phenomenon. 'Discourse' in this context doesn't refer solely to talk itself, it refers to talk that is constructed within the constraints of a social structure. DA can be applied to other kinds of data, such as written texts (Bryman 2012: 528) and images (Rose 2012: 195). CA and DA are not mutually exclusive; it can be helpful to integrate CA into DA for a more detailed analysis of talk or texts (Bryman 2012: 528).

Michael Corman, from the University of Calgary in Qatar, took a constructivist approach to DA in studying the way mothers talk about placements outside the home for their autistic children. Nine mothers from western Canada had taken part in semi-structured interviews in their homes for an earlier study. Corman extracted relevant sections from those interview transcripts to use as secondary data in investigating 'how their talk accounted for placement and their social reality surrounding placement' (Corman 2013: 1323). He used predetermined questions to orient himself as he analysed the data.

- What is the talk of participants accomplishing?
- Why is the subject matter being brought up now and in this way?
- How is participants' talk being used to make claims?
- How do participants make their talk persuasive?
- What discourses do participants invoke to talk about placement, and why? (Corman 2013: 1324)

This analysis allowed Corman to make visible the ways in which mothers constructed their own realities by talking about, and making meaning of, their experiences. This in turn enabled an increase in understanding of the mothers' stress factors and coping mechanisms.

Some researchers choose to gather talk from people in more natural settings.

In the year 2000, four dual-income American families with at least one child were asked to audio-record as many of their interactions as possible for one week. This led to over 450 hours of recordings, and the transcripts ran to over 1 million words. The study was designed by American researchers Deborah Tannen and Shari Kendall, and the aim was to find out how women and men talk at home and at work, and how they use language to balance work and family life. Part of the rationale for the methodology was that self-recording over such a long period would lead participants to become habituated to the recording device, and indeed the intimate nature of some of the data suggests that this did happen to some extent. However, this was not the whole story. Cynthia Gordon, a member of the research team, re-examined all the transcripts for evidence of times when talk focused on the recording device. She found that all participants focused on the recording device at times, giving it different roles such as 'burden', 'spy' or 'audience', and effectively using it as a resource within their interactions (Gordon 2013: 314).

Gordon's research is creative because she takes a fresh look at an aspect of the research process, recording of data, which is often taken for granted or viewed as neutral by researchers. Gordon's analysis shows that research participants have a very different perspective, which is helpful in enabling researchers to think differently about this basic tool of our trade.

Visual analytic techniques

Diagrams and maps can be particularly useful in data analysis to help you visualise your data and the ideas and relationships that develop as you work through the analytic process. Maps have been used in this way within a range of disciplines including geography, psychology, sociology, anthropology and education (Powell 2010: 539–40). Diagrams have been used in grounded theory analysis for many years (Strauss and Corbin 1998: 12) and are also relevant to other forms of data analysis. These visual techniques help the researcher to move from coding or theme identification to conceptualisation (Strauss and Corbin 1998: 218). They are also great vehicles for using, and stimulating, creativity and imagination (Strauss and Corbin 1998: 220).

UK researchers Charles Buckley and Michael Waring used diagrams at various stages of grounded theory studies of children's attitudes to physical activity (Buckley and Waring 2013). At the analytic stage, they found that creating diagrams helped them to generate, explore, record and communicate insights about their data. Drawing on the work of Clarke (2005), they also suggest that using diagrams in data analysis can help to uncover some otherwise hidden parts of the research process, and so rebut potential accusations of reductionism (Buckley and Waring 2013: 150). 'During the process of research, the use of diagrams can help the researcher make sense of relationships that may not have been previously explicit. In this way, they become an active part of the theory generation and not only support developing conceptualisation but also actively encourage clarity of thought.' (Buckley and Waring 2013: 152).

Diagrams can of course be created by hand, or using specialist diagram software such as Gliffy, or research analysis software that supports diagramming such as NVivo. Similarly, maps can be drawn by hand or using specialist mapping software such as Esri or Maptitude.

Analysing video data

Video offers a myriad of possibilities, and enormous challenges, to the data analyst. 'Video allows us to document time in a complex fashion: action presents different simultaneous layers of temporal conducts – such as talk, gestures, gaze, body movements, postures of all of the participants ... One of the challenges of video recording social action is precisely the continuous documentation of all of these layers of timed action – which is often impossible to achieve with one camera and difficult to solve with several' (Mondada 2012: 305–6). It is also impossible to transcribe everything that could possibly be relevant: all the physical movements and gestures, directions of gaze and eye contact, handling of material objects, use of technology, details of the environment and so on (Hammersley 2010: 566).

Jessica DeCuir-Gunby and her colleagues in America gathered video data from three cohorts of teachers in their longitudinal study of mathematics teachers' professional development. Mathematics lessons were video-recorded, then coded using a three-step process.

1 Lesson mapping – description of each lesson's organisation and structure, with categories based on teachers' interactions in the classroom, for context and to identify changes over time.
2 Lesson rubric coding – quantitative examination of teacher-initiated verbal communication in specific categories such as 'language matching' (teacher using child's own language) and 'illuminating thinking' (teacher drawing attention to and/or highlighting child's understanding), to capture the number of times each category was used by each teacher.
3 Transcription of verbal communication from the lesson rubric, to capture what was said within each category.

ANOVAs and Bonferroni tests were used to analyse quantitative data from this coding system and identify any significant differences between the three cohorts of teachers. Qualitative data was analysed using a five-step method for each individual lesson.

1 Use lesson mapping categories to provide structure and framework for the lesson.
2 Pair lesson rubric codings within events highlighted by lesson mapping.
3 Place comments from field notes within lesson mapping categories.
4 Match events of lesson with the teacher's statements from group interview.
5 Integrate first four data sources to create individual cases.

The quantitative analysis enabled DeCuir-Gunby and her colleagues to provide an overall view of what happened in the cohorts' classrooms, while the qualitative analysis enabled them to scrutinise each individual teacher and lesson (DeCuir-Gunby, Marshall and McCulloch 2012: 212). This mixing of methods also enabled the researchers to identify and describe several aspects of complexity within the data, such as instances of some teachers' data corroborating, complementing or contradicting other data (DeCuir-Gunby, Marshall and McCulloch 2012: 207).

The wealth of video freely available on internet sites such as YouTube means that scholars are increasingly turning to such sources for information and data (Kousha, Thelwall and Abdoli 2012: 1710). The analysis of video data enables researchers to examine aspects of social practice that it would be difficult or impossible to study in any other way. Examples include the way that architects use sketches and other drawings to help them think and communicate as they collaborate (Mondada 2012: 317–22) and the processes of informal interaction and tacit participation that enable people with different roles in emergency call centres to work together flexibly and effectively as they respond to the needs of people in crisis (Fele 2012: 281).

Mixed-methods analysis

As shown above, it is possible to use quantitative and qualitative analytic techniques in the same piece of research, and this can enrich your findings. For example, cultural consensus analysis, a quantitative method, can be combined with cultural modelling, a qualitative method (Fairweather and Rinne 2012). Cultural consensus analysis asks three key questions about sharing of culture and then assesses the patterns in the data using mathematical techniques (Fairweather and Rinne 2012: 477). Cultural modelling is based on DA, which enables researchers to understand participants' perspectives on thoughts, knowledge and the meaning of language, and is used to demonstrate and explain relationships between cultural elements in the data (Fairweather and Rinne 2012: 482). So, both analytic techniques are used to investigate the extent to which culture is shared, albeit in different ways, and using both together can give a more complete picture than using one alone (Garro 2000: 285).

> Reesa Sorin and her colleagues in Australia developed an analytical procedure using three different methods to analyse children's artworks. The first method was content analysis, a quantitative technique: the researchers developed categories for the salient features of children's drawings such as animals, houses and trees. The items in each category were counted for number and frequency. The other two methods were qualitative. One was interpretive analysis, in which categories were again identified, this time based on the mood or atmosphere of each drawing and the story the child told about their drawing. The other was developmental analysis, which suggests that stages in the development of children's artworks can be correlated with their ages. The researchers conclude that this combination of analytic methods can 'provide deep insights into young children's understandings' (Sorin, Brooks and Haring 2012: 29).

Q methodology offers another way of using statistical analysis with qualitative data about people's views, attitudes, beliefs and emotions (Ellingsen, Størksen and Stephens 2010: 395). A short **video** introducing Q methodology can be viewed online.

Alternatively, research can involve more than one type of quantitative analysis, or more than one type of qualitative analysis, conducted either concurrently, or consecutively in an iterative approach.

> Erica Halverson and her colleagues in America studied four youth media arts organisations across the US to investigate how video could be used to represent young people's identity. They describe video data as 'multimodal' because it contains still and moving images, colour, a range of sounds and silences,

sometimes text and so on. Halverson et al originally approached video analysis by starting with dialogue, but then they encountered a film that had no dialogue, which engendered their decision to develop a multimodal approach. Their aim was to create a multimodal analytic framework, not to analyse data in different chunks, but to reflect how the interaction of different chunks of data can create new meanings. Following the work of Baldry and Thibault (2006), they divided the film into 'phases and transitions', which were units of analysis that had some kind of internal consistency, for example through a type of shot, a consistent voiceover or the same music. Then they devised a coding scheme, based on the work of Bordwell and Thompson (2004), for each unit of analysis. This involved four broad categories based on filmmakers' key cinematic techniques:

1 mise-en-scène: anything visible within the camera's frame, such as setting and characters
2 sound: anything audible, such as dialogue and music
3 editing: the filmmaker's interventions that create the film
4 cinematography: the filmmaker's techniques for altering the image from that seen through the camera's lens.

Within each category, more detailed codes were developed, such as facial expressions, clothing, sound effects, flashback, freeze frame, lighting and close-up. Halverson et al say that using this system 'to describe the phases and transitions of the films resulted in the creation of multilayered filmic transcripts that allow us to consider each mode individually, as well as how they connect to one another to help youth consider issues of identity in their films' (Halverson et al 2012: 8).

Doing mixed-methods analysis well can be resource-intensive and time consuming, particularly in international research.

Anne Shordike and her colleagues in America, Thailand and New Zealand investigated the meanings of celebratory food preparation for older women in three different cultures, to find out what commonalities might exist across different cultural contexts. They developed a research design in which researchers from each country would gather, analyse and report on the topic from their own country, before they made comparisons between the countries. Data was gathered using three focus groups in each country in 2000–01, and was transcribed and analysed. Coding data collaboratively was difficult. A face-to-face meeting of researchers from all three teams in 2002 facilitated the development of nine initial codes, but it proved impossible to involve a Thai team member in the full coding exercise, which was done over several months by one researcher from New Zealand and one from America. Then the coding was reviewed by all team members, using electronic communication. The team planned for one researcher to write a memo about each code, incorporating data from all three countries, and e-mail it to all researchers for feedback. This also proved impossible, so researchers met again for two weeks in April 2005, intending to discuss each of the memos that had been written until everyone understood it and new insights had been generated. For each code, this required each country's researchers to present their own interpretation of their own data, and then a full discussion of the data under that code for all three countries. This process continued after the meeting, using videoconferencing. The process of identifying commonalities began at a meeting in October 2005 and took about 18 months, again with use of videoconferencing and another meeting towards the end of the process in early 2007. The research, including data analysis, was an effective collaboration (Shordike et al 2010: 351) but, as this summary shows, the data coding and analysis took around five years and a great deal of effort to complete.

A **presentation** by Professor Ray Cooksey about the analysis of quantitative and qualitative data with the support of technology can be viewed online.

Data integration

The trend of combining data and findings from different datasets has increased rapidly since the turn of the century (Ivankova and Kawamura 2010: 583; Hannes and Macaitis 2012: 405). The data and findings may be from a single mixed-methods study or from different studies, and may be qualitative, quantitative or both. One of the most challenging aspects of mixed-methods data analysis is integrating the findings from different datasets and/or different analytic techniques. As so often with new research methods, a variety of terms are used to describe the process of combining data and findings, including:

- data integration – usually within a mixed-methods study
- meta-analysis – usually for quantitative studies
- data synthesis – usually for qualitative studies
- meta-synthesis – for qualitative or quantitative studies
- evidence synthesis – for qualitative or quantitative studies
- systematic review – for qualitative or quantitative studies.

Data integration in mixed-methods research can be conducted for a number of reasons, such as to address a research question from a variety of perspectives or to bring together different parts of a phenomenon or process (Mason 2002: 33). Within a research project, data integration has three main purposes: triangulation of data, the development of richer analysis and the illustration of findings (Fielding 2012: 124). The aim is to synthesise equivalent or complementary findings and make further investigation of contradictory findings (Fielding 2012: 125). The precise methods of integration will vary, depending on the nature of the datasets, but there are some basic questions that are likely to apply in any case, such as:

1. How far can each of your datasets contribute to answering your research questions?
2. To what extent can your findings be brought together to create an explanatory narrative?
3. How much do the answers to 1 and 2 above benefit your research?

These kinds of questions can be difficult to answer, but there is no point integrating data just for its own sake, so it is important to ensure that integration is rigorous and meaningful (Mason 2002: 36).

Methods of combining data and findings from different studies usually start from the researcher's strategy for searching for, and identifying, studies that fit their criteria. Although this happens at an early stage of the research, it is included here because it is essentially an analytic process. Devising a search and identification strategy is quite a creative process, with many decisions to be made, such as:

- which criteria to use for inclusion or exclusion
- which search terms to use
- which databases and/or websites to search
- how to manage studies that don't fit with your inclusion/exclusion criteria.

The idea behind having predefined inclusion and exclusion criteria is to reduce researcher bias in the selection of studies (Petticrew and Roberts 2005: 10). However, as the selection criteria are defined by researchers they may themselves include bias (Kara 2012: 21). A short **video** about researcher bias can be viewed online. An initial question is how broad or narrow to make the criteria: broader criteria increase the likelihood of generalisability, while narrower criteria are likely to yield a more homogeneous evidence base (Salanti 2012: 81). Practical considerations also come into play here, as some selection criteria can yield hundreds of thousands of studies, which may encourage researchers to use narrower criteria.

You may choose to replicate an existing search and identification strategy, either because it has proved to be effective and would fit with your own research, or because you want to compare your research with a previous study and using the same strategy would facilitate this (Hannes and Macaitis 2012: 403). Or you may prefer to devise your own strategy. When you have selected your studies, you need to extract the relevant information and then re-analyse it as a dataset of its own, using suitable analytic tools.

Australian researchers Pat Bazeley and Lynn Kemp considered the metaphors used to describe integration in the research methods literature. These included:

- bricolage, mosaics and jigsaws – aiming for completion
- sprinkling and mixing/stirring – aiming for enhancement
- triangulation and archipelago – aiming to show that the whole is greater than the sum of its parts

- blending, morphing and fusion – aiming to explore through transformation
- conversation and DNA – aiming to explore through iterative exchange.

Bazeley and Kemp used their exploration of these metaphors within the research methods literature to define the following eight principles for data integration (Bazeley and Kemp 2012: 69).

1. There are many methods and techniques of integrating data.
2. Integration can start at any point in the research process.
3. Integration should happen at the earliest possible stage, certainly during analysis, and always before conclusions are made.
4. The level of integration must be commensurate with the aims of the research.
5. The research report should provide clear evidence of the ways in which each data element or finding depends on, or is enhanced by, others.
6. Data integration aims to obtain results that could not be obtained in any other way.
7. The research is written up around the topics it investigates and its findings, not around its methods.
8. If the requirements of other forms of publication, such as journal article word limits, make it difficult to include all the components of an integrated study, care needs to be taken to make sure the whole can be represented as well as the relevant parts.

Norwegian researcher Sofia Hussain conducted research in Cambodia that aimed to help the developers of prosthetic legs to obtain a deeper understanding of their users' needs. Hussain conducted semi-structured interviews with six Cambodian children who had prosthetic legs, incorporating 'child-friendly techniques such as drawing, photography, and role play' (Hussain 2011: 1430), and several follow-up interviews with three of those children. She also conducted group interviews with six professional rehabilitation workers and seven children who had no disabilities. Five adults who had been using prosthetic legs since childhood took part first in individual interviews and then in a group interview. Hussain also interviewed five Buddhist monks and four shamans, to find out more about cultural views of disability and health. An interpreter assisted the researcher, as most of the interviewees were Khmer speakers, and all interviews were recorded. The materials for analysis included audio tapes, field notes of interviews and observations, transcripts in English and Khmer, photographs and drawings. Hussain took a cyclical approach to her analysis, 'working from parts to the whole and back again', and 'looking for information that stands out, and might lead to a deeper understanding in relation to the lived experiences of those being interviewed' (Hussain 2011: 1431). This enabled the identification of themes, which were refined through discussion with a colleague. Hussain used reflective writing as a key part of her thematic analysis, viewing her material in the context of relevant literature and reflecting on the changes in her own understanding in the process.

This approach was drawn from the work of Gadamer (1975), who 'wrote that all parts of a text should be understood in the context of the entire text, and that the entire text should be interpreted within the framework of its parts' (Hussain 2011:1431). This analytic approach enabled Hussain to identify relevant cultural and social attitudes, and so to establish ways in which the developers of prosthetic legs, and support services such as NGOs operating locally whose staff fit prostheses, could improve the lives of children with disabilities in Cambodia.

 A **Huffington Post articl**e showing one way in which Sofia Hussain's research has been used is available online.

Data analysis using technology

Some researchers worry that a computer will take some of the control away from the researcher within the analytic process (Bazeley and Jackson 2013: 9, Odena 2013: 358) and make the process mechanical (Bazeley and Jackson 2013: 7). However, it can equally be argued that computer–assisted data analysis gives a researcher more control. For qualitative data, this is achieved by offering increased flexibility in coding and ensuring that researchers can rapidly retrieve every item with a given code. Also, it is still the researcher's job to assign names to codes and codes to data, and to derive meaning from the slices of data served up by the computer in response to the researcher's queries. For qualitative or quantitative data, computer-assisted analysis enables work with far bigger datasets than could be analysed by hand. We saw this earlier with the analysis of 600,000 tweets carried out by Tonkin, Pfeiffer and Tourte (2012); even more impressive is the analysis of 2.6 million tweets transmitted by 700,000 users of Twitter during the London riots that was carried out by just three researchers with the aid of computers (Procter, Vis and Voss 2013: 199). The computer is a tool to help the researcher, and just as it's usually easier to bang in a nail with a hammer than with your hand, it's easier to analyse most datasets with a computer than with a pen and paper.

Electronic data needs to be coded with meticulous care, and this can be quite a laborious process. Some computer programs offer automatic coding options so that, for example, you can assign the same code to all the text under the same heading in different documents in a single action (Bazeley and Jackson 2013: 109). This can speed up the process of coding, although it is useful only up to a point, because it is still the researcher's responsibility to define the automated codes, check which other codes may be needed and implement them, and interpret the coded data (Odena 2013: 358). Concentrating on the detail of the data while coding can help to reduce the impact of researchers' unconscious biases about broader themes in the data (Odena 2013: 365) and so can lead to interesting surprises at the analytic stage.

Once the coding is done, analysis is comparatively straightforward. However, whether analysing qualitative or quantitative data, it is essential that the researcher uses analytic techniques appropriately. You need to choose what to consider, compare or calculate, and those decisions should be based on a credible methodological rationale. It is not acceptable to run queries or calculations simply because the software enables you to do so (Cooper and Glaesser 2011: 45–6); you need to know why you're running those queries or calculations.

There are a large number of proprietary software packages to support different kinds of data analysis. Excel and SPSS (Statistical Package for Social Sciences) are probably the most common packages used for quantitative analysis, with the **open source R software** gaining popularity. For qualitative analysis, Atlas.ti and MAXQDA are popular, and there are a number of open source packages available (list on Wikipedia at the time of writing). You can also find packages for the analysis of specific types of data, such as observational or visual data. There are an increasing number of packages being adapted or designed to help with the analysis of large datasets (Cooper and Glaesser 2011: 31; Crowston, Allen and Heckman 2012: 523; Angus, Rintel and Wiles 2013: 261). And there are numerous providers of custom-built software if you can't find the functions you need in any off-the-shelf packages.

Few packages support the analysis of both qualitative and quantitative data, and at the time of writing perhaps the best-known software that does is NVivo. This enables you to import and code across a wide range of data sources, including documents you have created, documents created by others (in word processing or PDF formats), spreadsheets, text files (.txt), images, audio, video, web pages and social media (Facebook, Twitter, LinkedIn, YouTube and so on) (Bazeley and Jackson 2013: 195–209). NVivo is very effective for qualitative data analysis, and reasonably effective for quantitative data analysis (particularly surveys). And it is extremely effective for mixed-methods analysis, supporting a consistent approach to coding across all kinds of data source and so enabling coherent integrated analysis of different types of data (Bazeley and Jackson 2013: 213). Furthermore, NVivo can be useful in the building and development of theory. Grounded theory is often seen as particularly compatible with NVivo (for example, Hutchison, Johnston and Breckon 2010), but the software's modelling and other functions can also be helpful in working with other types of theory.

Transformative frameworks and data analysis

Data preparation, coding and analysis are the aspects of research that are perhaps most resistant to participation. At these stages, research work can be quite tedious, repetitive and time consuming, which puts some people off. There are many barriers to participation in research, and even within transformative frameworks, levels of participation vary considerably between one project and another (Chevalier and Buckles 2013: 174). Also, levels of participation can vary within a research project. Participation is often presented as static and binary – something people either do or don't do – but, in reality, participation fluctuates constantly alongside other demands of life (Jochum and Brodie 2013: 380). However, if people have been fully involved as co-researchers such that they feel the project is truly theirs as much as anyone else's, then they may be willing or even keen to go through the analytic process.

If you want to involve participants in data analysis, you'll need to make early decisions about gathering data and using an analytic process that can be accessible for your participants.

> As we saw in Chapter Five, Mary Ann Kluge and her colleagues in America and New Zealand (Kluge et al 2010) used video in their case study of Linda, a 65-year-old woman who had minimal experience of sport and didn't like exercise, yet decided to aim for master's level as a senior athlete. They gathered many hours of video footage, from Linda's first-ever training session to her competing in, and winning, a race at the Rocky Mountain Senior Games. The video footage was viewed several times by researchers and participant together, with the aim of recognising material that was visually significant and could be used to reflect the associated narrative. This collaborative process enabled the participant to verify as significant the themes identified by the researchers.

Some participants may need more support with analysing data than others, such as children, or people with learning disabilities (Nind 2011: 375). Whether or not participants have extra support needs, the key to maximising participation in the analytic phase is to make the process as accessible as possible. It may also help, if appropriate for your project, to integrate data analysis with data gathering, at least to some extent.

> Critical communicative methodology (CCM) is a particularly ethical type of participatory mixed-methods research that aims to identify and solve social problems through dialogue. A key aspect of communicative analysis is to identify a successful or 'transformative' case and interrogate it thoroughly. For example, a study of the economic crisis, aiming to find effective alternatives to the capitalist system, focused on the Mondragon Corporation, a very successful and ethical group of cooperatives. Mondragon was founded in 1955 and by 2008 had become Spain's third-largest industrial group by employees, with almost 100,000 staff. It works in industry, distribution, finance and knowledge and is successful in overcoming inequalities such as social exclusion, with a range of ways in which staff can participate in management and decision making. Mondragon was able not only to maintain but also to create employment during the economic crisis. The case of Mondragon was interrogated to find out what made it so successful and whether its success could be replicated. Statistical and interview data was gathered, coded and analysed with reference to identified barriers and enablers to social inclusion, within Habermas's 'system' and 'lifeworld' distinction, that is, the social/organisational or the personal/experiential. Identification of barriers helps to identify reasons why those barriers continue to exist, and identification

of enablers helps to show what may be transferred to other contexts (Redondo et al 2011: 282).

Arts-based data analysis

The arts offer many creative ways to enrich the analytic process. Here are just three examples: screenplay writing, I–poems and a mixed–methods arts–based approach using poems, photographs and diagrammatic metaphors.

Lisbeth Berbary, an American researcher, used screenplay writing as creative analytic practice in her feminist research. She studied discourses of femininity among young women in an American sorority (college students' social club for women). Berbary gathered data through participant and informal observation, in-depth and informal interviews and artefact collections. Her analysis began with coding against her research questions, but the resulting categorisation seemed unsatisfactory because it didn't reflect the complexity of her data. So she looked for a way to deconstruct her analysis and chose to write a screenplay, albeit one that is ethnographic rather than intended for production. Berbary structured her screenplay carefully to reflect the themes from her data. She used seven different settings from the university campus, taking details from her observational field notes and making changes only where necessary to protect participants' confidentiality. Four main characters were created as composites from research participants, differing from each other in as many ways as possible while remaining true to the data. Scenes were written showing settings, characters, dialogue, action, interaction, non-verbal communication and gesture. Berbary also included 'director's comments', which enabled her to include the connections she made between perspectives, themes and data. This 'writing inquiry' enabled illumination of sorority women's experiences of gender and femininity (Berbary 2011: 186).

Given that written text is so dominant in research outputs, it is perhaps not surprising that creative analytic practice is also dominated by written art forms.

I-poems are a way of identifying how participants represent themselves in interviews, by paying attention to the first-person statements in the interview transcripts. This technique was developed by Carol Gilligan and her colleagues in the 1990s and used more recently by UK researchers Rosalind Edwards and Susie Weller in their longitudinal research investigating change and continuity in young people's senses of self over time. The interview transcripts are carefully read to identify the ways in which interviewees speak about themselves, paying particular attention to any statements using the personal pronoun 'I'. Each instance of 'I' is highlighted, together with any relevant accompanying text that might help a reader to understand the interviewee's sense of self. These highlighted phrases are then copied out of the transcript and placed in a new document, in the same sequence, each instance beginning in a new line, like the lines of a poem. I-poems can be very helpful in identifying participants' senses of self by foregrounding the voice, or voices, that they use to talk about themselves. This is an adaptable technique that can be used with participants of different ages, genders, abilities and backgrounds (Edwards and Weller 2012: 206) although working with I-poems is quite time consuming, so they're best used with a small sample or sub-sample (Edwards and Weller 2012: 215).

It would also be possible to construct we-poems, they-poems and so on, if relevant for your dataset.

Researching complex human experience suggests, to some people, that they could reflect that complexity by mixing analytic methods.

Jennifer Lapum and her colleagues in Canada used arts-based analysis in their investigation of patients' experiences of open-heart surgery. Participants took part in two interviews after their operations, the first while they were in hospital but out of intensive care and the second when they had been home from hospital for 4–6 weeks. Between the two interviews, participants kept a journal of their experiences (Lapum et al 2011: 102). The multi-disciplinary research team used an arts-based method of analysing patients' stories. They began by imagining how patients felt physically and emotionally during their experiences. Patients' stories were presented in chronological order, so this was used as an organising framework. The framework had five phases: pre-operative, post-operative, discharge from hospital, early and later recovery at home. Within this framework, key words, phrases and ideas from the patients' stories were documented and categorised. These key words, phrases and ideas were used to form free-verse poems. The team also developed concepts for photographic images that would highlight the main narrative ideas of each poem. This process yielded several poems and photographic images. Reflective discussions about the poetry and images, drawing heavily on imagination, were used to seek fuller understanding of patients' experiences. In a second phase of analysis, the images were further developed and the poetic text refined so as to 'further illuminate the complexities, ambiguities, defining features, tensions, and sensory details' of participants' stories (Lapum et al 2011: 104). This was done through 'a process of iterative dialogue, systematic inquiry, visualization, concept mapping, and metaphorical interpretation' (Lapum et al 2011: 104). The researchers discussed, wrote, and drew their findings as visual and diagrammatic metaphors. This analytic technique was explicitly used to work towards a public exhibition that would be used to disseminate the research findings and that is discussed more fully in Chapter Nine.

 A **video output** from this research can be viewed online.

CONCLUSION

There are many ways to analyse primary and secondary data and to integrate different datasets, and more are being devised all the time. This means that, although parts of the process can be laborious and repetitive, there is still plenty of scope for creativity in data analysis. However, it is important to ensure that your analytic method produces findings that are firmly rooted in your data. It is equally important to ensure that your analysis and its results will be helpful in the next stages of the research process: writing, presentation, dissemination and implementation.

SEVEN

Writing for research

Introduction

Writing is the one art form with which all researchers must engage. Sadly, many researchers 'are not willing or able to write engaging prose' (Ellingson 2009: 57). Traditional research writing is 'depersonalized and alienating' (Gergen and Gergen 2012: 50) and some academics, in particular, write in such a 'dense and convoluted' style that their ideas are hard to grasp (Jones and Leavy 2014: 6). But it does not have to be like that. This chapter aims to help you write creatively and well. Also, a number of useful **resources to help you write well for research** are available online.

Good, creative research writing will always be:

- Clear, at every level, from each individual sentence to the overall structure
- helpful
- understandable
- free of waffle and jargon
- properly spelled and punctuated
- original, without clichés or plagiarism
- written with the requirements of its audience(s) in mind.

Good research writing will also have a clear narrative. Even the most quantitative, statistical research can be communicated only through stories made of words (Smith 2009: 99). Numbers in research are not neutral, they are value-laden communication devices that – like words – can be used in many different ways. However, the ways in which numbers are used to communicate are not always clear in and of themselves, because numbers do not 'carry within themselves everything that is needed to interpret their meaning' (Verran 2014: 118). Therefore, researchers using numbers need to explain how those numbers are being used, and interpret their meanings for their readers.

Australian researcher Helen Verran has identified three main ways in which numbers are used by researchers:

1 iconic numbers, used to order our social world, such as the calculation of Gross National Product; these numbers are generally accepted as correct by most people

2 symbolic numbers, used to represent value in a theoretical context, such as the headline ratio of a Social Return on Investment study

3 indexical numbers, used for 'an ongoing project of ordering and reordering effected partly in response to values that become calculable through the ordering moment' (Verran 2014: 123), such as the Global Peace Index, which is an annual calculation of the relative peacefulness of nations around the world.

Helen Verran suggests that 'researchers in the social sciences should know what they are doing with their numbers and how, and most importantly be able to articulate why they want to work with numbers in those ways' (Verran 2014: 123).

The UK Government Statistical Service (GSS) has produced some useful guidance on writing about statistics (GSS undated). It recommends choosing a descriptive title. The writer should understand the context for the research and the factors that could influence the findings, and should be able to explain these clearly for readers. The most important and relevant messages from the data should be summarised and highlighted. More detailed background information, such as methodological details or raw data, should be presented in appendices. It is useful to include other statistics for context, where possible: for example, if your data is collected locally, there may be parallel national figures that could indicate whether the local situation is below, above or on average. Overall, the GSS stresses the importance of good interpretive commentary that informs readers about the meaning and relevance of the data, rather than simply describing the data. It suggests that interpretation 'should explore relationships, causes and effects, to the extent that they can be supported by evidence ... and present a balanced picture.' (GSS undated: 14) The **GSS guidance** is available online.

While some quantitative researchers struggle to communicate their research in writing, so too do some artistic researchers. As this book demonstrates, many artistic researchers understand that their artistic practice is a form of research and that it can make a significant contribution to research. However, with the possible exception of the word-based arts such as poetry and storytelling, in the language-dominated world of the academy these practices often fail to be understood or recognised as legitimate research (Blom, Bennett and Wright 2011: 360). Yet writing itself is an art form, a creative process, and this will be discussed in more detail later in the chapter.

Writing occurs throughout the research process. Research proposals and plans; e-mails; funding applications; ethics applications; minutes of meetings; to-do lists – writing is a fundamental building block of research.

Sheila Henderson and her colleagues in the UK conducted qualitative longitudinal research for the Inventing Adulthoods project. They interviewed 121 people growing up in England and Northern Ireland up to six times each over 10 years. The process for turning the resulting huge volume of biographical information into comprehensible written accounts developed as the research progressed. After the first set of interviews, the researchers conducted straightforward thematic analysis and wrote a reasonably conventional account linking theory, research questions, findings and social policy (Henderson et al 2007). As the dataset grew, the researchers began to work towards writing individual case studies to show how participants' lives changed over time. Narrative analysis formed an intermediate step after the second set of interviews, and they built on this after the third set to write condensed 'case profiles' that showed at a glance how circumstances changed over time, and summarised key themes from interviews, researchers' notes and initial connections with the research questions. These case profiles then formed the bases for the case studies, which were structured to give a sense of chronological order while also focusing on four key biographical fields: work, play, education and family (Henderson et al 2012: 21).

The **Inventing Adulthoods website** provides more information about the project.

Ethics in writing for research

When you reach the writing stage, you develop a new set of responsibilities: to your potential readers, as well as to participants, researchers whose work you are building on and all the others who hold a stake in your research. For your readers, you need to write well and clearly, so as to help them read and understand your work as easily as possible. You need to do justice to your participants by ensuring that you represent your data accurately and interpret your findings fairly in your writing. And you need to be fair to researchers whose work you build on, by citing their work accurately and not plagiarising (Löfström 2011: 263).

There are many ethical decisions to be made in writing. For example, qualitative researchers often use direct quotes from participants in their writing. This is seen by some as an ethical approach because it gives participants 'a voice'. Most researchers will use a pseudonym, unless their participants object. But how do you choose a pseudonym? Is it best to choose a name that indicates the same gender, age, race and so on as the actual participant? Or not? Suppose your participant was called Wilfred Arthur Brown. What constitutes a good pseudonym? Arthur Wilfred Smith? Bilbo Baggins? Jamila Patel? Should you ask your participant to choose their own pseudonym? Are there contexts in which using a pseudonym will not protect participants' anonymity?

As we saw in Chapter Three, Danish researcher Stine Lomborg studied the ways in which Danish people use personal blogs and Twitter, and how those social media were integrated with their users' everyday lives. She gathered an archive consisting of six months of posts from several blogs and one month of tweets

> from several Twitter accounts. In writing up her data analysis, she realised that she needed to quote excerpts from some of the posts and tweets. However, this would compromise her participants' anonymity because entering a string of text from such an excerpt in any internet search engine would lead straight to the blogger or tweeter. The data was already, in a sense, in the public domain and it fell under the Danish Data Protection Agency's definition of 'non-sensitive information'. Nevertheless, Lomborg decided that it would not be ethical to compromise her participants' anonymity. Instead, she shared her write-up in draft with her participants and gave them the option to remove any direct quotes that they didn't want to share through her research (Lomborg 2012: 26).

There is huge scope for creativity here, and it may be useful to think about what you want your readers to understand and take from your research. But then, how ethical is it to try to influence your readers? Should you revert to trying to be somehow 'neutral'? Is that even possible?

Audience

Writing, while in one sense a solitary pursuit, is also a relational activity (Tierney and Hallett 2010: 683). Even a private personal diary is written by a current self for a future self. And any other form of writing will have at least one reader in mind, such as when you write an e-mail or a card for a single recipient. Research writing is likely to have several audiences, some at different stages of its development. For example, a dissertation may be critiqued by fellow students and supervisors before it is marked by examiners. An academic journal article may be critiqued by colleagues before it is assessed by an editor, reviewed by peer reviewers and eventually read by scholars and other interested people. Whenever you are writing, whatever you are writing, you need to keep your audience(s) in mind and write for them.

Feedback

Receiving feedback on your research writing, whether from a fellow student, supervisor, commissioner, colleague, peer reviewer or someone else, can be a daunting experience. A survey of 150 postgraduate students from a range of disciplines found that, for most of them, feedback took too long, arrived too late, was over-critical and didn't help them to improve their writing skills (Catt and Gregory 2006: 23). To use feedback creatively, seek it at an early stage, from someone who can and will discuss it with you to help you improve. But ask that person to give you their feedback in writing first, then take some time to read and digest the written feedback before moving into the discussion phase. Try not to be defensive; rather, be open to suggestions and ideas – although of course the final decision is yours. Good feedback, helpfully offered, can help you to improve your writing and your research work far more – and more creatively – than you could achieve alone.

Giving feedback is also a creative process. When giving feedback, you need to read someone's work carefully, at least twice, and make notes as you go. Don't spend ages correcting typos or grammar, just make a passing comment if there are a significant number of errors. Instead, think about what could be improved, and how this could be done. Is the narrative coherent? Does it flow well? Do the arguments make sense? Is the structure helpful? Are there any specific flaws such as unnecessary repetition or waffle? How can you help the writer to improve their work? Having said that, don't expect the writer to accept all your suggestions. The work is, after all, theirs not yours, so they have the final decision. Offering feedback is helpful, but doesn't entitle you to part-ownership of the writing work. A **video** presented by Nick Hopwood about how to give effective feedback on academic writing can be viewed online, and the principles and practices discussed have application beyond the academy.

The international Committee on Publication Ethics (COPE) published a set of **ethical guidelines for peer reviewers** in March 2013, which are freely available online, just five pages long and well worth consulting by anyone who is thinking of giving someone feedback on their work. The following are some of the key points.

- Make sure you have time to do a proper critique before you agree to take it on.
- Only critique work where you have the necessary expertise in the subject matter (unless the writer wants a critique from a layperson's perspective, or for some other reason).
- Read the work thoroughly.
- Make constructive comments about the text, not personal comments about the writer.
- Give your feedback within a reasonable length of time.
- Keep the work, and your feedback, confidential.

Fact versus fiction

Writing doesn't come naturally, because it isn't natural: it is a craft, a skill, that has to be learned. One aspect of the craft that novice writers often find hard to grasp is that every piece of good research writing will go through several drafts, and revision and editing are essential parts of the process (Becker 2007: 17). This can be an intensely creative practice, even for those producing academic writing (Lillis 2006: 31). Creativity is highly relevant to academic writing, even in 'hard science' subjects such as engineering (Ahearn 2006: 117).

Writing is creative in many ways, not only in creating sentences and paragraphs and meaning, but also in helping the writer to think creatively while they review, re-evaluate and refine their ideas as they write (Colyar 2009: 425–6). Given that writing is an integral part of research, and most research outputs are written, it seems odd that few books on research methods give advice on how to write (Murray 2011: 2). Those that do usually treat research writing as factual, non-fiction prose. Yet writers of fiction and non-fiction use many of the same skills (Stein 1998: 7), which suggests that even prose non-fiction may be more creative than it appears (Brien 2013: 35). For example, any piece of good writing, whether academic or romance or autobiography, will be written using a consistent 'voice' or persona. Finding the right 'voice' is part of the creative process of writing. Writing in English, which is rich in synonyms, means that we have choices to make in almost every phrase. A writer's choices must be guided by, and consistent with, the voice in which they are writing. And choices mean decisions – where, as we have seen, creativity resides. In some contexts, using fictional forms in research writing may be a sensible ethical choice, such as when it is vital to protect participants' identities because of the sensitivity of a research topic (Piper and Sikes 2010: 572). Indeed, it has been argued that the distinction between fact and fiction is not clear (Brinkmann 2009: 1390; Ellingson 2009: 66; Vickers 2010: 561) and that 'writers both beyond and within the academy have been blurring the fiction–nonfiction divide for centuries' (Leavy 2012: 517).

Patricia Leavy is now a full-time creative academic writer and her **website** has lots of useful information for people who want to write creatively in research.

Some writers of research have found that using the techniques of literary fiction helps to solve research problems at the writing stage, such as by showing 'other truths and different perspectives that were not available in the nonfiction realm' (Vickers 2010: 563). For example, the ethnographer Kay Inckle, in her investigation of gendered embodiment and body-marking practices informed by queer theory, and Helen Kara, in her PhD research into the emotion work of managers in public sector partnerships informed by social policy and organisation theories, reached similar conclusions about this, despite their very different areas of study. Both concluded that their research was best written using fictionalised accounts, rooted in the experience of real people, that portray actual but anonymised experiences and are directly applicable to real-life situations (Inckle 2010: 37; Kara 2013: 81). Both Inckle and Kara placed their fictional accounts within a conventional academic framework, but not all scholars have done so. For example, the ethnographer Jessica Gullion writes her study of health and natural-gas drilling in north Texas using a short abstract that leads into an entire article of creative non-fiction based on her field notes and in-depth interview transcripts (2013).

Katrina Rodriguez and Maria Lahman, from the US, investigated how messages from family and peers influence the ways in which Latina college students understand their intersecting ethnicity, class and gender, and the value of education. They chose to write up their findings as a full-length three-act play script titled *Las Comadres: Cuentame su Historia* ('Girlfriends: Tell Me Your Story'), made up of both direct quotes from interview and focus group transcripts, and fictional dialogue created by the researchers. The aim was to place participants at the centre of the research. 'Creating intersections of race, class, and gender in the dramatic script allow for a complex view of participants and their multidimensionality' (Rodriguez and Lahman 2011: 603). The original plan was to use only quotes from transcripts in the play script, but, used alone, these 'sounded flat and sanitised' (Rodriguez and Lahman 2011: 611). The researchers had to perform a difficult balancing act as they rewrote the text: making sure the words would work as performed dialogue, while maintaining the integrity of participants' experiences and messages. While this play has not been performed, the researchers did enlist the help of colleagues in reading the script aloud during the writing process, which helped to enhance the authenticity of the characters' dialogue and interaction.

Perhaps this is, at least in part, due to the communicative power of stories. Stories are an economical way to communicate ideas, emotions and experience directly and vividly, make sense of complex situations and share knowledge (Gabriel and Connell 2010: 507–8). There is evidence that reading fictional stories influences the way people feel and think (Djikic et al 2009: 27). Yet, creative writing has traditionally been seen as separate from academic writing; but more recently this division has been described as 'perplexing' by academic writers (Young and Avery 2006: 97) and 'falsely separated' from the creative writing side (Lasky 2013: 16). And indeed researchers today are being much more creative with their writing. They are telling research stories through a wide range of prose and non–prose forms, including poetry, dialogue, vignettes, play scripts, screenplays and memoir. Some researchers argue that this is an entirely legitimate way to convey social scientific truths about human experience (for example, Brinkmann 2009: 1381). Others go further, calling for research to be written in 'aesthetic, literary forms turning the reading of research into an experience in itself' (Finlay 2012: 29).

Kitrina Douglas and David Carless are UK researchers who are interested in how sport and exercise can contribute to recovery from severe and enduring mental illness. As part of their research, they set up and ran a nine-week golf programme for men with severe and enduring mental health problems. They analysed the resulting data using thematic analysis and then narrative analysis, but neither technique proved adequate to communicate the 'richness and complexity' of the data to the researchers' satisfaction (Douglas and Carless 2010: 337). The researchers then turned to writing as a form of analysis, and experimented with poetic representation, autoethnography, songwriting, creative non-fiction and ethnographic fiction (Douglas and Carless 2010: 338). Like all research methods, each of these has advantages and disadvantages. Douglas and Carless learned from this process that the methods of data analysis and presentation chosen by researchers have an impact on the types of knowledge they produce and also have a reciprocal influence on the researchers themselves, in terms of the types of researchers they become (Douglas and Carless 2010: 351; see also Barone and Eisner 2012: 5).

A short performative **video** based on the research of Douglas and Carless, and that shows some of the ways alternative styles of writing can be used, can be viewed online.

Researchers are also acknowledging the limitations of writing. For a start, it's not possible to tell everything that could be told (Lemert 1999: 440), so every writer has to be selective. For a second thing, writing is not able to convey the totality of human experience (Barbour 2012: 67; Romanyshyn 2013: 5), although words can 'pin experience to meaning, at least temporarily' (Lockford 2012: 236). Some writers argue that traditional academic writing conveys less about human experience than more creative approaches (for example, Tamas 2010; Kara 2013). And it is certainly the case that creative approaches such as fiction evoke more emotion in readers than non-fictional writing, even when the level of interest is the same (Djikic et al 2009: 27).

Academic writers usually wear a mantle of certainty (Vannini 2013: 447). There is a convention in academic writing that authors should reveal some of their uncertainties, such as the problems they encountered during the research process, and some of the limitations of their research. But even this is cloaked in a sense of certainty: as if everything that could be revealed has been revealed. The words 'author', 'authority' and 'authoritative' are closely linked. This effect is partly created by the passive voice so common in academic literature, which conveys events as if they were fixed and unarguable: 'Potential participants were given a copy of the leaflet and an opportunity to discuss the research and question the researcher. Those who agreed to take part were then asked to sign a consent form.' This is partly because the passive voice is a legacy from traditional research methods, within which the researcher was supposed to be a fulcrum for the research process rather than part of that process. It is also because the passive voice uses a form of the past tense, which gives the impression that we are dealing with fixed facts, rather than acts, speech, experience and events that are open to interpretation (Vannini 2013: 447). Some academic authors now choose to use the present tense for a more active voice, which allows the process being described to unfold within the narrative as if it is happening before the reader's eyes (Vannini 2013: 447). It also allows the researcher's involvement in the research to be made clear: 'I give a copy of the leaflet to potential participants, and offer them the opportunity to discuss the research and ask me questions. If they agree to take part, I ask them to sign a consent form.'

Journals

One tool in the researcher's box that has the potential to be very creative is the research journal. The kind of reflective thinking required to keep a research journal has been found to promote creativity (Cohen and Ferrari 2010: 71), so, for researchers wishing to be more creative, a journal can be very helpful. There are several types of research journal, including:

- field journal – originally used by ethnographers as a daily diary
- reflexive journal – borrowed from health and social care, in which the researcher exercises 'self-surveillance' (Alaszewski 2006: 12) to help develop and improve their research skills
- arts-based journal – for example, based on poetry (Slotnick and Janesick 2011: 1353) or sketched cartoons
- photo-journal – where visual images are important, such as in tourism research
- audio journal – useful for researchers who can't carry much equipment, or who have difficulty using a pen or keyboard
- video journal – helpful for researchers who want to make a fuller record than is possible with text, images or audio alone
- online journal – this can be mixed-media, including text, images, audio, video, hyperlinks and so on; a number of researchers now keep research journals online in the form of weblogs.

Journals can be entirely private, for the researcher's own use; entirely public, as in an openly accessible blog; or part private, part public. The latter case could, for example, be a journal initially intended to be private that the researcher later decides to harvest for data to use as part of the project, some of which may end up being quoted in the final report or other output. Or a researcher could keep a public online journal, plus a separate offline journal for confidential and sensitive material, as well as odd jottings and notes that are too unformed for public view.

Slotnick and Janesick (2011) suggest that researchers can use journals in a number of ways, including:

- to help them clarify and articulate the purpose of their research
- to reflect on their own thinking patterns, with the aim of increasing their understanding of the ways they do – and can – work
- to reflect on their own role, to gain a fuller understanding of its meaning and possibilities
- to reflect on, and thereby gain a fuller understanding of, participants' responses
- to vent emotions such as frustration
- as data for analysis to 'create cohesive, coherent, and deeply textured analysis' through writing (Slotnick and Janesick 2011: 1354)

Blogs

Researchers are increasingly using blogs to write about their research. Blogs can be used at a late stage in the research process for dissemination (Mewburn and Thomson 2013: 1111). They can also be used throughout the process as an online equivalent to a field journal, although of course omitting any confidential or private content, as a blog is in the public domain (Vannini 2013: 448–9). If comments are enabled, or blogs include the researcher's e-mail address (or it can easily be found online), the researcher can gather feedback, ideas and suggestions during the process, which can be very helpful for the research (Vannini 2013: 449). Blogs can even help researchers to recruit participants, by giving details of what kind of persons will be needed, where and when (Vannini 2013: 449).

Blogs are content heavy and demanding of time, and so are probably easier to manage as a field journal equivalent than for dissemination alone (see Chapter Nine for more information on setting up and managing a blog). But the actual writing process is reasonably straightforward. A compelling blog post will be 500–700 words in length and well written, in plain English and with a good narrative arc. It is useful to embed hyperlinks for readers to click on if they want more information, but the blog post should stand alone so that time-poor readers can take something from it without having to click on the links.

Poetic writing

We have seen that poems have been used to support data analysis. They are also used in writing research. This can be done in a range of ways. Poetry can be formed or extracted from data, like the I-poems constructed by Edwards and Weller (2012) as discussed in Chapter Six. Speech is often as close to poetry as to prose (Carter 2004: 10), yet written speech is usually represented in prose. For example, the following is a piece of data from my PhD, a quotation spoken, in fact, by me:

> I think that applies to all, all research methodologies, really, because it's, I mean one of the things about this is that it is novel, it does, you know, it is thinking out of the box, but it will create its own box, in time, if it goes on, in the way that interviewing has done and you know focus groups have done.

If I render this quotation word for word as a poem, it reads as follows:

I think that applies to all
All research methodologies, really
Because it's
I mean one of the things about this is
That it is
Novel
It does
You know
It is thinking out of the box
But it will create its own box
In time
If it goes on

In the way that interviewing has done
And
You know
Focus groups have done

Poems, demonstrably, make people feel and think differently (Dark 2009: 182–3). I contend that the 'poem' above has a different effect on the reader than the prose quotation, even though it contains the same words in the same order. There may be a couple of reasons for this. First, precisely transcribed speech often reads rather badly, like rambling, ill-formed prose. This gives the reader a negative perception of the speaker, because the speaker's words are set out on the page like properly written prose, while in fact they are transcribed speech (Mark Miller 2013: personal communication). If the speaker's words are set out like a poem, with one unit per line, the meaning and impact are clearer; perhaps because, as we have seen, spoken language has more in common with poetry than with prose (Carter 2004: 10). Second, setting out this spoken language as if it were a poem highlights some of the devices that speakers and poets both use for effect, such as repetition and rhythm (Swann 2006: 10, 44). It is not in any sense a 'good' poem, but it could, in some contexts, be a useful one.

Kate Connelly was part of a research team investigating the lives of people on welfare benefits in Victoria, Australia. She noticed that the recordings and transcripts comprising the research data were poetic in nature, with speakers using devices such as pauses, repetition and changes in tone or volume for emphasis. Connelly decided to re-present participants' voices in poetic form, with the aim of creating emotional connections between their stories and her readers. This reader found the poems to be powerfully affecting when read from the page, and Connelly reports that several of her colleagues were moved to tears by reading them aloud (Connelly 2010: 32). She concludes that the poems have potential as a tool for use in social policy (Connelly 2010: 39).

Poetic representation in research writing is most commonly seen in the form of free verse. However, there are exceptions. For example, the American researcher Darlene Drummond used traditional forms of poetry, including the villanelle, rondeau and roundel, to depict the intra-racial experiences of White college women. Drummond used these traditional forms to 'address serious issues of racial identification, identity negotiation, and enactment' and 'employs the principles of variation, alliteration, and rhyming to underscore the impact of various ethnicities and nationalities in making Whiteness visible within the United States' (Drummond 2011: 332).

Collaborative writing

Researchers regularly collaborate, which can increase creativity, particularly when they come from different disciplinary backgrounds. Perhaps more creatively still, some researchers now co-write with their participants. There are several ways of doing this, from simply adding a participant's name or pseudonym to the list of authors, to full-scale collaboration.

> Carolyn Ellis and Jerry Rawicki's relationship began as researcher and interviewee, when she interviewed him as part of a larger study of Holocaust survivors in America. During the initial interviews, Ellis decided to do a small number of follow-up interviews with survivors who were interested in talking further about their experiences, one of whom was Rawicki. Ellis wrote drafts of Rawicki's stories and made initial interpretations, then they worked together to edit and revise the stories, 'passing them back and forth numerous times over a two-year period during 2009–2011' (Ellis and Rawicki 2013: 367). They use the present tense and a literary style with the aim of engaging readers' emotions as well as their thoughts. Initially, Ellis assumed that Rawicki would tell the stories and she would provide the analytic interpretations. However, Rawicki challenged Ellis's interpretations and offered many of his own, while Ellis used all the details and analytic insight provided by Rawicki to help tell his stories. Ultimately, their roles overlapped to such an extent that they have now co-written several publications, some with Ellis and at least one with Rawicki as lead author.

Many of Carolyn Ellis's **interviews** with Jerry Rawicki are available on YouTube.

Mixed-methods writing

It is possible to use several different writing techniques, even within one short journal article. This can be confusing, difficult to read and understand, but, if done well, can be very effective.

> Ben Clayton is a British lecturer and researcher who chose to write up some of his findings from two related but separate research projects using a combination of techniques from fiction, creative non-fiction and traditional academic writing. He had conducted an ethnographic study of male football (soccer) players, and a study of students' experiences of learning about 'gender and difference' in sports-related courses, at a British university (Clayton 2010: 373). Some of the participants in the first study were also participants in the second. Clayton's write-up was framed by traditional academic writing, with an abstract, a scene-setting, contextualising introduction and a conclusion. In between came 'the tale', a story of a 10-minute classroom interaction informed by empirical data. This tale was framed by creative non-fiction-type prose in the third person, interspersed with

fictionalised scenes incorporating standard elements of fiction writing such as dialogue, speech tags, description and sensory writing. Clayton's intention was to 'show' his readers, rather than 'tell' them about, some aspects of masculinity and the gender relations of male, football-playing students.

It is also possible to add visual elements to text, such as by using different fonts.

Rosemary Reilly, a Canadian researcher studying the effect of violent trauma on communities, used a range of techniques, including creative non-fiction and poetic transcription, in her writing about the murder of a young girl. Her aim was to 'communicate the depth of grief, loss, and disconnection' as well as the difficulty of researching trauma (Reilly 2011: 599). The paper begins with a conventional academic voice, then moves to the researcher as narrator in creative, non-fiction style. Some of the narrator's words are set out as poetry, some as prose, although the voice is consistent throughout. Two research participants are each given their own voice, set out as poetry, introduced by name (using pseudonyms) and each in a different font, which is different again from the font used for the researcher's voice. For this reader, Reilly's mixed-methods writing achieved her aims.

More and more researchers are choosing to use other forms of representation alongside their words. This has long been done in quantitative research, with tables, charts and diagrams forming an integral part of many articles and books. Historically, it has been less common in qualitative research, perhaps partly because of the higher printing costs of pictures, perhaps because they are seen as less valuable than words within the academy (which seems odd, in contrast with the journalist's dictum that 'a picture is worth a thousand words'). It can be more difficult to achieve formal publication of mixed-methods accounts of research (Ellingson 2009: 61). Also, if not carefully constructed, these texts can be incoherent and exhausting to read (Ellingson 2009: 61). However, if done well, mixed-methods accounts can both tell and show, by combining a rich evocation of an experience with a critical view (Ellingson 2009: 61).

UK researcher Helen Owton used narrative poetry and artwork, alongside conventional academic prose, to show and tell readers about her research into sport and asthma. Her aim was to align and unite these three methods so as to enrich the reader's experience of her narrative by explicitly evoking 'emotional and visceral' responses to add to the inevitable cognitive ones (Owton 2013: 600). For Owton, this is important because asthma is a sensory experience and sport is an embodied activity, so her view is that 'Narrative poetry and art might help explore personal and shared bodily-felt sensory experiences of asthma' (Owton 2013: 602). For me (asthmatic and not very sporty), her approach was effective, perhaps in part because she is a published poet and a skilled artist.

It is difficult to write a report or article about research involving embodied methods (Cherrington and Watson 2010: 278). This is partly because academic writing rarely uses the vocabulary of embodiment, apart from a few metaphorical usages such as 'standpoint' or 'perspective', with visual words being heavily dominant and few words evoking the other main senses of hearing, touch, smell or taste. Yet, 'people's knowledge of themselves, others and the world they inhabit, is inextricably linked to and shaped by their senses' (Sparkes 2009: 23–4). And this includes other senses such as movement and rhythm (Sparkes 2009: 27). Fiction and poetic writing techniques encourage sensory writing, while analytic, non-fiction techniques, conventionally used to report research, make it difficult to convey sensory experience (Vannini et al 2010: 380). Yet it is hard to judge whether fictionalised or poetic writing conveys information effectively, as these writing techniques are specifically designed to evoke individual emotional responses. New digital technologies have a great deal of potential for adding extra dimensions to writing, such as a soundtrack, images, animation, film and other ways to engage the senses more fully (Sparkes 2009: 33). However, as yet, this potential has barely begun to be realised. Some books and journals, for example Robson (2011) and *Qualitative Research in Sport and Exercise* vol 2 no 2 (2010) (and, of course, this book too), contain links to websites where extra resources, colour images and video clips can be viewed, but in terms of the potential of digital technologies to add extra dimensions to writing, this is barely scratching the surface. In the meantime, researchers are doing all they can to add extra dimensions to their writing on the page.

Karen Barbour is a Pākehā (white) dancer and researcher from New Zealand who aims for 'methodological fusion between my autoethnographic writing and solo contemporary dance practices' (Barbour 2012: 67). Her paper begins with a conventional academic abstract, keywords and short introduction. Then there is an 'activity', in two columns; the left-hand column contains instructions for a yoga-type exercise and the right-hand column contains an academic commentary. Then there is a paragraph of creative non-fiction, followed by a photograph of the author engaging in the first activity. Then a second activity with commentary; a paragraph of creative non-fiction; and a photograph of the author engaging in the second activity. This format is used three more times, and the paragraph of (presumably) creative non-fiction before the fifth photograph is in te reo Maori (the language of New Zealand's indigenous people), which is not translated. An endnote for this paragraph explains that the author's intention is to 'draw attention to the way in which understanding other languages provides opportunities to know and communicate embodied experiences in different ways' and 'to highlight that' te reo Maori is 'a living treasure' (Barbour 2012: 71). A final section of the paper is written in conventional academic language, and then ends with a short poem that the author asserts contains some of the sentiments also included in the te reo Maori piece. Then come the acknowledgements, a final photograph of the author dancing, the usual declarations about conflicts of interest and funding, end notes, references and so on. I found it quite difficult to

> digest and understand Barbour's work while moving back and forth between these registers, although the concluding section did a good job of bringing together the apparently disparate points made in the body of the article.

Within Ellingson's methodological framework of crystallisation, outlined in Chapter Four, she describes this kind of mixed-methods account as 'integrated crystallization'. This refers to 'a written and/or visual text consisting of multiple genres' (Ellingson 2009: 97). For Ellingson, this refers solely to qualitative research, but I would contend that quantitative research could also be included, certainly within a mixed-methods project, and perhaps, for some research, alone.

How to write better for research

It often seems to be assumed that researchers can write. Writing is rarely dealt with as part of research training, and many how-to books about research say nothing about writing skills, although two recent exceptions are Robson (2011: 509–13) and Bryman (2012: 684–707). Yet some people find it very difficult to write research, and it can be even harder to admit to having problems with writing (Murray 2009: 2–3).

Many people cite lack of time as a major barrier to the writing process (Murray 2009: 34), but there are many ways to manage time effectively for writing, such as setting goals, making a plan, learning to write in short bursts and establishing writing habits and routines (Murray 2009: 69–85). Also, it's easier to claim lack of time than to own up to feelings of fear and inadequacy, which may sometimes be the bigger obstacles. What novice writers don't know is that all writers have these feelings, but more experienced writers have, on the whole, learned to manage them – by writing (Becker 2007: 56).

Language itself may be part of the problem. The English language can be 'hopelessly fuzzy' (Smith 2009: 94), with many words that can be descriptive, evaluative, predictive or explanatory, depending on how they are used. Think of the word 'kind'. 'She is a kind person' – descriptive. 'She gave me her gloves to warm my hands because she is kind' – explanatory. 'She is kind, so I like her' – evaluative. 'She will help me; she is a kind person' – predictive. There are probably hundreds, maybe even thousands, of other words in the English language that are similarly flexible. This is a gift to rhetoricians, but a challenge to writers, who need to work with all the resources of grammar and structure at their disposal if they are to write clearly.

However, writers of research have a great advantage over many other writers. Writing is an integral part of research work at every stage, from planning to analysis. Therefore, by the time you reach the point of writing a research output such as a report or dissertation, you will have already written thousands of words. Some of this will be ready to use as it stands – a paragraph here, a couple of paragraphs there – while other parts can form a basis for sections of your writing.

You rarely have to start from the proverbial blank sheet of paper (or screen), so there should be no reason for you to suffer from 'writer's block'.

It is true that some parts of research writing are harder than others. Writing recommendations for an evaluation, or constructing an argument for a thesis or journal article, are challenging parts of the process. The way through these difficulties is to keep writing, reading, thinking and writing again. Some people find it helpful to set themselves a daily or weekly word count for the first draft, and a page count at the editing stage. As we have seen, it is also helpful to keep your reader(s) in mind, as this is the key to finding the 'voice' you want to use. 'Voice' is a term from fiction writing that is also applicable to non-fiction (Morgan 2011: 128). The 'voice' of a narrative you write is not quite the same as your own voice (Neale 2009: 181), which is partly because written grammar is rather different from spoken grammar (Carter 2004: 10). It is also because you will want to write persuasively.

The language of persuasion is known as rhetoric. Rhetoric is sometimes derided or dismissed as being too far removed from reality – and indeed, when rhetoric becomes spin, where people such as politicians use language to give a positive gloss to negative news, there is some justification for that view. But the true meaning of rhetoric is to help your audience to comprehend your message through the use of clear language and understandable meaning, using the best possible combinations of words to convey your argument (Greenwell 2009: 196).

Writing research is about identifying links and connections, and interpreting them for your readers. There will be links and connections within the research, such as between your research questions and your data, and beyond the research, such as between your findings and the findings of other relevant research. Interpretation is a crucial part of research work. Anything you feature within your writing – a table, a quote, a graph, an image – needs to be interpreted for your readers, to tell them what is significant or important or relevant. Don't assume they can and will decode a table or an image just like you will; point out which figures in the table, or elements in the image, are worthy of their notice, and explain why.

CONCLUSION

This chapter has covered a range of creative writing techniques. One key question is: which method of writing to use? Thinking about your audience's requirements will help you to decide. Commissioners of contract research are unlikely to be impressed by a poetic presentation; most research participants will not appreciate lots of technical language; academic conference delegates generally prefer writing that is both stimulating and accessible. But, ultimately, decisions about writing methods are highly creative decisions that should not be taken lightly, but should be thoroughly thought through.

EIGHT

Presentation

Introduction

All researchers will need to present their research to at least one audience, such as a written report for commissioners, a PowerPoint presentation for stakeholders or a dissertation or thesis for examiners. Presentation is a form of dissemination, but usually requires the researcher to be present, while on the whole dissemination happens through media that people can access independently, ranging from academic journals to art exhibitions to websites. Dissemination will be covered in Chapter Nine.

Most research is presented through the written word (Jones 2006: 68; Watson 2009: 528). Yet conventional presentation techniques, such as written research reports, or conference papers read out word for word, can be stultifyingly dull (Cutcher 2013: 39). If we want to make our research have an impact, we need to present it in ways that audiences appreciate (Tracy 2010: 838; Kirk 2012: 32; Jones and Leavy 2014: 3). Luckily, there are many creative ways to make your research presentations more engaging, such as visual, performative and other arts-based techniques (Gergen and Gergen 2012: 12, 25–6). However, as with all creative research methods, it's essential to make sure you choose methods of presentation that suit your purposes and are appropriate for your audience(s), rather than using a method just because someone you admire has used it or because it appeals to you.

Just as research methods should be chosen because they are most likely to help answer research questions, so methods of presenting and disseminating research should be chosen because they are most likely to help convey the key messages of the research to the audience(s) (Kelleher and Wagener 2011: 826). This chapter and the next are designed to help you think creatively about possibilities for presentation and dissemination. When you have been immersed in a research project, it can be difficult to step back and think about the needs of individuals and groups for whom your work, or its findings, are news. Yet, it is essential always to keep your audience(s) in mind. Consider questions such as the following:

- What is the audience's demographic profile? Consider factors such as: age range, status (whether professional, community or other), gender balance, ethnicities.
- Are there cultural factors you should take into account?
- What emotional response(s) to your findings do you anticipate? Will your audience be interested, bored, hostile, welcoming? Or a mixture?

- How attentive do you think your audience will be? Are they likely to be riveted by your fascinating findings? Or distracted by hunger, Facebook or other preoccupations?

Answering these kinds of questions will help you to design your presentations to meet your audience's needs. For example, take the cultural question. It is important to remember that particular colours and shapes may have different meanings in different cultures (Evergreen 2014: 106–7). For example, in Europe red means 'danger', as in 'red alert', and is often used for traffic warning signs. In China, however, red means good luck. In some cultures, a circle is just another shape, while for others, such as the indigenous peoples of Canada, the circle is a sacred shape to be treated with reverence (Blodgett et al 2013: 319). So, in preparing presentations, it helps to understand the cultural relevance for your audience of shapes and colours.

If you can't answer questions about your audience precisely, use intelligent guesswork. Knowing your audience will help you to choose suitable methods of presentation, at appropriate levels of detail, using relevant imagery and so on.

Good practice in research presentation suggests that more than one method should be used at a time. For example, a written report should contain charts or pictures, or a spoken presentation should be accompanied by images or video. Even a simple illustration can be useful, in adding another dimension to the presentation of research. An image or video clip can liven up a statistical presentation and make the research seem more relevant or real, while a graph or chart can clarify specific aspects of complex qualitative data (Fielding 2012: 127). Juxtaposing text and images enables you to present more of the complexity of research (Mandlis 2009: 1358).

The ethics of presentation

Over ten years ago Paul John Eakin (2004: 1) stated that very little had been written about the ethics of presentation, and not much has changed since then. Yet, all presentation both reveals and conceals (Tamas 2009: 617). As researchers aspiring to be both creative and ethical, we need to consider both sides of any presentation we create: what does it reveal, and what does it conceal? Methods of presenting research are no more neutral or value free than any other research methods (Ellingson 2009: 6).

In every aspect of research, we need to care for our participants' confidentiality and anonymity. This can cause particular difficulties for the presentation of research.

As we saw in Chapter Five, UK researcher Jacqui Gabb conducted mixed-methods qualitative research into family life in northern England. Family life is generally regarded as very private in Western societies, and family research has to achieve a careful balance between worthwhile social investigation and intrusion into people's personal spaces and relationships. This caused significant problems in presenting the research to participants. While it is easy to protect someone's identity from strangers reading a research report, it is virtually impossible to conceal their identity from other family members doing the same. Case studies were key to Gabb's comprehensive analytical strategy. Gabb acknowledges that this caused some of her ethical problems, but thought that the benefits of the method outweighed the disadvantages (2010: 468–9). In the end, she published just one case study, of a family whose only child was already aged 17. The family were themselves reflexive, open and welcoming of new insights, and, even then, the case study was carefully edited.

However, some participants want to be seen in research presentations, which may conflict with the researcher's tenet that participants' anonymity should always be preserved (Wiles et al 2012: 45). Where participants want to be shown and heard, researchers have a responsibility to accept and work with this, albeit with an eye to safeguarding and the minimisation of harm (Wiles et al 2012: 45–6).

Presentation within transformative frameworks can also be ethically challenging.

UK researcher Victoria Foster conducted participatory research with a Sure Start programme (a UK government initiative to support families with pre-school children in deprived areas). Her participants decided that they wanted to present the research as a pantomime. Foster took care to involve her participants fully in every stage of the research process. However, she was not able to persuade or enable them to reflect critically on the research findings. As a result, the performance, in Foster's view, was skewed towards the positive and ignored some of the negative but very real problems in the Sure Start programme, such as tensions between service users and programme staff. Reflecting on this ethical problem in order to learn for future projects, Foster was unsure whether she would challenge the story her participants wanted to tell, thinking that this might compromise the participatory methodology (Foster 2013: 47). However, she was sure that, on another occasion, she would include an element of discussion with the audience after the performance, thinking that this 'would enable more critical reflection of the findings' (Foster 2013: 48).

Here again, you gain a new level of responsibility: to your audience(s). It is particularly important to be clear about who your audience(s) are (Kirk 2012: 33).

Responsibility to participants is not limited to ensuring their anonymity and confidentiality. It is important to remember that 'Reframing our participants' words within our theoretical frames benefits us far more than them, and may even serve to harm participants' (Ellingson 2009: 37). Fortunately, some presentation methods are specifically designed to be ethical. One example is ethnodrama, a form of 'reality theatre' based on participants' reports that is designed to highlight social (in)justice and provoke social action. There has long been a link between theatre and activism/social justice movements, such as through the work of

Ernesto Boal in the 1970s, who used drama performances in public places to support political resistance, inviting people who found themselves spectating to take part in the drama and so breaking down the barrier between 'performers' and 'audience' (Gergen and Gergen 2012: 162). Gergen and Gergen have called for 'performative social science' to be a 'center of social critique and political action' (Gergen and Gergen 2012: 37).

> Jasjit Sangha and her colleagues studied the lived experience of workers in precarious jobs in Toronto, Canada, most of whom were women and immigrants. The researchers chose to present their findings using ethnodrama. They wanted to convey the complexity of their participants' experiences, bring those experiences vividly to life and show how workers in precarious jobs struggled and managed to navigate their difficult working lives. The ethnodrama was made up of six short scenes, with three scenes showing women working in a call centre, supermarket and garment factory, followed by three more in the same settings but focusing on the workers' resistance (Sangha et al 2012: 288). Minimal props and costumes were used. Casting was intentionally disruptive, for example a woman of colour played a male manager called Tom, to both challenge stereotypes and show how roles in the workplace, rather than personal attributes, create certain responses and behaviours (Sangha et al 2012: 294–5). The ethnodrama was created by a group of researchers and refined over two years as a result of the researchers' experiences of performing the ethnodrama and receiving feedback from their audiences. This method of presenting research findings proved accessible to non-academics, and thought-provoking for all types of audience. It also benefited the researchers, who found that creating and performing the ethnodrama enriched their analysis and expanded their 'understanding of how academic research should be represented and understood' (Sangha et al 2012: 295).

Heather Mosher is a public ethnographer, a discipline that straddles the divide between academic and public communities. Public ethnographers aim to disseminate their work as widely as possible through public media such as film, blogs and magazines. Within this, Mosher is particularly concerned about accurate re-presentation of participants' and researchers' voices within the research. She suggests four key questions to consider when planning to present public ethnography:

'1. How does the research, including the report, give voice to participants?
2. Is the selected communication medium for reporting/disseminating research adequate for presenting the plural structure, multiple voices, views, departures, and agreements leading to multiple possible actions and interpretations?
3. Does the report make clear the researchers' positionality (in relation to politics, intentions, etc) in order for audiences to understand the process through which data were interpreted and represented?

4. How have community members been involved in reviewing the material with the researcher and challenged researchers' interpretations and representations of them?' (Mosher 2013: 435)

Mosher suggests that considering these questions carefully, and taking any resulting action that may be necessary, will help to ensure high-quality presentation of research.

Ethical presentation of research data is presentation that gives the audience the best chance of understanding and remembering the information you wish to convey. Researchers who focus on this as they prepare presentations are likely to make full use of, rather than to misuse, their authorial power and control. It helps if researchers can remain reflexively aware of the details they choose to include and leave out, and of the consequences of their decisions (Ellingson 2009: 39).

When we present research, it is not possible to reveal everything about that research. We can show that research is messy and complex, but we cannot show all the mess or every facet of the complexity. Presentation is necessarily partial, a story we tell – but, if it is a good story, it will engage, instruct and entertain. And I would argue that it is unethical to tell poor-quality stories: it does no justice to our participants and wastes the time of our audiences. Storytelling skills are not the same as writing skills (McKee 1998: 27). As we saw in Chapter Seven, writing skills are essential for research at all stages of the process. But for presentation and dissemination, storytelling skills are also essential, being 'the creative conversion of life itself to a more powerful, clearer, more meaningful experience', whether in prose, poetry, drama, film, dance or any other form of presentation (McKee 1998: 27). As stories are economical ways to communicate experience, ideas and emotions, and effective in making sense of complexity, they are particularly valuable at times of information overload (Gabriel and Connell 2010: 507).

It is also necessary to present enough information to enable audiences to judge research for themselves. We are all subject to a wide range of cognitive biases, such as confirmation bias, which causes us to ignore evidence that contradicts what we believe, and hindsight bias, which makes us see an event as more predictable when it has already taken place than we would have done beforehand. We cannot identify our own cognitive biases, but we may be able to detect those of others (Kahneman, Lovallo and Sibony 2011: 52). However, we will be able to do this only if we are given enough information. Therefore, ethically, researchers should strive to present enough information to enable audiences to identify those cognitive biases that may have affected the research.

One activity that does not enhance presentations is reading aloud. Reading a presentation is guaranteed to bore your audience (Cutcher 2013: 39; Evergreen 2014: 5). There may be justification for reading a short part of your presentation, such as a poem, brief excerpt from a novel or a piece of spoken data. If you choose to do this, don't display it on screen until you have finished reading, because most people can read much faster than you can speak (Evergreen 2014: 22). Otherwise, speak from very brief notes, designed simply to help you keep track of the structure of your talk, and tell your story in your own words. If this sounds like a daunting prospect, think about how often you tell stories to colleagues in the course of your work; all you need to do is draw on those same everyday skills. An instructive short **video** about how *not* to present research, and another with five top tips for good-quality presentation, can be viewed online.

Arts-based research often aims for authenticity and integrity in presentation, rather than absolute truth (for example, Parker 2004: 70–1; Carroll, Dew and Howden-Chapman 2011: 629).

UK researcher Cate Watson presented a paper focusing on constructions of the 'home–school partnership' at a research seminar on professional development for inclusion in education. Watson's paper centred on the narrative of a child being diagnosed with Attention Deficit Hyperactivity Disorder, from the mother's perspective. As the mother saw it, her son's diagnosis was the consequence of a series of trivial events, beginning with him forgetting his school tie. Watson scripted a set of satirical scenes, quoting the mother's narrative, adding her own interpretations, with some parts fictionalised, but all based on the mother's experience. The intention was to use satire to highlight the absurdity within the rational; to question where the 'madness' actually lies. In her presentation, Watson asked members of the audience to play the roles in the scripts. Feedback from the audience suggested that this was a powerful and effective way to present the issues (Watson 2011: 402).

Whatever type of presentation you are making, one key rule is to keep it as simple and straightforward as possible. To this end, it can be useful to write a short summary of what you want to convey – a single sentence for a graph or chart, a brief synopsis for a verbal or dramatic presentation – and use it to help you stay on track.

Data visualisation – dos and don'ts

Visualising data effectively is not easy (Kirk 2012: 12) but it is important, because the use of visual methods will help your audience(s) to understand and remember what they read or hear in your presentation (Evergreen 2014: 18). Here are some examples of presentation of differing levels of quality. First, let's consider the following presentations of fictional data about the favourite holiday activities of 1,500 researchers.

Table 8.1: Data presentation #1

Favourite holiday activity	Number of researchers
Spending time with family	157
Sightseeing	118
Lying on beach	242
Watching TV or DVDs	105
Trying new foods and drinks	219
Sleeping	379
Reading fiction	103
Physical activities	9
Checking e-mail	47
Working or studying	121

Table 8.1 contains the data, but it's not very user friendly. It's hard to see what conclusions could be drawn. You may be able to pick out that physical activities are unpopular with researchers on holiday, but it's not easy to spot much else at a glance. Let's try a different format.

Table 8.2: Data presentation #2

Favourite holiday activity	Number of researchers	Percentage
Sleeping	379	25%
Lying on beach	242	16%
Trying new foods and drinks	219	15%
Spending time with family	157	10%
Working or studying	121	8%
Sightseeing	118	8%
Watching TV or DVDs	105	7%
Reading fiction	103	7%
Checking e-mail	47	3%
Physical activities	9	1%

Table 8.2 is easier to understand and interpret because the data is ranked in the second column from favourite to least favourite activity, and percentages are given as well as the total numbers. So we could add a paragraph of analysis, such as:

> The key finding from this research is that researchers love to use holidays to catch up on sleep – and don't like to do physical activities. This causes concern about the implications for researchers' health, although of course it may be that, when not on holiday, researchers

do lots of physical activity and that is what leaves them so tired. It is a cause for concern that only 10% of researchers prefer to spend time with their families; this suggests a need for more research into the relationship between research work and the quality of family life. Also, over 10% of researchers seem to favour work-type activities while on holiday – working, studying or checking e-mail – and, overall, this data suggests that researchers' work–life balance needs attention.

Ranking numerically is only one option for sorting data. In some cases it may make more sense to sort alphabetically, for example if you're comparing data from different countries, so that readers can quickly find the countries that interest them. There is also the option to present data visually. The following figures present some examples based on the data used above (colour versions are available online).

Is Figure 8.1 a 'good' graph?

Figure 8.1: Graph

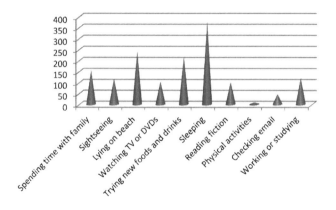

No. The axes are clearly labelled, but the graph has no title and the data is not ranked. It's easy enough to pick out the highest and lowest figures, but hard to differentiate clearly between others – the triangular shape of the column gives you little idea of where it actually ends.

Let's look at a few more bad examples. Figure 8.2 is a pie chart.

Figure 8.2: Pie chart

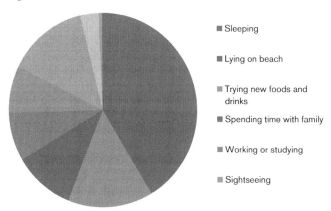

This is really hopeless, even in colour, and almost illegible in black and white. The smallest 'slice' is barely visible. There is no title and the legend includes only six of the ten categories. Pie charts are occasionally useful when there are a small number of categories, such as when you want a visual way to represent a percentage of a whole. But generally they are best avoided, as they ask far too much of the reader.

The bubble graph in Figure 8.3 is equally abysmal.

Figure 8.3: Bubble graph

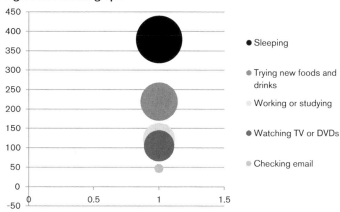

Again, it contains only half of the categories; the horizontal axis is incomprehensible and the vertical axis starts at minus 50, which makes no sense. Also, most humans are not good at judging area (Evergreen 2014: 8), which is a strong argument against using area-based graphics such as pie charts and bubble graphs.

The block graph in Figure 8.4 is perhaps the worst offender of all.

Figure 8.4: Block graph

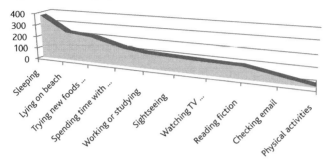

This graph presents the data as continuous, when it's not. Also, three of the labels on the horizontal axis are truncated, ending in an ellipse so their full meaning is unclear. And it's in a bizarre kind of 3D, although the extra perspective is of no practical use. Generally, more complication just makes life harder for your reader. Two-dimensional presentations, on paper or screen, should generally be kept in two dimensions, and variations in colour, shape and so on should be used to help readers visualise multi-dimensional data (Kelleher and Wagener 2011: 823).

In my view, the best way to present this data visually is through a straightforward bar chart (Figure 8.5).

Figure 8.5: Bar chart

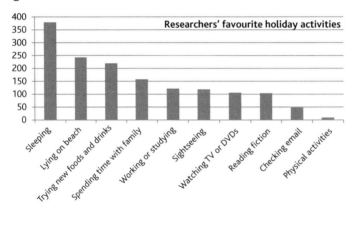

Figure 8.5 is a better graph. While you still can't pick out the exact figures, you can get a much clearer idea of the relationships between the different categories. The data is ranked, and the graph has a title. Together with Table 8.2 above, this would make a reasonably competent presentation.

These graphs were all created using Excel software. As discussed in Chapter Six, with respect to data analysis software, they provide a good illustration of why it is important to understand the capabilities of the software you're using and how to achieve the effects you want, rather than simply selecting options that the software can provide.

Drawing on the work of Kelleher and Wagener (2011) and Evergreen (2014), some basic elements that are common to all good presentations include:

- legible text, images, graphics and so on
- a combination of visual and textual/verbal elements
- predominantly essential information – no 'chart junk', that is, unnecessary and superfluous elements
- non-essential information used only where necessary for emphasis
- metaphors
- simple visualisation, where it is used
- headings noticeably different from other elements
- use of headings to direct the reader and formatting to set the order of information
- clear fonts, used consistently
- no more than three fonts per presentation
- most text printed in black on a white background
- careful and consistent use of colour, with sequential shades of one colour for sequential data, and contrasting colours to emphasise major variations
- no more than two contrasting colours.

Graphs and charts

When you're working with numbers and statistics, it is an essential research skill to identify the key messages and present them appropriately for your audience (Laux and Barham 2012: 1). This kind of data visualisation brings together arts and science skills (Kirk 2012: 12). It can be useful to start with a summary overview of the main messages, perhaps making contextual comparisons with relevant regional, national or international findings, and then home in on details specific to your research and likely to be of interest to your audience. **Guidance on the presentation and dissemination of statistics** from the UK's Government Statistical Service is available online.

Graphs and charts are often helpful for presenting quantitative data (Robson 2011: 422). Most people are familiar with basic graphs such as:

- bar chart – usually comparing frequency and distribution of nominal or ordinal data, for example the number of people in socioeconomic bands (bars are separated from each other)
- histogram – usually comparing frequency and distribution of interval data, for example the number of people in each income bracket (bars are adjacent to each other)

- pie chart – to show relative proportions, such as the percentages of employees in each role within a company
- line chart – for correlations between two variables, such as age and weight
- scattergraph – to give an overview of the relationship between two variables.

Line charts and scattergraphs can be useful for comparing different conditions. For example, a line chart could be used to compare the number of service users presenting with a particular problem over two 10-year periods, one decade being represented by a red line, the other by a blue line. A scattergraph could be used to show relationships between three variables, such as the body weight, age and gender of research participants, with body weight and age on the two axes, and each participant plotted using a diamond for a man and a star for a woman.

Let's say the scattergraph in Figure 8.6 is showing the relationship between the length of someone's nose, in millimetres, and their annual income, in thousands of dollars. We can see that there is, broadly, a positive relationship between nose length and annual income, that is, the longer someone's nose, the higher their income is likely to be. However, there are some exceptions; some people with comparatively short noses still have comparatively high incomes, and vice versa. And this tells us that there is more to the relationship between nose length and income than meets the eye.

Figure 8.6: Scattergraph

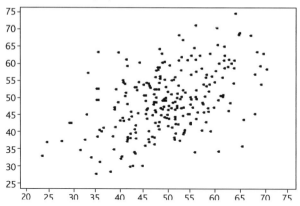

Annotation can be useful to help direct the reader to important information, such as by identifying outliers and highlighting their significance. Colour and/ or shape can be used to highlight important or extra elements. For example, in the scattergraph in Figure 8.6, if you wanted to add the element of gender (and were happy to regard gender as a binary characteristic), you could use red for men and blue for women, or squares for men and circles for women.

More complex types of chart include forest plots, funnel plots and slopegraphs. There are also many other kinds of simpler graphs and charts available, such as column graphs, area graphs, doughnut charts and radar charts. A short video showing how best to work with graphs and charts can be viewed in a **live presentation** online.

Diagrams, infographics and maps

Diagrams can be useful for presenting qualitative or mixed-methods research, as they offer the option to show complex and simultaneous relationships more clearly than text or narrative (Buckley and Waring 2013: 149). Diagrams can be helpful for researchers working in teams, to present aspects of their work to each other in the course of the project (Buckley and Waring 2013: 163), as well as for researchers to present their methods and findings to various audiences. They are particularly useful for conceptualisation (Buckley and Waring 2013: 168), although some researchers worry that diagrams can be reductive. But for others, diagrams in conjunction with other forms of communication, such as text, allow deeper understanding for broader audiences than text alone does (Buckley and Waring 2013: 169). Even if you love diagrams, though, one word of warning: don't be seduced into using too many, because diagrams are most effective when they really have something to add to the presentation (White et al 2014: 397).

Some types of diagram, such as the flow chart and spidergram, are well known. Others, such as the schematic diagram, which shows the elements of a system or process, are less well known but no less useful. Anthropologists offer other types of diagram that may be useful beyond the boundaries of the discipline, such as the kinship diagram, which shows a participant's relationships with other people in his or her family, whether created or ended by birth or death, marriage or divorce, or other types of attachment or separation (Chang 2008: 82). There is also the 'culturegram', used by autoethnographers to display the different facets of their own identity, with categories such as gender, ethnicity, race, nationality, religion and so on (Chang 2008: 97–8).

There are an infinite number of possible diagrammatic representations of research findings, which makes diagrams a very creative way to present aspects of research. However, the sheer range of possibilities can make the production of diagrams daunting to contemplate. A useful way to approach this is to think about what you want the diagram to achieve and to ensure that your diagram fits with both your data and your theoretical stance (Mason 2002: 170–1).

'Infographic' is short for 'information graphic', that is, a particular kind of diagram that is designed to present complex information clearly. A good infographic will tell a story about some useful or interesting data or findings, helpfully supported by visual information in an appealing and relevant style. A **website** is available with dozens of examples of good infographics.

There are some excellent online tools to help you create infographics, such as Piktochart and infogr.am. Infographics can be animated, and **some examples of**

animated infographics, including a wonderful **TED talk by Hans Rosling**, can be viewed online.

Diagrams and infographics are good for showing connections and explanations, while maps are most helpful for showing relationships, particularly if there is a geographic component. Maps are also useful for representing other aspects of research, including data and ideas (Powell 2010: 539; Newman 2013: 228). Maps can offer greater levels of complexity than diagrams.

American researchers Kimberly Powell and Peter Aeschbacher taught field research to an interdisciplinary group of students. They spent a month studying development strategies in the El Chorrillo neighbourhood in Panama City. This fieldwork involved a lot of conventional mapping, but they also wanted to map the lived experience of the neighbourhood's residents. Most of the residents were poor, and many were immigrants from Central and South America, the West Indies and Africa. Powell and Aeschbacher encouraged their students to use visual research methods and to push the boundaries of traditional mapping methods. As a result, three of the students developed 'collage maps'. Brian Squires, a student of landscape architecture, used collages of photographs superimposed on a transect map of the waterfront, and framed the photographs in different colours (blue for 'positive' and red for 'negative') to make clear visual links. Gillian Speers, a student of integrative arts, used photographs to document the layers and textures of the neighbourhood, supported by interviews to investigate the way women perceived architectural spaces and defined space in and around their homes. She used the photographs to make collage maps that she called 'reflective maps', to show the confusion she felt as an outsider in the community (Powell 2010: 550). Trieste Lockwood, an interdisciplinary arts student, used photographs, sketches, tissue paper and text to create collage maps of residents' experiences of music. Collage is a particularly powerful method for acknowledging ambiguity and multiple perspectives, as well as non-linear and multi-sensory dimensions, in the presentation of research (Powell 2010: 543).

Many examples of diagrams, infographics and maps can be found online.

Conferences and meetings

Traditionally, research has been presented in written or spoken prose. The convention is that, to do this well, you should tell an understandable story with a clear narrative arc. However, presenting research in this way can occlude much of the complexity and messiness of the research process. In recent years, researchers in the arts and humanities have been experimenting with ways to convey more of the multifaceted totality of the research experience to their audiences. For some researchers, drawing on techniques such as poetry (Prendergast, Leggo and Sameshima 2009), staged storytelling with digital installations (Cutcher 2011, cited in Cutcher 2013: 39), dance (Blumenfeld-Jones 2006, cited in Cutcher

2013: 39) and even mediaeval musical forms (Gadow 2000; Humphries 2012), enables them to offer a fuller, richer insight into the matters under investigation.

Presenting research in traditional 'non-fiction' prose is as much of a created construct as presenting research through haiku, sonata form or a patchwork quilt (Watson 2011). For many researchers it makes no sense to privilege traditional forms of research presentation. The quest now is to find methods of presentation that will do as much justice as possible to each individual piece of research. This offers considerable scope for creativity.

> Janice Fournillier, a Trinidadian scholar in America, found a conceptual framework very helpful in presenting her research into the experiences of immigrant women in US higher education. Her own heritage is one of slavery, and when she moved to study in the US at the age of 50 she found it painful to experience the 'divide and rule' culture of higher education, where most of the power is held by white people and it can feel very risky for people of colour to speak authentically. After some years, she received an invitation to participate in a conference with a theme of 'the plantation'. This offered a conceptual framework for her own research: the 'plantation system', with its masters and slaves. For Fournillier, this offered a direct parallel with the academy. She performed her presentation, using a stream-of-consciousness type of monologue spoken in a Trinidadian dialect. She also incorporated the Caribbean musical form of calypso, choosing a highly regarded traditional song that describes the horrors of slavery and the search for freedom through rebellion. Fournillier asked her audience to participate in a call-and-response style, to make her performance more interactive. Viewed from one angle, this could look like a whole lot of risks to take in the context of an academic conference. However, it was evidently very effective, as 'the audience responded lustily and shook their heads and shed a tear after hearing the presentation' (Fournillier 2010: 59).

Others have also noted that arts-based performance can enable greater connection with audiences than traditional lecturing does (Douglas 2012: 530; Gergen and Gergen 2012: 161). In the UK, some researchers are even presenting their work through stand-up comedy, for example through the Bright Club movement (Ridley-Ellis 2014: 57). A short **video** example of academics performing at a Bright Club event can be viewed online.

Mixed-methods presentation

Live presentations use mixed methods almost by definition, with something to see and something to hear. This may simply be a person speaking, or a speaker using visual aids. These don't have to be technologically generated. Designers such as Jose Duarte, from Colombia, and Nadeem Haidary, from America, have shown that everyday household objects can be used to help people visualise research findings. For example, you could use tall glasses filled with liquid to different levels to represent the bars on a bar chart. This would be particularly powerful if you could use a liquid relevant to your findings. So, if you were researching the relationship between economic well-being and stress levels in dairy farmers, you could use milk; if you were researching factors affecting injury and death in road traffic accidents, you could use fake blood. Of course, precision will be difficult if you are pouring liquids in front of a live audience – or blowing up balloons to different sizes, or drawing a map by hand – but Duarte says on his website (viewed 8.10.14) that, while you need to attend to proportion, accuracy is much less important than conveying a clear idea. More on **Duarte's and Haidary's work** can be viewed online.

Also, information can be presented in a variety of ways in the same document.

> Arianne Reis is an Australian researcher who studied conflict between hunters and 'trampers' (aka hikers, ramblers or bushwalkers) in outdoor environments in New Zealand. She chose to use photographs in a written presentation in three different ways. First, she embedded photographs in the text, with words printed across part or all of the picture, in an attempt to provoke an emotional response, although she had no wish to try to dictate what that emotional response – or any meaning drawn from it by the reader – might be. Second, she used photographs to represent some particularly vivid memories from her fieldwork, to support the points she was discussing. Third, she used photographs to illustrate other people's experiences, some of which were actually her participants' photographs. These were used adjacent to (but not overlaid by) quotes, with the intention of giving the reader more insight into the nature of her participants' experiences. Taken in total, Reis's aim was to 'add layers of meanings and emotions' to the written narrative she had produced (Reis 2011: 15).

As stated in Chapter Seven, Karen Barbour is an autoethnographer and a contemporary dancer. She too used photographs in the presentation of her research, but in a very different way from Arianne Reis. Barbour writes: 'My aim in dancing is to embody through autoethnographic performance that which I am unable to write on the page. The aim in this article is to playfully represent my embodied methodologies and some of my "findings" through creative writing and images of performance' (Barbour 2012: 67). Her article includes six 'images' or photographs, each more or less blurred, presumably to convey a sense of movement. Barbour is trying to do something extremely difficult: to convey aspects of the experience of dance in writing. I have a great deal of respect for Barbour's attempts to span this enormous gulf, although I don't think they entirely succeed. It is really hard to express something in one medium and then communicate that through a very different medium (Gergen and Gergen 2012: 166). Dance would perhaps be better represented using another medium, such as video (Kousha, Thelwall and Abdoli 2012: 1710), perhaps with some overlaid text. A **video presentation** of research by Rosemary Reilly can be viewed online that uses photography, text, voice, music and art and that, in my view, is more effective in conveying aspects of the experience of research participants – in this case, users of a community arts studio. However, Barbour's article was formally published in a journal, so it will presumably it help her academic career, while Reilly's video is self-published on YouTube, so presumably it won't, even though it may reach many more people overall.

I think this illustrates another potential problem with some creative research methods, and perhaps particularly the arts-based methods. Because many art forms are difficult to communicate in writing – and writing is the primary communication method of the academy – attempts that fall short run the risk of being condemned as self-indulgent. There are arguments against this, as we saw in Chapter Two, but at the present time arts-based presentation of research does remain a risk, both within and beyond the academy. For example, in the case of the pantomime performance mentioned above from UK researcher Victoria Foster's participatory research with a Sure Start programme, the national Sure Start evaluation team didn't want to see the pantomime – or even the video that was made – accepting only a short summary. However, local community members and programme staff received the pantomime warmly, finding it powerful and authentic, and the video was well received by academic communities (Foster 2013: 49). So every researcher considering arts-based methods needs to decide whether using those methods is worth the risk – or, perhaps, which of their audiences to prioritise.

To some extent, perhaps the risk can be reduced by using a semi-formal technique with a semi-formal name, such as infography (not to be confused with infographics). Traditional research texts set out to frame and orchestrate the reader's experience, while infography aims to enable more interactive reading, in order to stimulate creative thought and discussion.

Michael Atkinson is a Canadian researcher who made an ethnographic study of fell running in England. Fell running is off-road, countryside running that includes steep ascents and descents, and obstacles including woodland, streams and rivers. Atkinson presents part of his research using infography, that is, photographs of fell runners in action alongside short quotations from field notes and interviews. Atkinson asserts that 'the representation of bodies with only "limited" analysis encourages/forces/challenges readers to connect with the photo in order to make sense of them' [sic] (Atkinson 2010: 119). Among other things, infography is:

- easy and enjoyable to read
- fluid and dynamic in its integration of words and pictures
- able to reveal information that other methods might conceal
- open to multiple readings (Atkinson 2010: 120).

So, although infography is a recognised method of presenting research using arts-based techniques, it is a method with considerable scope for creativity and requiring no great artistic skill to use it effectively.

Arts-based presentation

Some researchers evidently do think it is worth risking some negative reactions in order to present their work using arts-based methods. For example, Kimberly Dark is an American professor of sociology and a professional performance poet. She uses poetry to present research to a range of audiences within and beyond the academy. This gives her work 'a broader reach' than either her research or her poetry would have on their own (Dark 2009: 173). Her work also has a much more profound impact on her audiences because of the combination of research and poetry presented in person. 'I have experienced how audiences are moved in ways that are deeper than language can convey ... Research-poetry represents an ability to bring what truly connects people into the forefront while the social critique remains an ever-present backdrop' (Dark 2009: 184). A **video** by Kimberly Dark talking about presentation through performance, with particular relevance to autoethnography, can be viewed online.

Kitrina Douglas is a British professional golfer, researcher and songwriter. She writes songs from her data and research experiences, and performs them to present her research to academic and other audiences. For Douglas, writing songs is like a reflective analytic technique that uses a largely wordless process to reflect on the non-verbal aspects of research: 'I wasn't attending to what we "actually" talked about, but rather the spirit of the interaction, the chemistry, of something shared that went unsaid' (Douglas 2012: 527). Douglas created a performance to explore her songwriting journey that included some of her songs and that has been presented at academic conferences in New Zealand, the US and Britain. At the close of the British presentation, as usual the chairperson invited comments or questions, but the audience remained silent for a prolonged period. 'It seemed that what delegates wanted was further time to reflect, and to remain within the space created by the performance ... the discussions that eventually flowed suggested that the songs did indeed facilitate ... deep reflection' (Douglas 2012: 531). This suggests that musical presentations of research may offer a way for a researcher to communicate non-verbal aspects of their experience to their audiences. You can find out more about this by viewing the online **video** of Kitrina Douglas's research-based song 'Gwithian Sands'.

I would contend that the above presentations were so effective because both researchers were skilled in research and performance poetry or songwriting. You may remember the debate around the use of arts-based methods in research that was reviewed in Chapter Two: some researchers argue strongly for only those skilled in artistic techniques to use them in research, while others believe everyone has a right to use artistic techniques. While I can see the arguments on both sides, at the point of presentation there may be a stronger case for the need for artistic skill. Yet the counter-argument also holds true, to some extent.

> Lisbeth Berbary, an American researcher investigating the gender-related experiences of sorority women who we first met in Chapter Six, used an ethnographic screenplay to present her data. An 'ethnographic screenplay' is written using standard screenplay writing techniques, but not to production standard, thereby allowing more flexibility in its narrative. This approach enabled Berbary to depict complex characters acting and interacting in specific settings, effectively showing readers her participants' experiences, rather than telling them. The ethnographic screenplay rendered Berbary's research accessible to her participants, many of whom reported that they enjoyed reading her work, and to non-academic readers, who were surprised by its readability. For Berbary, this approach 'encourages involvement, inspires curiosity, creates inclusivity, and constructs depictions that remain in the thoughts of readers in ways that traditional representations sometimes do not' (Berbary 2011: 195).

For some artist researchers, arts-based presentation offers an opportunity to develop and use new artistic skills.

> You may remember from Chapter Five that Judith Davidson is an American researcher who is skilled in sewing, spinning, weaving and felting. She conducted an autoethnographic study of her post-tenure experience by analysing her own diaries, and presented her findings at an academic conference in the form of an interactive art exhibition with nine pieces of art that she had created, based on her findings. Although she is an experienced artist, this was the first time she had ever curated an exhibition. The art she displayed was mostly mixed-media collage and sculpture, made primarily from textiles, including a felted prayer bowl with a sign inviting conference delegates to write a prayer for someone they cared about who needed help and to place it in the bowl. The process of creating this exhibition added unexpected dimensions to Davidson's analysis. She had to decide how to place her artworks for viewing, which made her 'think about the new meanings created by juxtaposition' and change her ideas about 'the meanings I thought they conveyed' (Davidson 2011: 97). Several of the artworks needed framing, which required Davidson to define their edges, so as to fix their meaning (Davidson 2011: 97). For Davidson, exhibiting research as art makes sense, because they both seek for their outputs to be 'viewed, discussed, and absorbed' (Davidson 2011: 97).

Mitchell et al (2011) conducted a three-year impact evaluation of the effect on audiences of dramatic performances based on research findings, specifically dementia research. They found seven types of impact:

1. seeing things differently
2. recognising and acknowledging truths
3. people locating themselves in a wider context
4. reactions eliciting embodied metaphors (for example, 'it was like a slap in the face')
5. meaningful learning
6. greater understanding of different perspectives
7. reminder and affirmation of personal knowledge.

The researchers concluded that dramatic performances make research findings more accessible for audiences from a range of backgrounds, and are likely to create changes in the understanding of audience members (Mitchell et al 2011: 390).

Some research may not seem very dramatic, but even research on topics such as health and safety can usefully be translated into theatrical performances for presentation. For example, a report of research into school safety in America was adapted for the stage, thereby enabling 500 new teachers to engage with the findings and recommendations of the research (Goldstein and Wickett 2009: 1565). The staging was carefully designed to make the audience feel involved, almost part of the action (Goldstein and Wickett 2009: 1564). It is highly likely that this form of presentation had much more impact on its audience than a more conventional PowerPoint or paper presentation.

Poetic presentations, too, can have a significant impact on their audiences.

> Penelope Carroll, Kevin Dew and Philippa Howden-Chapman, in New Zealand, used research-based poetry to represent the realities of participants living in marginal housing such as tents, buses, sheds, vans, garages and caravans. They interviewed rural and urban dwellers and began by conducting a thematic analysis of the transcripts. Then they identified phrases and sentences from the interviews that illustrated something unique to the participant's perspective or their life events, or illustrated a theme from the analysis. These were noted alongside descriptions from field notes, and were then arranged into poetic stanzas, with the aim of 'remaining true to the flow and meaning of participants' narratives and focusing on what appeared to be central in their narratives' (Carroll, Dew and Howden-Chapman 2011: 628, citing Clarke et al 2005). This approach was appreciated by participants, who told the researchers they had accurately captured the realities of their lives. It also enriched the research from the researchers' perspective, as the poems 'provided context for the thematic analysis, created empathy which allowed for a felt sense of the phenomenon and not merely a detached cognitive understanding, and afforded an alternative framework for insight into the complexities of informal housing in Aotearoa/New Zealand' (Carroll, Dew and Howden-Chapman 2011: 629).

 A **video** of a presentation by Dr Karlo Mila, New Zealand academic and poet, can be viewed online.

As Breheny tells us, poetry's use of metaphor means that poems can enable us to 'explore the social patterning that structures individual lives' (Breheny 2012: 157). Drawing on narrative theory, Breheny suggests that this can work on three levels:

1. individual – the personal story that someone tells
2. interpersonal – the relationship between the storyteller and their audience
3. public – stories of social life that are publicly available (Breheny 2012: 157).

On this basis, the use of poems to present research can have a range of purposes, including:

- to represent the multiplicity of the self shifting through space, place and time
- to represent the nature of human existence: disorganised, fluid and inconsistent
- to explore topics in which a prominent feature is time
- to represent any number of accounts that are similar in outline but different in detail
- to highlight the role of character within a narrative
- to use that/those character(s) to represent different facets of experience and perspective
- to show how embodied, discursive and social aspects of an experience cannot be separated from one another (Breheny 2012: 157–8).

Poetic presentation is a form of interpretation, by a researcher, of the experiences of their participants as portrayed in their data. Because poetry is such a condensed form of presentation, it may prompt further interpretation from its listeners or readers. This may be at Breheny's individual level, enabling understanding of the individual's story; at her interpersonal level, beginning a dialogue about what the poem might mean; or at her public level, enquiring about the contextual circumstances that made this social project possible (Breheny 2012: 165).

Canadian researcher Lane Mandlis is a transsexual researcher with a professional background in art and design. His research into transphobic violence engaged with feminist post-structural theory. In the process of writing a seminar paper, he began to understand the extent to which that theoretical stance excluded his experience and his self. He chose to express his resulting feelings of powerlessness by cutting the text of his paper into phrases, which he presented in the shape of a river flowing across each page. He used 'fragmented tangents of thought' (Mandlis 2009: 1357) to form the banks of the river, and added images and drawings that he describes as 'strong depictions of liminal positions; empowered representations of transformation; positive cultural symbols of transition' (Mandlis 2009: 1357). The paper grew physically as well as conceptually, as he added cellophane tape so that his words could both spill off, and be contained within, standard-sized pages. The result is a multi-directional, multi-layered presentation, showing something of the complex relationships between disenfranchisement and power.

Presentation using technology

The technologies most commonly used for presenting research findings are film and video, with accompanying audio soundtracks.

American researcher Sarah Franzen conducts ethnographic research on community-based rural development. She uses a range of methods, including participant observation, interviews, oral histories and ethnographic filmmaking. This is an 'ongoing cyclical process' in which Franzen makes films collaboratively with her participants, and questions audiences at viewings to find out how they construct and interpret knowledge and meaning from the film (Franzen 2013: 421). She supports and enables her participants to direct and edit short films for three audiences: the participants themselves, other farmers and rural organisers and other stakeholders in rural development, including universities and government. The films are presented to small groups, from a handful to 50 audience members at most, to facilitate feedback and discussion. This approach enables Franzen to use the films to communicate and produce knowledge at the same time. It also helps her to learn more about how different audiences understand and interpret information provided by film, which in turn renders her better able to communicate and share knowledge with such audiences by film. This is a form of public scholarship that 'involves more than providing public access to academic knowledge; it involves collaborative knowledge production and emphasizes audience reception and engagement with scholarship' (Franzen 2013: 420).

The ethnodrama produced by Sangha et al, outlined in Chapter Three, was recorded and put into DVD format (Sangha et al 2012: 295). This enabled members of the research team to re-present their research findings in different contexts for different purposes, such as by using the ethnodrama as a teaching tool for students.

As we saw in Chapters Five and Six, Mary Ann Kluge and her colleagues in America and New Zealand used video in their case study of Linda, a 65-year-old woman who had minimal experience of sport and didn't like exercise, yet decided to aim for master's level as a senior athlete. They gathered many hours of video footage, from Linda's first-ever training session to her competing in, and winning, a race at the Rocky Mountain Senior Games. Linda also kept a journal of her thoughts and feelings about her sports-related experiences. The researchers also used video to present their findings, working with Linda to select and edit footage into a 23-minute film. This film was narrated by Linda using three techniques: straightforward voice-over, recounting excerpts from her journals and live accounts from the original recordings. The aim was to produce a film with significant levels of authenticity and credibility (Kluge et al 2010: 286).

Another option for presentation using technology is the webinar, or online seminar. There are a variety of technologies, many of them free to use in basic form, which enable tens or hundreds of people worldwide to take part in an interactive online session. Webinars can be recorded for later dissemination. Time differences and technical malfunctions can cause problems (Armstrong 2014: 22), but webinars are a very useful and cost-effective way to present research to a global audience.

CONCLUSION

This chapter has given a flavour of some of the many creative ways in which researchers can present their findings and results. Presentation is important, but one researcher – or even a team of researchers – can reach only a comparatively small number of people through direct presentation: tens, maybe hundreds, occasionally perhaps thousands over time. Dissemination can, in theory at least, reach millions of people, and creative ways of doing this are the topic of the next chapter.

NINE

Dissemination, implementation and knowledge exchange

Introduction

Dissemination of research is essential to inform people of your findings and conclusions and to build the global knowledge base. There is a strong argument for it being unethical *not* to disseminate research, especially any research that is publicly funded. However, dissemination methods are under-reported in the methods literature (Vaughn et al 2012: 32). The purpose of this chapter is to help fill that gap.

As we saw in Chapter Eight, presentation is a form of dissemination, but usually requires the researcher to be present, while on the whole dissemination happens through media that people can access independently, ranging from academic journals to art exhibitions. There are of course areas of overlap between presentation and dissemination: for example, research can be presented online and therefore, in effect, be disseminated at the same time.

Historically, creative approaches to dissemination were in the minority (Jones 2006: 67). More recently, research has begun to be disseminated in a range of creative ways, including art exhibitions (for example, Davidson 2012), graphic novels (for example, Dahl et al 2012), films (for example, Kluge et al 2010), DVDs (for example, Franzen 2013), cartoons (for example, Bartlett 2013), drama performances (for example Kontos and Naglie, 2009) and novels (for example, Leavy 2012). Each of these has been used in projects focusing on a range of subjects. For example, static or animated cartoons have been used for dissemination in projects focusing on subjects including HIV/AIDS (Petersen et al 2006), youth violence (Vaughn et al 2012) and dementia activism (Bartlett 2013). While these creative methods focus on arts-based dissemination and dissemination using technology, they can also be used for disseminating mixed-methods and transformative research.

Academics are often seen as people who communicate in a rarefied and specialist way that is accessible only to other academics, such as through expensive conferences or subscription-only academic journals that require impenetrable language to be used in particular ways. Yet, more and more academics are taking a creative approach to dissemination using popular media. This chapter provides many examples of creative dissemination methods. However, one word of caution: it is always important to think of your audiences and to choose the methods of dissemination that are most likely to transmit your messages to them effectively

(Finlay 2012: 28; Souza 2014: 83). In some cases, this will mean using more traditional dissemination methods. It is important not to let a fascinating new method seduce you away from good research practice.

Ethics in creative dissemination and implementation

In these final stages of your research process, if you disseminate your work in the public domain you are responsible to every potential reader or viewer. Alternatively, if you are required to sign over the ownership of your work to a commissioner, funder or institution you may have no control over its dissemination (a situation I regard as unethical, particularly if it results in research not being disseminated at all). Dissemination is an ethical act in itself, and you should plan a dissemination strategy at the start of your research project, in order to ensure that your findings reach as many members of suitable audiences as possible. Knowledge exchange is a particularly ethical form of dissemination and is covered in more detail later in this chapter.

Online and other media

A blog can be quickly and easily set up using a hosting provider such as Blogger or Wordpress. However, if you are tempted to start a blog, it is worth thinking through some of the pros and cons before you put finger to keyboard. I kept a blog from 2005 to 2009 (now deleted), and started another while I was writing this book, so I can tell you that blogs are content-heavy and demanding of time. Can you commit to producing a well-written and interesting 500- to 700-word post at least once a week, responding to comments and e-mails daily and publicising your blog through a variety of channels? This is probably the minimum requirement for a blog to succeed in gaining and keeping readers – and unless you have readers, you are not actually disseminating your work or ideas.

A number of people do use blogging to disseminate research. Mewburn and Thomson analysed the content of 100 academic blogs and found that 40% of them contained research dissemination (Mewburn and Thomson 2013: 1111). If you are going to use a blog for dissemination, it is helpful to link with the wider blogging community, using blog-to-blog links, networks of blogs – for example, the well-established science blogging networks such as scientificblogging.com (Shanahan 2011: 903) or newer networks such as the public ethnography network e.m.a.c. at publicethnography.net – or blog aggregators such as the Huffington Post (Vannini 2013: 449). This will mean making time to read other blogs in your field – which is worth doing, in fact, before you start your own (Webster 2014: 75). If you decide that you don't want to start a blog of your own, you could consider writing a guest post here and there for other people's blogs (Campos-Seijo 2014: 102) – many bloggers are delighted to find people to provide their content from time to time, as long as it's well written and relevant. It is also useful to link your blog or guest posts with other social media platforms, such as your

Twitter account, Pinterest, Tumblr or whatever you prefer to use. And do, always, add a copyright statement to protect your work and ideas (Lantsoght 2014: 26).

If you can manage all this alongside your other commitments, there are rewards to be gained. Blogging can be particularly useful for sharing ideas and receiving feedback (Vannini 2013: 449). Newer blog platforms, such as Medium, are bridging the gap between the length of a conventional blog post and the brevity of a tweet (and, no doubt, by the time you read this, other options will be available too). Alongside Twitter and other social media, blogging enables conversations to be conducted regardless of geographical location, time zone, discipline or status. This can be enormously useful for the pursuit of knowledge. Also, blogging can enable communication about scholarly work to cross the boundaries of the academy.

> Ed Yong is an award-winning science writer, journalist and blogger based in the UK. In 2010 he wrote a blog post disseminating the work of Zhao et al that had just been published in the academic journal *Nature*. This work showed that some chickens could be gynandromorphic, that is, have an equal balance of male and female cells. Yong received comments on the post from a range of people, including a scientist who was one of the authors of the original paper, and a farmer who had a gynandromorphic chicken on his farm and wanted to know more about his unusual bird. Yong put the scientist and the farmer in touch with each other, which led to a full-scale collaboration. The farmer recorded observations, took photographs, arranged for blood samples to be taken and shared all this data with the scientist. The collaborators also kept Yong informed of their progress, which meant that he, in turn, could inform his readers (Shanahan 2011: 911–13).

YouTube also enables communication about scholarly work (Barrett 2014: 23). It is the third most popular website after Google and Facebook and has been used for dissemination since it was founded in 2005. There are now thousands of research projects being disseminated via YouTube, and it's probably not surprising that there is a steady increase in the citation of YouTube videos in research articles (Kousha, Thelwall and Abdoli 2012: 1710). A **video** is available on YouTube, presented by UK researcher Melissa Terras, about how to disseminate research using social media.

> As we saw in Chapter Eight, Penelope Carroll, Kevin Dew and Philippa Howden-Chapman in New Zealand used research-based poetry to represent the realities of participants living in marginal housing such as tents, buses, sheds, vans, garages and caravans. The poems were recorded onto CDs. It was not possible to arrange for participants to make the recordings themselves, so readers were chosen with voices that more or less matched the participants. The voices of those in marginal housing are rarely heard in discussions of housing and health in New Zealand, but these poems were heard by academics, policy makers and the general public (Carroll, Dew and Howden-Chapman 2011: 628).

Podcasts, webcasts and recorded webinars (see Chapter Eight for information on webinars) are also useful ways to disseminate research online. Podcasts are static audio files that are easy to create and upload to the internet using technology available on most laptops and smartphones (Blake 2014: 67). They can be used to add value to other forms of dissemination, for example by telling listeners why a research project came to be done, or what has happened since an article was written. A webcast is a real-time online broadcast of a presentation, which is a little more complicated, but conference and other venues may have facilities for doing this. The URLs for podcasts, webcasts and recorded webinars can be disseminated using social media such as blogs and Twitter.

Finally, you can curate resources relevant to your research online – that is, collect and present those resources, including links to your own blogs, podcasts and so on, in an appealing way. There are various ways of doing this, such as setting up a dedicated website or other web presence, perhaps using a tool such as Bundlr or Pinterest, or using an online curation tool such as Storify. There are dozens of free and helpful resources for online curation. Creating a specialist online library of relevant resources in this way can also be useful for your own future reference (Westbury 2014: 106).

Mainstream media

If you want to disseminate research through the mainstream media, you will need to write a press release (for newspapers, radio and TV) or a pitch (for magazines). A press release is a one-off piece of writing that can be sent to as many newspapers, radio and TV stations as you like, all at the same time. A pitch should be individually written, or at least carefully tailored, for each magazine you send it to. Whatever medium you're aiming at, it will be helpful to have some good-quality photos available to accompany your article (Crofts 2002: 91).

If you want to disseminate your work through magazines, you should be prepared to write an article yourself. Do be aware that magazines commission articles months in advance of publication, so, for example, if your research focuses on Diwali, you would need to pitch it to editors early in the calendar year (Formichelli and Burrell 2005: 71).

You will need to begin work on your pitches by researching each potential title. Some will have guidelines for writers, which will be available either online or by e-mail from one of the commissioning editors. If you can get hold of these, read them carefully and do exactly as they say. You will also need to read several copies of the magazine, paying attention to the types and lengths of articles, the writing style(s) used and the advertisements, which can tell you a great deal about the magazine's readership. Make sure that no article on a similar topic has been published by the magazine or any of its direct competitors in recent months. When you have a clear idea about the magazine's readership and the editor's likely requirements, you can begin to prepare a pitch.

Preparing a pitch for a magazine

- Aim for three short paragraphs.
- The first paragraph should answer the six key journalist's questions – who, what, when, where, how, why? – and do this in a way that is clearly targeting the magazine's readership.
- The second paragraph should explain the story more fully, with some juicy details.
- The third paragraph should demonstrate why you're the best person to write this article for the magazine.
- Don't bother saying how wonderful you think the magazine is; just make sure your pitch oozes understanding of the publication.
- Write well, using plain English.
- In your writing, 'show, don't tell' wherever possible; try to bring your research to life for the reader.
- Say what kind of article you are proposing to write, and how long you intend it to be.
- E-mail the pitch, with the proposed article title and your name in the subject line.
- Include your phone number – ideally your mobile – and make sure you're available at any time to answer questions, as editors often work to very tight schedules and this can make the difference between your research being disseminated or not.
- If you have published similar articles before, attach copies as examples.
- Don't give the editor a timescale or deadline for their response.

If you're new to magazine journalism, it may be useful to write your article before you send in your pitch. Of course, you may decide that you don't want to use your time that way, in case the editor doesn't accept your suggestion – which is more likely than not. However, if the editor does come back to you, he or she will usually want a quick response. So if you don't want to write the article upfront, make sure you'll be able to do a good job at short notice, otherwise you will have wasted both time and opportunity.

When you're ready to send in a pitch, find the name, direct phone number and personal e-mail address of the relevant editor. You may be able to find these on the internet, or you may have to ring the magazine (Formichelli and Burrell 2005: 66). Don't send your pitch to 'The Editor', which is a sure sign of an amateur. Identifying the appropriate person and contacting them by name makes it much more likely that they will take your idea seriously.

Make sure that you're easy to contact and able to respond quickly, as editors work at high speed (Perrin 2014: 44). If you don't hear from the editor after pitching, you can ring or e-mail them after a week or two to chase it up (Formichelli and Burrell 2005: 64). If you e-mail, forward your original e-mail with the new message, to save the editor hunting for it. Editors do receive a lot of pitches, so it's entirely possible that yours has just been overlooked. Be polite, not pushy, and don't try to persuade them if they say 'no'; you can always pitch the article to a different magazine. A **web page** is available with more tips for successful pitching.

If the editor does come back to you to commission the article, make sure that you write down any further instructions or suggestions they offer. You are likely to be given a deadline; if you can't meet it, be honest and ask for more time. Be as professional as you can: write the article well and quickly, and don't keep ringing or e-mailing the editor with questions. Take care to write in the style the publication uses: for example, if they write about 'non-profits', don't use 'charities'. Also, write to the required length; don't write more than a handful over or under the word count you're given. If you find that you're unsure about something, use your own networks first, and only contact the editor as a last resort.

If you're lucky enough to have two editors come back to you for similar articles, don't just forge ahead, or you will risk alienating them forever. Accept the commission from the one whose magazine you most want to publish in (or the one who got back to you first, if relevant). Then tell the other editor what has happened and suggest a twist to the article that would be appropriate for their publication while making it sufficiently different from the first one.

When you've written your article, the editor may well ask for changes. This can mean a lot of changes or just a few tweaks – and either way, they will want them done quickly. Once the changes have been made and the article has been accepted for publication, it will be worked on by a sub-editor, who is responsible for making sure that your article is in the magazine's own style. It is very unlikely that your article will be printed using exactly the same wording that you sent to the magazine, so it's essential that you make it clear if there are any expressions that must be used or avoided, such as terms that might have particular sensitivity for your participants.

Alternatively – or in addition – you may choose to send out a press release about your research, giving the key points and suggesting that a journalist might like to find out more. A press release is similar to a pitch: you're aiming to capture someone's interest and leave them wanting more. However, a press release has a slightly different format from a pitch. Also, rather than being tailored for one magazine, a press release can be sent to as many newspapers, radio and TV stations as you like.

Preparing a Press Release

- Do not simply send out an abstract or executive summary to editors.
- Aim for 250 words, 500 at most.
- Begin by using the classic journalist's prompts: who, what, when, where, how, why.
- Explain why your research is news, that is, what is new, unique, original, and/ or timely and why it is relevant to people today.

- Keep the headline short and attention grabbing.
- Make the content compelling and persuasive.
- Write in the third person and use plain English.
- Don't use superlatives.
- In your writing, 'show, don't tell' wherever possible; try to bring your research to life for the reader.
- You can include a quotation or (at the most) two, from yourself and/or other people, but make sure they are from people who will be available and willing to be interviewed by a journalist if necessary, and always include their name and role or job title.
- Edit carefully before sending.
- Give your credentials at the bottom, in a single sentence.
- Include your phone number – ideally your mobile – and make sure you're available at any time to answer questions, as journalists often work to very tight schedules, and this can make the difference between your research being disseminated or not.
- Send the release in the body of an e-mail, as plain text, rather than as an attachment; the subject line should begin with the words 'PRESS RELEASE'.
- Include a photo or other image, if relevant and publishable; make sure images are low resolution, so the e-mail won't be too large.
- All your press releases should be sent at the same time. They can either be marked 'for immediate release' or be 'embargoed until [date and time]'. The latter can be useful to give journalists time to prepare, but don't embargo for more than a few days at most, or your release may be forgotten.

There are lots of **examples of press releases** available online.

If a newspaper, radio or TV editor takes up your press release, they will prepare the story themselves, although they may want to interview you (and/or other relevant people, possibly those you quoted, possibly their own sources) for more information. Again, they are likely to edit your work – sometimes to the point where it's almost unrecognisable – and they may, in the end, not use it after all (Crofts 2002: 91–2).

Bear in mind that journalistic ethics are, in some ways, different from research ethics. For example, journalists generally see it as unethical to use a pseudonym for an informant, as news is based on real people's actual experiences. This is occasionally waived for articles on very sensitive subjects, but that is rare, and on the whole editors don't like to use pseudonyms. So if you're interested in disseminating any or all of your findings through the mainstream media, plan for that from the outset; make sure that your participants are aware of and support your plans; and, if necessary, also seek approval from your ethics committee. Phillip Vannini asks his participants to check his written submissions at different stages for accuracy and appropriateness (Vannini 2013: 450), which is worth considering as an approach if it would be workable in the context of your own research.

Arts-based dissemination

Visual arts, creative writing, textile arts and performance arts have all been used to disseminate research. Some researchers have created works of art and exhibited them in public spaces. The aim is to increase public engagement with research; to find an audience beyond the specialist academics and practitioners who might read a journal or attend a professional conference. Sometimes this has worked well (for example, Calver 2012), sometimes not so well (for example, Pahl, Steadman-Jones and Pool 2013). If you have little or no artistic skill, it may help you to involve someone who does – although Pahl and her colleagues did this, so it's clearly no guarantee of success; however, it should at least add another dimension of interpretive skill.

Arts-based dissemination often incorporates technology. For example, virtual quilts have been used online for purposes as diverse as reconciliation between nations and fundraising for charity. A virtual quilt exists on a website, with a front page which looks like a quilt (usually a grid of square blocks), and clicking on any block or 'patch' leads through to another page (sometimes called the 'stuffing' or 'batting') that holds information and perhaps other links. Lori Koelsch constructed a prototype virtual quilt as a way of disseminating information from interviews with participants in her research into the unwanted and unlabelled sexual experiences of young women. This enabled her to 'present participant data as both unique and part of a larger whole' (Koelsch 2012: 823). The surface of Koelsch's quilt – aka the homepage – is a block of brightly coloured squares with traditional patchwork designs, some squares bearing a woman's name. A viewer can click on any named square to find out more about that woman's story, which includes a narrative as well as hyperlinks exploring 'additional threads' of her situation (Koelsch 2012: 826), such as potentially useful resources about legal information, alcohol use and so on. Koelsch's virtual quilt is not online, for ethical reasons, but she suggests that future research projects could use this method for simultaneous data construction and dissemination within a participatory framework. A virtual quilt 'can be viewed, adjusted, criticized, and built by many' (Koelsch 2012: 825), and can be linked in with resources, debates, information, social media and so on. It is a living text, fluid, connected and accessible (Koelsch 2012: 828).

American researcher Abigail Schoneboom exhibited her sociological research in an arts centre in Scotland, as an interactive multimedia installation about work–life balance called Project Skive. The installation included six light-hearted stories about six English workers with excellent work records who were also very good at 'skiving', a playful practice for wasting or creatively reclaiming time in the workplace. For example, one would set up fake meetings with her colleagues so they could sit on comfortable sofas and catch up on gossip; another would write posts for his personal blog or do the *Guardian* crossword. At the suggestion of the arts centre curator, visitors were invited to enter their own 'skives' into a live internet database. Some of these were highly creative, including writing satirical songs and building bicycles out of bamboo, while others were more mundane, such as reading newspapers online. This method of exhibiting research increased its accessibility, inclusivity and social relevance (Schoneboom 2010: 14) as well as enabling new sociological insights (Schoneboom 2010: 12), partly by using the process of interactive dissemination to gather new data.

Project Skive is accessible online.

Canadian researcher Lane Mandlis's paper-based presentation of his research on transphobic violence, discussed in Chapter Eight, included cut-up text, images, drawings and cellophane tape. This was unsuitable for dissemination because it was too fragile and could be engaged with by only one person at a time (Mandlis 2009: 1361). Mandlis, who has a professional background in art and design, converted his presentation into an art installation. The focus was a bathroom, a 'space of transformation' (Mandlis 2009: 1366) where, in an intimate, private space, a public self is created. One of Mandlis's key aims was to focus on complexity. Words from his original presentation, and newly constructed drawings, were taped onto transparent shower curtains that hung like a maze for viewers to negotiate. White walls behind the shower curtains were covered with perpendicular graffiti, offering a layered effect to viewers moving through the maze and encouraging them to 'glean different levels of meaning based on their own understandings and interpretations' (Mandlis 2009: 1364). Two mirror panels were used, covered in text but not obscured, so that viewers could see their own reflections and those of other viewers, effectively placing them within the installation. Shower mats underfoot made the floor uneven and multi-textured, adding another dimension to the viewer's experience. The installation was accompanied by a weblog that advertised the work through pictures and podcasts, enabled some engagement with the installation by people who were not able to visit the actual gallery and provided another form of engagement with the installation through online discussions.

A **newspaper article** about Mandlis's exhibition can be read online.

A few academic journals are willing to let researchers present their work in entirely artistic form (Rodriguez and Lahman 2011: 604), with just a brief, context-setting abstract to position the reader. For example, Monica Prendergast presented 'a fragment of arts-based inquiry' as a poem in the journal *Qualitative Inquiry* (Prendergast 2009b), and Jocene Vallack presented her research into life as a university student in Tanzania as the script for a play in the journal *Creative Approaches to Research* (Vallack 2012). But most journal editors and reviewers look for a less experiential, more academic article, in which overt connections are made between any artistic presentation, social theory and professional practice.

Mercilee Jenkins, an American professor of communication studies, poet and playwright, presented her research in the form of a full-length play. *The Fabulous Ruins of Detroit* is based on 'the author's autoethnography, oral histories, archival materials, and the imaginative re-creation of actual events' (Jenkins 2010: 90). The play was staged in Chicago, Phoenix, San Francisco and Detroit, and was selected for the 2008 Theatre Bay Area Playwrights Showcase (Jenkins 2010: 103).

UK researcher Kip Jones spent four years researching the lives of older gay people in rural England and Wales. He used the findings as the basis for a film script and, during its writing, he developed the concept of a 'fictive reality' (Jones 2013: 10). This is 'conceived as the ability to engage in imaginative and creative invention while remaining true to the remembered realities as told through the narrations of others' (Jones 2013: 10). Jones was able to secure funding to engage a professional film company and director to produce the film, *Rufus Stone*, which had its premiere in Bournemouth in 2011 and went on to win two awards at the 2012 Rhode Island International Film Festival. This is a highly creative way of disseminating research and has the potential to reach a very wide audience.

Kip Jones' website contains information about the research and making of *Rufus Stone*.

Patricia Leavy, an American researcher and novelist, spent 10 years interviewing young women about identity issues, including sexuality, body image and relationships, and teaching a range of courses on subjects including gender and sexuality. She drew on these experiences in writing a novel for women, *Low-Fat Love*, with the aim of helping her female readers to reflect on their own self-perceptions and how these might affect their relationship choices. The novel has proved very useful in undergraduate teaching with both female and male students, generating 'rich and powerful conversations' (Leavy 2012: 522). Writing a novel may be beyond the powers of most of us, but Leavy's work usefully demonstrates the importance of disseminating research in ways that will appeal to those we want to influence, if it is to have any impact (Watson 2011: 402).

Patricia Leavy's website contains information about her novels.

Mixed methods of dissemination

It is arguable that most of the methods of dissemination reviewed in this chapter are, to some extent, mixed. Methods of dissemination can be mixed within one public exhibition, installation or production – and this can then be further disseminated using technology.

As we saw in Chapter Six, Jennifer Lapum and her colleagues in Canada used arts-based techniques to study patients' experiences of open-heart surgery. The multi-disciplinary research team spent over a year planning, designing and preparing an exhibition of their findings, alongside patients and health practitioners. Their aim was 'to develop a dissemination method that could immerse audiences in patients' experiences, such that they intimately feel the emotional, psychosocial, and embodied effects of heart surgery', in order to 'underscore the salience of humanistic health care practices' (Lapum et al 2011: 103). The researchers designed a 1,739-square foot installation, including 35 photographic images and 13 poems, exhibited on layered textile compositions that hung within the installation. The poems were constructed from interview data and patients' journals to illustrate 'the key narrative components' (Lapum et al 2011: 106). The photographic images were 'constructed with close attunement to patients' perspective of their world' (Lapum et al 2011: 106). The installation was arranged so that viewers would follow a one-way route through seven sections: departure for hospital, pre-operative, operating room, post-operative, leaving the hospital, home and the aftermath. The operating room was at the centre, and throughout, aesthetic elements such as light, colour and texture increased and reduced in intensity to reflect the changes in patients' experiences. Textures included the cool and clinical, such as metals, and the warm and organic, such as fabrics, to highlight the contrast between hospital and home. The route viewers took through the installation was twisting and winding, echoing the uncertainty felt by open-heart surgery patients. The aim was to give viewers the opportunity to imagine what it might be like to undergo open-heart surgery and to 'employ emotional and aesthetic cognitive faculties in their interpretation of research' (Lapum et al 2011: 112).

A **video presentation** of the above research was further disseminated through YouTube.

Some researchers use a number of different ways to disseminate their findings. For example, Janice Fournillier, a Trinidadian scholar who conducted insider research into immigrant women's experiences in the US higher education system, disseminated her work in a variety of ways, including an encyclopaedia entry, a book chapter and an autoethnographic paper (Fournillier 2010).

As we saw in Chapter Eight, Sarah Franzen is a public ethnographer in the US who is interested in the ways in which audiences engage with scholarship. She worked with participants to create ethnographic films that could be disseminated in various ways: online, for example via YouTube; on DVDs; or through private or public screenings to audiences of various sizes. One problem with disseminating research online or through DVDs is that the output is viewed remotely, which doesn't give the researcher much opportunity to gather reactions from their audiences. So Franzen chose to present her work at small screenings with audiences of no more than 50 people – although she also disseminated her research by giving DVDs to participants so that they could share them with families and friends if they wished, and by providing online versions for stakeholders who had their own websites (Franzen 2013: 422). This mixed-methods approach to presentation and dissemination enabled Franzen to 'receive feedback, interpretations, and corrections, which build upon my research data while contributing to the knowledge of participants and audiences involved' (Franzen 2013: 424). It also enabled her to disseminate her work more widely than she could have done through presentations alone.

Within Ellingson's methodological framework of crystallisation, outlined in Chapter Four, she uses the term 'dendritic crystallization' to refer to the use of multiple methods of dissemination. For example, a researcher might publish a journal article, a book chapter and a newspaper feature, write and perform in a play and present at a conference, all based on one research project. The form of any presentation carries a message, as well as its content, and it is worth bearing this in mind when deciding how to present and disseminate your work, because the more closely you can align the message of the form with the message of the content, the more powerful your message will be (Gergen and Gergen 2012: 113). Dendritic crystallisation is another form of mixed methods, and can help researchers to say more about their work than they could through one method alone, as well as to reach multiple audiences, which can be very satisfying (Ellingson 2009: 128–9).

Dissemination in transformative research

Traditionally, research is concerned to disseminate its findings as far and wide as possible, outwards from those involved in the research process. Conversely, transformative research is particularly concerned to disseminate its findings among the participants of that research and their communities (Vaughn et al 2012: 30). This can be done using any method that is accessible to those people and communities and is aligned with the ethos and aims of the research. For example, we saw in Chapter One that Amy Blodgett and her colleagues in Canada conducted participatory action research with a decolonising agenda in their investigation of the sport experiences of young indigenous athletes who were moving off reserves to take part in sport. The research team, which included academic and indigenous researchers, decided to ask participants to create mandala drawings for them to use as data. At the suggestion of the indigenous researchers, some of the findings were disseminated through the mandalas being printed on a community blanket to form a collective narrative that could be displayed publicly at the youth centre. This enabled sport and recreation staff to use the mandalas as educational tools for young indigenous athletes who were considering moving off the reserve to take up sport opportunities – partly to explain what that experience is like, and partly to encourage young people to pursue their dreams (Blodgett et al 2013: 324).

Nicole Vaughn and her colleagues in Philadelphia, America conducted community-based participatory research into youth violence, in communities where youth homicide was five times the national average. They used traditional methods to disseminate their findings through academic communities, at conferences and through formal publication, and looked for alternative methods that would be effective for disseminating their findings to participants and their communities. They began by working up eight vignettes from the data, then linking these with 55 evidence-based tips for reducing youth violence. These were positively received by the community, but community members were less impressed with the researchers' plans to disseminate through the local paper, pointing out that young people would not read information written in newspapers. One community member suggested creating a comic strip for the local paper, as something that might be more appealing to young people. So the researchers asked some local young people whether they thought this would work, and they said that animated cartoons, disseminated online, would work better. Young people were then involved in an iterative process of choosing a professional artist to work with, reviewing storyboards produced by the artist, voicing characters and advising on which online platforms to use for dissemination. These young people were rewarded for their input through cinema tickets, travel tokens and refreshments, as well as advice from the professional artist on careers in media art and animation. On the young people's advice, the animations were disseminated through YouTube and Facebook. Static advertisements were also developed, with the help of young people, and placed on local public transport vehicles, bearing the web links for the animations. This whole process was slow and time consuming, which made it difficult at times for the academic researchers to manage their own time and budget constraints. Young people and older community members did not always see eye to eye, so there was a balancing act to be performed. However, overall, this participatory dissemination strategy made a positive contribution to youth development and capacity building within participants' communities (Vaughn et al 2012: 31).

The **Facebook page** for the above research contains links to the animations.

Implementation

If research is conducted simply to increase knowledge for its own sake, then dissemination alone is enough. However, research designed to identify ways to improve a situation will be wasted if the knowledge generated is not used in practice. 'Implementation' means 'putting research into practice', and 'implementation science', the study of methods for putting research into practice, is a form of research in itself (Eccles and Mittman 2006). This is a fairly new field that is developing in recognition of the finding that, in fields such as healthcare, interventions that were found to be effective were not being used to improve patient outcomes.

'Implementation' is a term used in the UK and Europe, while other countries and continents use different names. For example, American health researchers may use the term 'translational research', which refers to ways of implementing laboratory and clinical research within applied healthcare (Drolet and Lorenzi 2011). Some Canadian health researchers call this 'knowledge translation' (Straus, Tetroe and Graham 2011). There are dozens of other terms with no common definition (Tugwell, Knottnerus and Idzerda 2011: 1). However, there is general agreement that implementation is both necessary and complicated. A **webinar** about dissemination and implementation research is available online.

The UK has a unique procedure for assessing national statistics against a code of practice (Laux and Pont 2012: 5). The aim is to ensure that statistical information gathered within the UK is usefully implemented, because 'Statistics realise their full potential only when they are used in ways that serve the public good' (Laux and Pont 2012: 3). The code of practice contains 75 specific requirements that must be implemented by over 200 bodies that produce official statistics in the UK. The first programme of assessment ran from 2009 to 2012, and within it the assessment team reviewed about 250 published reports containing approximately 1,100 sets of statistics. The programme identified five main areas for improvement.

1. Improve the quality of the text that is written to support statistical information.
2. Increase understanding of the actual or potential use of statistics.
3. Improve documentation of sources and methods.
4. Where possible, maximise the use of existing administrative data, for example from hospitals or schools.
5. Improve comparability of statistics between the four UK administrations (England, Wales, Scotland and Northern Ireland).

Now that we know what needs to be done to implement research, the big question is, *how* should that be done? The topic of writing good text to accompany statistical information was covered in Chapter Seven. There is also considerable scope for creativity in how to increase understanding of the use of statistics in research, maximise the use of existing administrative data, and improve the comparability of statistics. I suggest that this also applies to qualitative data. It is beyond the scope of this book to explore these processes in detail, but it would be useful to consider how they might apply in relation to the implementation of your own research. **Online guidance** produced by the UK's National Statistician may help if you want to investigate this further.

There are many obstacles to the implementation of research findings (Straus, Tetroe and Graham 2011: 7). For example, Canadian researchers Janice Du Mont and Deborah White, whose literature search strategy was highlighted in Chapter Four, studied the implementation of rape kits in cases of sexual assault around the world. Rape kits are standardised methods for gathering evidence of sexual assault that are used in criminal justice systems worldwide. However, they are often not used successfully. Du Mont and White found three main reasons for this: incompetence of professionals, contempt for women reporting rape and corruption in professional settings (Du Mont and White 2013: 1234). So while the rape kits have been implemented to the extent that they are in common use around the world, they are not being fully implemented, due to social and structural factors. In a more localised example, Swedish researchers Andersson and Kalman studied interactions between care managers, care workers and residents in care homes for older people. They found that differing perspectives, knowledges and understandings of seemingly everyday concepts such as 'time' and 'care' presented serious barriers to the implementation of social and institutional policies (Andersson and Kalman 2012: 70).

Laura Damschroder and her colleagues in America developed the Consolidated Framework for Implementation Research (CFIR). They looked for theories about how to put research into practice and found 19, one of which was itself based on almost 500 pieces of literature (Greenhalgh et al 2004, cited in Damschroder et al 2009) and 18 of which had been published in peer-reviewed journals; the 19th was included because of its scope and depth. The researchers then assessed the constructs, or concepts, on which each theory was based, within five domains: characteristics of the intervention, outer setting (that is, wider context), inner setting (that is, within the institution concerned), characteristics of individuals involved and the process of implementation. Thirty-seven constructs were identified in total, with between 4 and 12 in each domain; each construct appeared in at least two of the 19 theories. Each of the 19 theories aimed to enable effective implementation. However, when Damschroder et al compared the constructs used in each theory, they found that each of the 19 was missing important constructs that had been included in other theories. This led them to create the CFIR, which describes all the domains and constructs in detail, and so can be used to guide the process of implementation.

The CFIR is not a rule book for implementation. In fact there is not, and cannot be, any such thing. Every situation is different, and a creative approach to implementation is needed. But there are some guiding principles, so, if your research is intended to generate improvements,

- start planning your implementation process from a very early stage
- try to use your research to identify features of the subject under investigation that make it more (or less) effective in generating improvements
- draw on the CFIR for constructs that will be helpful in the context within which you are working

- be aware of the possibility of unexpected barriers to or enablers of implementation, and aim to address problems and maximise opportunities as soon as possible
- keep a record of what influenced implementation, whether positively or negatively, and how and why these factors operated.

One big enabling factor for implementation is to root the research firmly in its context. Participatory frameworks can be particularly useful here. A **short video** on participatory research and implementation can be viewed online.

Knowledge exchange

Even within participatory frameworks, dissemination and implementation are both activities that are done by researchers to or for others. Knowledge exchange is a more egalitarian approach that implies a two-way process of sharing knowledge between researchers, practitioners, service users and other interested people.

The process of knowledge exchange is dynamic, social and complex (Ward et al 2011: 298). Knowledge exchange is embedded within transformative research frameworks at all stages of the research process (Gagnon 2011: 28), but in other paradigms is more often seen as something that happens after findings have been established. Either way, it is not feasible to exchange all knowledge, because different people have different knowledges and different understandings of knowledge (Martin, Currie and Lockett 2011: 214). This can make attempts at knowledge exchange rather like attempts at conversation between people who don't speak each other's languages. Time pressures are another barrier (Martin, Currie and Lockett 2011: 216). So it makes sense to prioritise the knowledge you wish to exchange, and to encourage others to do the same. Whether you are working within a transformative research framework or not, it may help to work out how to do this by first agreeing on the problem that needs solving, or on what needs to change (Ward et al 2011: 302).

Knowledge exchange increases the likelihood that 'research findings will be used and ... the research ... will achieve a greater impact' (Gagnon 2011: 28). Gagnon identified four factors that can help knowledge exchange to succeed:

1. a team of people who are experienced and competent in both research and knowledge exchange partnerships
2. a plan for working together, with specified roles, named responsibilities and regular reviews
3. a process for developing a shared understanding, language and perspective on the problem or issue at hand
4. a strategy for ensuring that trust among the team is built and maintained and for resolving any conflicts that arise (Gagnon 2011: 28–9).

Even if full-scale knowledge exchange proves too difficult or time consuming, it makes considerable sense to involve research participants and potential research users in working out how to disseminate and implement research (Gagnon 2011: 25).

A **website** is available about knowledge exchange, and an **animation** and a **presentation** on the topic can also be viewed online.

CONCLUSION

Dissemination is not an optional extra, it's an integral part of research. Without dissemination, research has little value or relevance. The ultimate aim of dissemination is for your research and its findings to take on a life of their own and be disseminated further by other people talking and writing about your work. For this to happen, it helps to ensure there are easy 'take-aways' for your readers or viewers (Nespor 2012: 458). For example, it's advisable for any abstract of a journal paper, or executive summary of a research report, to contain at least one sentence summarising a key finding or findings. Equally, any drama performance or film should include one or more soundbites giving the same kind of summary. For example, the dramatic performance of the research into school safety discussed in Chapter Eight finished with several characters in turn each speaking the sentence 'How can we do our part?' (Goldstein and Wickett 2009: 1565). The performance was designed to convey the message that school safety is everyone's concern, and this ending was chosen to leave that key question resonating in the ears and minds of audience members, and so inspire them to discuss the message of the performance and take responsibility for its implications within their lives. So, when you're planning your dissemination, think about what you want your readers or viewers to remember. How can you encapsulate that in memorable language?

TEN

Conclusion

Traditional research methods were, of course, creatively devised, but in use their aim was to avoid creativity. They advocated a procedural approach and valued hard facts and replicability. By contrast, creative research methods advocate a considered approach, and value contextual specificity. This book has shown that a creative approach to research methods is not only widespread but also now recommended for use in many areas of the social sciences, humanities and neighbouring fields.

If you take away just one learning point from this book, it should be that knowledge, experience and skills from almost any arena can make a useful contribution to research (Gergen and Gergen 2012: 49; Jones and Leavy 2014: 6). To do research well, of course, you need a good understanding of its basic principles and practice: research ethics, how to plan research, gathering and analysing data and so on. But all sorts of other knowledge and experience can be helpful too. Do you practise judo? Renovate steam trains? Know how to prune an apple tree? I have no idea about any of those subjects – but I will bet that people who do could make useful contributions to research.

Marco Gemignani is a trained counsellor and psychology researcher working in America. In his research on refugees from the former Yugoslavia, he analysed the phenomenon of countertransference, well known to counsellors and psychotherapists, to enhance his interview data. Countertransference is 'the influence of the patient on the therapist in the here and now of the clinical relationship' (Gemignani 2011: 704), which manifests as emotional reactions for the therapist (or researcher), most of which are unpredictable (Gemignani 2011: 703). While not every researcher will be a trained counsellor or psychotherapist, anyone can identify and examine their own emotional reactions to participants. Gemignani suggests that doing this will have a range of benefits for researchers and their research, including:

- increased sensitivity and empathy
- better rapport with participants
- deeper reflexive analysis
- improved self-awareness and performance
- richer experience
- more creativity (Gemignani 2011: 705).

Doing this is not without risk, as increasing awareness of emotional reactions can leave people open to vulnerability. However, Gemignani's view is that 'the

> potential for personal engagements, heartfelt interpretations, collections of complex data, and nuanced analyses well-justifies the risk' (Gemignani 2011: 707).

Taking a creative approach can be particularly useful when research doesn't go well, or doesn't go according to plan, or obstacles are encountered. For example, creativity can be useful when recruitment strategies don't work (McCormack et al 2012), when data integration plans don't bear fruit (Lunde et al 2013) or when the shyness of researchers threatens to cause problems (Scott et al 2012). And of course, even creative methods can go wrong. Here is a cautionary tale from a doctoral researcher who found herself having to be extra creative when the creative method she originally chose didn't work as planned.

Denise Turner's PhD research offers an interesting example of what she calls 'meandering methodologies' (Turner 2014). Her aim was to improve practice following sudden and unexpected child death. A social worker and bereaved parent herself, she chose to do this by exploring the experience of other bereaved parents. She was attracted to the Biographic Narrative Interpretive Method (BNIM), which was developed by German sociologists exploring accounts from Holocaust survivors. This method is based on interviewing, and takes quite a structured approach to both the interviews and the data analysis. Turner found this method useful for the interviews, which – as we saw in Chapter Five – are structured through a single question; this worked well, enabling bereaved parents to tell their stories in their own terms. Turner then transcribed the interviews and tried to condense them into the complex structure of documents prescribed by the BNIM, but this proved unhelpful and in the end she used only one part of the suggested structure. The documents she produced were presented to panels of three people for discussion as part of the analytic process. Panel members were known to Turner but were not specialists in the research topic. The BNIM suggests that small chunks of data from a small number of interviews should be presented to the panels, but Turner struggled with this, feeling that such an interventionist approach to her data would inevitably alter the 'reality' presented by her participants and that selection raised ethical issues of inclusion and exclusion. In the end, she went with her instincts rather than the BNIM's instructions and presented large chunks of data from five of her eight interviews to the panels. For many panel members, the data elicited acute emotional responses, something the BNIM methodology had not led Turner to expect and that neither Turner nor her ethics committee had foreseen. Ultimately, between the structured nature of the BNIM and the unexpected difficulties faced by the panels, Turner became distanced from her data. She sought a new method to repair this breach and chose to use the Listening Guide developed by Doucet and Mauthner, which recommends multiple readings of data from different perspectives. This enabled her, in effect, to become a 'one-woman panel', reading from her own perspectives as bereaved parent, social worker and researcher.

Research is a political activity, and creativity is also political (Gauntlett 2011: 19). Therefore creative research methods can be a contentious topic. More than once in my research career I've suggested a creative method and been told, 'No, we'd better play it safe.' Which implies that creativity is dangerous. And perhaps it is – for people's careers in particular, and for social science in general (Gergen and Gergen 2012: 47) – although mostly, in my opinion, it's dangerous for the status quo. There is a very real danger that people who use creative methods will find ways to express themselves, learn and have fun.

The subtitle to this book is 'A Practical Guide'. The book has aimed to help you by including a wealth of examples of creative research methods in practice, and to offer ideas and inspiration, as well as an overview of current debates and some 'dos and don'ts' about various approaches to research. But creativity in research is indisputably context specific. It depends on: the skills, knowledge and abilities of the individuals involved; when and where the research is conducted; and other contextual factors (see Chapter Four for fuller discussions of context). The key point – which has been made several times in this book, and which bears repeating – is that methods must flow from research questions, and not the other way around. No step-by-step instructions can be given for your own particular research. What this book has done is guide you through the process, providing ideas and provoking thought at every stage. Maybe your own work will feature in the next edition. Who knows?

References

Aarsand, P. and Forsberg, L. (2010) Producing children's corporeal privacy: ethnographic video recording as material-discursive practice. *Qualitative Research* 10(2) 249–68.

Adamson, S. and Holloway, M. (2012) Negotiating sensitivities and grappling with intangibles: experiences from a study of spirituality and funerals. *Qualitative Research* 12(6) 735–52.

Ahearn, A. (2006) Engineering writing: replacing 'writing classes' with a 'writing imperative'. In Ganobcsik-Williams, L. (ed) *Teaching academic writing in UK higher education: theories, practices and models*, 110–23. Basingstoke: Palgrave Macmillan.

Ahram, A. (2011) The theory and method of comparative area studies. *Qualitative Research* 11(1) 69–90.

Alasuutari, P. (2009) The rise and relevance of qualitative research. *International Journal of Social Research Methodology* 13(2) 139–55.

Alaszewski, A. (2006) *Using diaries for social research*. London: Sage.

Allen, A. and Thomas, K. (2011) A dual process account of creative thinking. *Creativity Research Journal* 23(2) 109–18.

Allen, L. (2011) 'Picture this': using photo-methods in research on sexualities and schooling. *Qualitative Research* 11(5) 487–504.

Allen, Q. (2012) Photographs and stories: ethics, benefits and dilemmas of using participant photography with Black middle-class male youth. *Qualitative Research* 12(4) 443–58.

Anderson, J., Adey, P. and Bevan, P. (2010) Positioning place: polylogic approaches to research methodology. *Qualitative Research* 10(5) 589–604.

Andersson, K. and Kalman, H. (2012) Methodological challenges in the implementation and evaluation of social welfare policies. *International Journal of Social Research Methodology* 15(1) 69–80.

Angus, D., Rintel, S. and Wiles, J. (2013) Making sense of big text: a visual-first approach for analysing text data using Leximancer and Discursis. *International Journal of Social Research Methodology* 16(3) 261–7.

Archer, B. (1995) The nature of research. *Co-design*, January, 6–13.

Armstrong, C. (2014) Webinars. In Daly, I. and Brophy Haney, A. (eds) *53 interesting ways to communicate your research*, 21–2. Newmarket: The Professional and Higher Partnership Ltd.

Arvidson, M. and Kara, H. (2013). Putting evaluations to use: from measuring to endorsing social value. Third Sector Research Centre, Working Paper 110, University of Birmingham.

Atkinson, M. (2010) Fell running in post-sport territories. *Qualitative Research in Sport, Exercise and Health* 2(2) 109–32.

Bahn, S. and Weatherill, P. (2012) Qualitative social research: a risky business when it comes to collecting 'sensitive' data. *Qualitative Research* 13(1) 19–35.

Barber, B., Boote, J., Parry, G., Cooper, C. and Yeeles, P. (2012) Evaluating the impact of public involvement on research. In Barnes, M. and Cotterell, P. (eds) *Critical perspectives on user involvement*, 217–23. Bristol: The Policy Press.

Barbour, K. (2012) Standing center: autoethnographic writing and solo dance performance. *Cultural Studies – Critical Methodologies* 12(1) 67–71.

Barnes, M. and Cotterell, P. (2012a) Critical and different perspectives on user involvement. In Barnes, M. and Cotterell, P. (eds) *Critical perspectives on user involvement*, 225–33. Bristol: The Policy Press.

Barnes, M. and Cotterell, P. (2012b) User involvement in research. In Barnes, M. and Cotterell, P. (eds) *Critical perspectives on user involvement*, 143–7. Bristol: The Policy Press.

Barone, T. and Eisner, E. (2012) *Arts based research*. Thousand Oaks, CA: Sage.

Barrett, E. (2014) Share a conference paper using YouTube. In Daly, I. and Brophy Haney, A. (eds) *53 interesting ways to communicate your research*, 23–4. Newmarket: The Professional and Higher Partnership Ltd.

Bartkowiak-Theron, I. and Sappey, J. (2012) The methodological identity of shadowing in social science research. *Qualitative Research Journal* 12(1) 7–16.

Bartlett, R. (2013) Playing with meaning: using cartoons to disseminate research findings. *Qualitative Research* 13(2) 214–27.

Batey, M. (2012) The measurement of creativity: from definitional consensus to the introduction of a new heuristic framework. *Creativity Research Journal* 24(1) 55–65.

Bazeley, P. and Jackson, K. (2013) *Qualitative data analysis with NVivo*. London: Sage.

Bazeley, P. and Kemp, L. (2012) Mosaics, triangles, and DNA: metaphors for integrated analysis in mixed methods research. *Journal of Mixed Methods Research* 6(1) 55–72.

Beck, J., Belliveau, G., Lea, G. and Wager, A. (2011) Delineating a spectrum of research-based theatre. *Qualitative Inquiry* 17(8) 687–700.

Becker, H. (2007) *Writing for social scientists: how to start and finish your thesis, book, or article* (2nd edn). Chicago: University of Chicago Press.

Belzile, J. and Öberg, G. (2012) Where to begin? Grappling with how to use participant interaction in focus group design. *Qualitative Research* 12(4) 459–72.

Beneito-Montagut, R. (2011) Ethnography goes online: towards a user-centred methodology to research interpersonal communication on the internet. *Qualitative Research* 11(6) 716–35.

Benozzo, A. (2011) An experienced academic becomes participant in a training course: an autoethnography of emotion and learning. *Creative Approaches to Research* 4(1) 19–32.

Berbary, L. (2011) Poststructural writerly representation: screenplay as creative analytic practice. *Qualitative Inquiry* 17(2) 186–96.

Bhana, A. (2006) Participatory action research: a practical guide for realistic radicals. In Terre Blanche, M., Durrheim, K. and Painter, D. (eds) *Research in practice: allied methods for the social sciences*, 429–42. Cape Town: University of Cape Town Press.

Biggs, S. (2009) New media: the 'first word' in art? In Smith, H. and Dean, R. (eds) *Practice-led research, research-led practice in the creative arts*, 66–83. Edinburgh: Edinburgh University Press.

Blake, L. (2014) Podcasting. In Daly, I. and Brophy Haney, A. (eds) *53 interesting ways to communicate your research* 67–8. Newmarket: The Professional and Higher Partnership Ltd.

Blee, K. and Currier, A. (2011) Ethics beyond the IRB: an introductory essay. *Qualitative Sociology* 34: 401–13.

Blodgett, A., Coholic, D., Schinke, R., McGannon, K., Peltier, D. and Pheasant, C. (2013) Moving beyond words: exploring the use of an arts-based method in Aboriginal community sport research. *Qualitative Research in Sport, Exercise and Health* 5(3) 312–31.

Blom, D., Bennett, D. and Wright, D. (2011) How artists working in academia view artistic practice as research: implications for tertiary music education. *International Journal of Music Education* 29(4) 359–73.

Boccagni, P. (2011) From rapport to collaboration … and beyond? Revisiting field relationships in an ethnography of Ecuadorian migrants. *Qualitative Research* 11(6) 736–54.

Boehner, K., Gaver, W. and Boucher, A. (2014) Probes. In Lury, C. and Wakeford, N. (eds) *Inventive methods: the happening of the social*, 185–201. Abingdon: Routledge.

Bolton, E., Vorajee, Z. and Jones, K. (2005) The verismo of the quotidian: a biographic narrative interpretive approach to two diverse research topics. *Narrative, Memory and Everyday Life*, http://eprints.bournemouth.ac.uk/5354/1/Chapter_2_-_Everton_Bolton__Zaheera_Essat_and_Kip_Jones.pdf (viewed 20 October 2014).

Botha, L. (2011) Mixing methods as a process towards indigenous methodologies. *International Journal of Social Research Methodology* 14(4) 313–25.

Bourgois, P. (2002) *In search of respect: selling crack in El Barrio*. Cambridge: Cambridge University Press.

Bowen, G. (2009) Document analysis as a qualitative research method. *Qualitative Research Journal* 9(2) 27–40.

Bowtell, E., Sawyer, S., Aroni, R., Green, J. and Duncan, R. (2013) 'Should I send a condolence card?' Promoting emotional safety in qualitative health research through reflexivity and ethical mindfulness. *Qualitative Inquiry* 19(9) 652–63.

Bradbury-Jones, C., Taylor, J. and Herber, O. (2014) Vignette development and administration: a framework for protecting research participants. *International Journal of Social Research Methodology* 17(4) 427–40.

Braye, S. and McDonnell, L. (2012) Balancing powers: university researchers thinking critically about participatory research with young fathers. *Qualitative Research* 13(3) 265–84.

Brearley, L. and Hamm, T. (2009) Ways of looking and listening: stories from the spaces between indigenous and non-indigenous knowledge systems. In Grierson, E. and Brearley, L. (eds) *Creative arts research: narratives of methodologies and practices*, 33–54. Rotterdam: Sense Publishers.

Breheny, M. (2012) 'We've had our lives, we've had our lives': a poetic representation of ageing. *Creative Approaches to Research* 5(2) 156–70.

Briassoulis, H. (2010) Online petitions: new tools of secondary analysis? *Qualitative Research* 10(6) 715–27.

Brien, D. (2013) Non-fiction writing research. In Kroll, J. and Harper, G. (eds) *Research methods in creative writing*, 34–55. Basingstoke: Palgrave Macmillan.

Brinkmann, S. (2009) Literature as qualitative inquiry: the novelist as researcher. *Qualitative Inquiry* 15(8) 1376–94.

Brittain, I. and Green, S. (2012) Disability sport is going back to its roots: rehabilitation of military personnel receiving sudden traumatic disabilities in the twenty-first century. *Qualitative Research in Sport, Exercise and Health* 4(2) 244–64.

Broussine, M. (2008) The seductive qualities of creative methods: critical awareness. In Broussine, M. (ed) *Creative Methods in Organisational Research*, 33–49. London: Sage.

Bryman, A. (2012) *Social research methods* (4th edn). Oxford: Oxford University Press.

Brzinsky-Fay, C. and Kohler, U. (2010) New developments in sequence analysis. *Sociological Methods & Research* 38(3) 359–64.

Buckley, C. and Waring, M. (2013) Using diagrams to support the research process: examples from grounded theory. *Qualitative Research* 13(2) 148–72.

Burgin, C., Silvia, P., Eddington, K. and Kwapil, T. (2012) Palm or cell? Comparing personal digital assistants and cell phones for experience sampling research. *Social Science Computer Review* 31(2) 244–51.

Burns, C. and Conchie, S. (2012) Measuring implicit trust and automatic attitude activation. In Lyon, F., Möllering, G. and Saunders, M. (eds) *Handbook of Research Methods on Trust*, 239–48. Cheltenham: Edward Elgar.

Burraston, D. (2011) Creativity, complexity and reflective practice. In Candy, L. and Edmonds, E. (eds) *Interacting: art, research, and the creative practitioner*, 107–18. Faringdon: Libri Publishing.

Burton, J. (ed) (2013) Understanding Society innovation panel wave 5: results from methodological experiments. *Understanding Society* Working Paper Series: 2013-06.

Calver, M. (2012) In winter look patiently around the edges of pools: re-writings between art and social science. *Creative Approaches to Research* 5(2) 47–57.

Campos-Seijo, B. (2014) Guest blogging. In Daly, I. and Brophy Haney, A. (eds) *53 interesting ways to communicate your research*, 101–2. Newmarket: The Professional and Higher Partnership Ltd.

Čančer, V. and Mulej, M. (2013) Multi-criteria decision making in creative problem solving. *Kybernetes* 42(1) 67–81.

Candy, L. (2011) Research and creative practice. In Candy, L. and Edmonds, E. (eds) 33–59. *Interacting: Art, Research and the Creative Practitioner*. Faringdon: Libri Publishing.

Carroll, P., Dew, K. and Howden-Chapman, P. (2011) The heart of the matter: using poetry as a method of ethnographic inquiry to represent and present experiences of the informally housed in Aotearoa/New Zealand. *Qualitative Inquiry* 17(7) 623–30.

Carter, R. (2004) *Language and creativity: the art of common talk.* London: Routledge.

Catt, R. and Gregory, G. (2006) The point of writing: is student writing in higher education developed or merely assessed? In Ganobcsik-Williams, L. (ed) *Teaching academic writing in UK higher education: theories, practices and models,* 16–29. Basingstoke: Palgrave Macmillan.

Chang, H. (2008) *Autoethnography as method.* Walnut Creek, CA: Left Coast Press, Inc.

Cherrington J. and Watson B. (2010) Shooting a diary, not just a hoop: using video diaries to explore the embodied everyday contexts of a university basketball team. *Qualitative Research in Sport, Exercise and Health* 2(2) 267–81.

Chevalier, J. and Buckles, D. (2013) *Participatory action research: theory and methods for engaged inquiry.* Abingdon: Routledge.

Childers S. (2012) Against simplicity, against ethics: analytics of disruption as quasi-methodology. *Qualitative Inquiry* 18(9) 752–61.

Christensen, P. et al (2011) Children, mobility, and space: using GPS and mobile phone technologies in ethnographic research. *Journal of Mixed Methods Research* 5(3) 227–46.

Clark A., Holland C. and Ward R. (2012) Authenticity and validity in community research: looking at age discrimination and urban social interactions in the UK. In Goodson L. and Phillimore J. (eds) *Community research for participation: from theory to method.* Bristol: Policy Press.

Clayton, B. (2010) Ten minutes with the boys, the thoroughly academic task and the semi-naked celebrity: football masculinities in the classroom or pursuing security in a 'liquid' world. *Qualitative Research in Sport, Exercise and Health* 2(3) 371–84.

Clegg, B. and Birch, P. (1999) *Instant creativity.* London: Kogan Page.

Coget, J.-F. (2014) Dialogical inquiry: a qualitative method for studying intuition in the field. In Sinclair, M. (ed) *Handbook of research methods on intuition,* 176–87. Cheltenham: Edward Elgar.

Cohen, J. and Ferrari, J. (2010) Take some time to think this over: the relation between rumination, indecision, and creativity. *Creativity Research Journal* 22(1) 68–73.

Coles, K. (2013) Forward, wayward: the writer in the world's text, at large. In Kroll, J. and Harper, G. (eds) *Research methods in creative writing,* 155–74. Basingstoke: Palgrave Macmillan.

Collingridge, D. (2013) A primer on quantitized data analysis and permutation testing. *Journal of Mixed Methods Research* 7(1) 81–97.

Colyar, J. (2009) Becoming writing, becoming writers. *Qualitative Inquiry* 15(2) 421–36.

Connelly, K. (2010) 'What body part do I need to sell?' Poetic re-presentations of experiences of poverty and fear from low-income Australians receiving welfare benefits. *Creative Approaches to Research* 3(1) 16–41.

Cooper, B. and Glaesser, J. (2011) Using case-based approaches to analyse large datasets: a comparison of Ragin's fsQCA and fuzzy cluster analysis. *International Journal of Social Research Methodology* 14(1) 31–48.

COPE (2013) Ethical Guidelines for Peer Reviewers, www.publicationethics.org/ files/Ethical_guidelines_for_peer_reviewers_0.pdf (viewed 20 October 2014).

Corman, M. (2013) How mothers talk about placement of their child with autism outside the home. *Qualitative Health Research* 23(10) 1320–32.

Corvellec, H. (ed) (2013) *What is theory? Answers from the social and cultural sciences.* Copenhagen: Liber CBS Press.

Cotterell, P. and Morris, C. (2012) The capacity, impact and challenge of service users' experiential knowledge. In Barnes, M. and Cotterell, P. (eds) *Critical perspectives on user involvement*, 57–69. Bristol: The Policy Press.

Creswell, J. and Plano Clark, V. (2010) *Designing and conducting mixed methods research*. London: Sage.

Crofts, A. (2002) *The freelance writer's handbook: how to make money and enjoy your life*. London: Piatkus Books.

Crowston, K., Allen, E. and Heckman, R. (2012) Using natural language processing technology for qualitative data analysis. *International Journal of Social Research Methodology* 15(6) 523–43.

Cunsolo Willox, A. et al (2012) Storytelling in a digital age: digital storytelling as an emerging narrative method for preserving and promoting indigenous oral wisdom. *Qualitative Research* 13(2) 127–47.

Cutcher, A. (2013) [In]accessibilies: presentations, representations and re-presentations in arts-based research. *Creative Approaches to Research* 6(2) 33–44.

Czymoniewicz-Klippel, M., Brijnath, B. and Crockett, B. (2010) Ethics and the promotion of inclusiveness within qualitative research: case examples from Asia and the Pacific. *Qualitative Inquiry* 16(5) 332–41.

Dahl, S., Morris, G., Brown, P., Scullion, L. and Somerville, P. (2012) *Somewhere nowhere: lives without homes.* Salford: University of Salford Housing and Urban Studies Unit.

Damschroder, L., Aron, D., Keith, R., Kirsh, S., Alexander, J. and Lowery, J. (2009) Fostering implementation of health services research findings into practice: a consolidated framework for advancing implementation science. *Implementation Science*, http://www.implementationscience.com/content/4/1/50.

Dark, K. (2009) Examining praise from the audience: what does it mean to be a 'successful' poet-researcher? In Prendergast, M., Leggo, C. and Sameshima, P. (eds) *Poetic inquiry: vibrant voices in the social sciences*, 171–86. Rotterdam: Sense Publishers.

Davidson, J. (2011) The journal project. *Qualitative Inquiry* 18(1) 86–99.

Davis, C. (2013) *SPSS for allied sciences: basic statistical testing.* Bristol: The Policy Press.

Davis, J., Normington, K., Bush-Bailey, G., Bratton, J. (2011) Researching theatre history and historiography. In Kershaw, B. and Nicholson, H. (eds) *Research methods in theatre and performance*, 86–110. Edinburgh: Edinburgh University Press.

de Bono E. (1999) *Six Thinking Hats.* London: Penguin.

DeCuir-Gunby, J., Marshall, P. and McCulloch, A. (2012) Using mixed methods to analyze video data: a mathematics teacher professional development example. *Journal of Mixed Methods Research* 6(3) 199–216.

Degarrod, L. (2013) Making the unfamiliar personal: arts-based ethnographies as public-engaged ethnographies. *Qualitative Research* 13(4) 402–13.

DeMeulenaere, E. and Cann, C. (2013) Activist educational research. *Qualitative Inquiry* 19(8) 552–65.

Denzin, N. (2014) *Interpretive autoethnography* (2nd edn). London: Sage.

Denzin, N. and Giardina, M. (2006) Introduction: ethical futures in qualitative research. In Denzin, N. and Giardina, M. (eds) *Ethical futures in qualitative research: decolonising the politics of knowledge*, 9–43. Walnut Creek, CA: Left Coast Press, Inc.

Denzin, N. and Lincoln, Y. (2011) *The Sage handbook of qualitative research* (4th edn). Thousand Oaks, CA: Sage.

Dias, R. (2010) Concept map: a strategy for enhancing reading comprehension in English as L2. In Sánchez, J., Cañas, A., Novak, J. (eds) *Proceedings of Fourth International Conference on Concept Mapping*, 29–33. Viña del Mar, Chile.

Dippo, C. (2013) Evaluating the alternative uses test of creativity. *Proceedings of the National Conference on Undergraduate Research (NCUR) 2013*. University of Wisconsin La Crosse, WI. 11–13 April 2013.

Dixon, S. (2011) Researching digital performance: virtual practices. In Kershaw, B. and Nicholson, H. (eds) *Research methods in theatre and performance*, 41–62. Edinburgh: Edinburgh University Press.

Djikic, M., Oatley, K., Zoeterman, S. and Peterson, J. (2009) On being moved by art: how reading fiction transforms the self. *Creativity Research Journal* 21(1) 24–29.

Donmoyer, R. (2012) Can qualitative researchers answer policymakers' what-works question? *Qualitative Inquiry* 18(8) 662–73.

Douglas, K. (2012) Signals and signs. *Qualitative Inquiry* 18(6) 525–32.

Douglas, K. and Carless, D. (2010) Restoring connections in physical activity and mental health research and practice: a confessional tale. *Qualitative Research in Sport, Exercise and Health* 2(3) 336–53.

Drolet, B. and Lorenzi, N. (2011) Translational research: understanding the continuum from bench to bedside. *Translational Research* 157(1) 1–5.

Drummond, D. (2011) White American style in rhyme. *Qualitative Inquiry* 17(4) 332–3.

Du Mont, J. and White, D. (2013) Barriers to the effective use of medico-legal findings in sexual assault cases worldwide. *Qualitative Health Research* 23(9) 1228–39.

Dumitrica, D. and Gaden, G. (2009) Knee-high boots and six-pack abs: autoethnographic reflections on gender and technology in Second Life. *Journal of Virtual Worlds Research* 1(3) 3–23.

Durré C. (2008) Texts in parallel: art research as allegory. *Creative Approaches to Research* 1(2) 35–44.

Duxbury, L. (2009) Ways of analysing: from reverie to reality. In Grierson, E. and Brearley, L. (eds) *Creative arts research: narratives of methodologies and practices*, 55–64. Rotterdam: Sense Publishers.

Eakin, P. (2004) Introduction: mapping the ethics of life writing. In Eakin, P. (ed) (2004) *The ethics of life writing*, 1–16. Ithaca, NY: Cornell University Press.

Eccles, M. and Mittman, B. (2006) Welcome to Implementation Science. *Implementation Science*, http://www.implementationscience.com/content/1/1/1 (viewed 20 October 2014).

Edwards, D. (2008) *ArtScience: creativity in the post-Google generation*. Cambridge, MA: Harvard University Press.

Edwards, R. and Weller, S. (2012) Shifting analytic ontology: using I-poems in qualitative longitudinal research. *Qualitative Research* 12(2) 202–17.

Einwohner, R. (2011) Ethical considerations on the use of archived testimonies in Holocaust research: beyond the IRB exemption. *Qualitative Sociology* 34: 415–30.

Eldén, S. (2013) Inviting the messy: drawing methods and 'children's voices'. *Childhood* 20(1) 66–81.

Ellingsen, I., Størksen, I. and Stephens, P. (2010) Q methodology in social work research. *International Journal of Social Research Methodology* 13(5) 395–409.

Ellingson, L. (2009) *Engaging crystallization in qualitative research: an introduction*. Thousand Oaks, CA: Sage.

Ellis, C. (2004) *The ethnographic I: a methodological novel about autoethnography*. Walnut Creek, CA: AltaMira Press.

Ellis, C. and Rawicki, J. (2013) Collaborative witnessing of survival during the Holocaust: an exemplar of relational autoethnography. *Qualitative Inquiry* 19(5) 366–80.

Ellis, C., Adams, T. and Bochner, A. (2011) Autoethnography: an overview. *Forum: Qualitative Social Research* 12(1) Art. 10.

Engman, A. (2013) Is there life after P<0.05? Statistical significance and quantitative sociology. *Quality and Quantity* 47: 257–70.

Evans, B., Coon, D. and Ume, E. (2011) Use of theoretical frameworks as a pragmatic guide for mixed methods studies: a methodological necessity? *Journal of Mixed Methods Research* 5(4) 276–92.

Evans, J. and Curtis-Holmes, J. (2005) Rapid responding increases belief bias: evidence for the dual-process theory of reasoning. *Thinking & Reasoning* 11(4) 382–9.

Evergreen, S. (2014) *Presenting data effectively: communicating your findings for maximum impact*. Thousand Oaks, CA: Sage.

Fairweather, J. and Rinne, T. (2012) Clarifying a basis for qualitative generalization using approaches that identify shared culture. *Qualitative Research* 12(4) 473–85.

Farnsworth, J. and Boon, B. (2010) Analysing group dynamics within the focus group. *Qualitative Research* 10(5) 605–24.

Fele, G. (2012) The use of video to document tacit participation in an emergency operations centre. *Qualitative Research* 12(3) 280–303.

Fielding, N. (2012) Triangulation and mixed methods designs: data integration with new research technologies. *Journal of Mixed Methods Research* 6(2) 124–36.

Finlay, L. (2011) *Phenomenology for therapists: researching the lived World*. Chichester: Wiley-Blackwell.

Finlay, L. (2012) Debating phenomenological methods. In Friesen, N., Henriksson, C. and Saevi, T. (eds) *Hermeneutic phenomenology in education: method and practice*, 17–37. Rotterdam: Sense Publishers.

Fleischmann, P. (2009) Literature reviews: an example of making traditional research methods user focused. In Sweeney, A., Beresford, P., Faulkner, A., Nettle, M. and Rose, D. (eds) *Survivor research*, 82–97. Ross on Wye: PCCS Books.

Fletcher, G. (2013) Of baby ducklings and clay pots: method and metaphor in HIV prevention. *Qualitative Health Research* 23(11) 1551–62.

Forceville, C. (2012) Creativity in pictorial and multimodal advertising metaphors. In Jones, R. (ed) *Discourse and creativity*, 113–32. Harlow: Pearson Education Limited.

Formichelli, L. and Burrell, D. (2005) *The renegade writer: a totally unconventional guide to freelance writing success*. Oak Park, IL: Marion Street Press.

Foster, V. (2013) Pantomime and politics: the story of a performance ethnography. *Qualitative Research* 13(1) 36–52.

Fournillier, J. (2010) Plus ça change, plus c'est la même chose: an Afro Caribbean scholar on the Higher Education Plantation. *Creative Approaches to Research* 3(2) 52–62.

Fournillier, J. B. (2011). Working within and in-between frames: An academic tourist/midnight robber and the academy. *Qualitative Inquiry*, 17(6), 558–67.

Franz, A., Worrell, M. and Vögele, C. (2013) Integrating mixed method data in psychological research: combining Q methodology and questionnaires in a study investigating cultural and psychological influences on adolescent sexual behaviour. *Journal of Mixed Methods Research* 7(4) 370–89.

Franzen, S. (2013) Engaging a specific, not general, public: the use of ethnographic film in public scholarship. *Qualitative Research* 13(4) 414–27.

Freeman, M. (2011) Validity in dialogic encounters with hermeneutic truths. *Qualitative Inquiry* 17(6) 543–51.

Friedemann, M.-L., Mayorga, C. and Jimenez, L. (2010) Data collectors' field journals as tools for research. *Journal of Research in Nursing* 16(5) 453–65.

Frost, N. et al (2010) Pluralism in qualitative research: the impact of different researchers and qualitative approaches on the analysis of qualitative data. *Qualitative Research* 10(4) 441–60.

Frost, N. and Elichaoff, F. (2010) Feminist postmodernism, poststructuralism, and critical theory. In Ryan-Flood, R. and Gill, R. (eds) *Secrecy and silence in the research process: feminist reflections*, 42–72. Abingdon: Routledge.

Fryer, M. (2012) Some key issues in creativity research and evaluation as seen from a psychological perspective. *Creativity Research Journal* 24(1) 21–8.

Gabb, J. (2010) Home truths: ethical issues in family research. *Qualitative Research* 10(4) 461–78.

Gabriel, Y. and Connell, N. (2010) Co-creating stories: collaborative experiments in storytelling. *Management Learning* 41(5) 507–23.

Gadow S. (2000) Philosophy as falling: aiming for grace. *Nursing Philosophy* 1: 89–97.

Gagnon, M. (2011) Moving knowledge to action through dissemination and exchange. *Journal of Clinical Epidemiology* 64: 25–31.

Galasiński D. and Kozłowska O. (2010) Questionnaires and lived experiences: strategies of coping with the quantitative frame. *Qualitative Inquiry* 16(4) 271–84.

Gale, M. and Featherstone, A. (2011) The imperative of the archive: creative archive research. In Kershaw, B. and Nicholson, H. (eds) *Research methods in theatre and performance*, 17–40. Edinburgh: Edinburgh University Press.

Galvin, K. and Todres, L. (2012) The creativity of 'unspecialisation'. In Friesen, N., Henriksson, C. and Saevi, T. (eds) *Hermeneutic phenomenology in education: method and practice*, 107–18. Rotterdam: Sense Publishers.

Gangadharbatla, H. (2010) Technology component: a modified systems approach to creative thought. *Creativity Research Journal* 22(2) 219–27.

Garro, L. (2000) Remembering what one knows and construction of the past: a comparison of cultural consensus theory and schema theory. *Ethos* 28(3) 275–319.

Gauntlett, D. (2007) *Creative explorations: new approaches to identities and audiences.* Abingdon: Routledge.

Gauntlett, D. (2011) *Making is connecting: the social meaning of creativity, from DIY and knitting to YouTube and Web 2.0.* Cambridge: Polity Press.

Gemignani, M. (2011) Between researcher and researched: an introduction to countertransference in qualitative inquiry. *Qualitative Inquiry* 17(8) 701–8.

Gergen, M. and Gergen, K. (2012) *Playing with purpose: adventures in performative social science.* Walnut Creek, CA: Left Coast Press.

Gergen, M. and Jones, K. (2008) Editorial: a conversation about performative social science. *Forum: Qualitative Social Research* 9(2) Art. 43.

Gidron, B. (2013) The (continued) search for an appropriate name for the third sector. *Voluntary Sector Review* 4(3) 303–7.

Gieseking, J. (2013) Where we go from here: the mental sketch mapping method and its analytic components. *Qualitative Inquiry* 19(9) 712–24.

Gillard, S., Borschmann, R., Turner, K., Goodrich-Purnell, N., Lovell, K. and Chambers, M. (2012) Producing different analytical narratives, coproducing integrated analytical narrative: a qualitative study of UK detained mental health patient experience involving service user researchers. *International Journal of Social Research Methodology* 15(3) 239–54.

Gillen, J. (2006) Child's play. In Maybin, J. and Swann, J. (eds) *The art of English: everyday creativity*, 157–208. Basingstoke: Palgrave Macmillan.

Gilliat-Ray, S. (2011) 'Being there': the experience of shadowing a British Muslim hospital chaplain. *Qualitative Research* 11(5) 469–86.

Gobo, G. (2011) Glocalizing methodology? The encounter between local methodologies. *International Journal of Social Research Methodology* 14(6) 417–37.

Godin, B., Lane, J. and SUNY (2011) Research or development? A short history of research and development as categories. *Online paper*. www.csiic.ca/PDF/Gegenworte.pdf (viewed 20 October 2014).

Goldstein, T. and Wickett, J. (2009) Zero tolerance: a stage adaptation of an investigative report on school safety. *Qualitative Inquiry* 15(10) 1552–68.

Gómez, A., Puigvert, L. and Flecha, R. (2011) Critical communicative methodology: informing real social transformation through research. *Qualitative Inquiry* 17(3) 235–45.

González-López, G. (2011) Mindful ethics: comments on informant-centered practices in sociological research. *Qualitative Sociology* 34: 447–61.

Gordon, C. (2013) Beyond the observer's paradox: the audio-recorder as a resource for the display of identity. *Qualitative Research* 13(3) 299–317.

Grant, M. and Booth, A. (2009) A typology of reviews: an analysis of 14 review types and associated methodologies. *Health Information and Libraries Journal* 26 91–108.

Gravestock, H. (2010) Embodying understanding: drawing as research in sport and exercise. *Qualitative Research in Sport, Exercise and Health* 2(2) 196–208.

Green, J. and Hart, L. (1999) The impact of context on data. In Barbour, R. and Kitzinger, J. (eds) *Developing focus group research: politics, theory and practice*, 21–35. London: Sage.

Greenwell, B. (2009) Rhetoric and style. In Neale, D. (ed) *A creative writing handbook: developing dramatic technique, individual style and voice*, 196–209. London: A & C Black Publishers Ltd.

Grierson, E. and Brearley, L. (2009) Ways of framing: introducing creative arts research. In Grierson, E. and Brearley, L. (eds) *Creative arts research: narratives of methodologies and practices*, 1–15. Rotterdam: Sense Publishers.

Grishin, S. (2008) Uncertainty as a creative force in visual art. In Bammer, G. and Smithson, M. (eds) *Uncertainty and risk: multidisciplinary perspectives*, 115–26. London: Earthscan.

Groom, R., Cushion, C. and Nelson, L. (2012) Analysing coach-athlete 'talk in interaction' within the delivery of video-based performance feedback in elite youth soccer. *Qualitative Research in Sport, Exercise and Health* 4(3) 439–58.

GSS (undated) *Writing about statistics*. London: Government Statistical Service.

Guiney Yallop, J., Naylor, K., Sharif, S. and Taylor, N. (2010) Exploring identities through poetic inquiry: heartful journeys into tangled places of complicated truths and desires. From Wright, W., Wilson, M. and MacIsaac D (eds) *Collected Essays on Learning and Teaching* Vol III 27–32. Canada: STLHE/SAPES.

Haigh, C. and Jones, N. (2007) Techno-research and cyber-ethics: challenges for ethics committees. *Research Ethics Review* 3(3) 80–3.

Halkier, B. (2010) Focus groups as social enactments: integrating interaction and content in the analysis of focus group data. *Qualitative Research* 10(1) 71–89.

Hall, J. and Ryan, K. (2011) Educational accountability: a qualitatively driven mixed-methods approach. *Qualitative Inquiry* 17(1) 105–15.

Halverson, E., Bass, M. and Woods, D. (2012) The process of creation: a novel methodology for analyzing multimodal data. *The Qualitative Report* 17(21) 1–27.

Hammersley M. (2009) Challenging relativism: the problem of assessment criteria. *Qualitative Inquiry* 15(1) 3–29.

Hammersley, M. (2010) Reproducing or constructing? Some questions about transcription in social research. *Qualitative Research* 10(5) 553–69.

Hammond, S. and Cooper, N. (2011) Participant information clips: a role for digital video technologies to recruit, inform and debrief research participants and disseminate research findings. *International Journal of Social Research Methodology* 14(4) 259–70.

Hanna, P. (2012) Using internet technologies (such as Skype) as a research medium: a research note. *Qualitative Research* 12(2) 239–42.

Hannes, K. and Macaitis, K. (2012) A move to more systematic and transparent approaches in qualitative evidence synthesis: update on a review of published papers. *Qualitative Research* 12(4) 402–42.

Hansen, F. (2012) One step further: the dance between poetic dwelling and Socratic wonder in phenomenological research. *The Indo-Pacific Journal of Phenomenology* 12: 1–20.

Hart C (2001) Doing A Literature Search. London: Sage.

Harvey, L. (2011) Intimate reflections: private diaries in qualitative research. *Qualitative Research* 11(6) 664–82.

Harvey, W., Wilkinson, S., Pressé, C., Joober, R. and Grizenko, N. (2012) Scrapbook interviewing and children with attention-deficit hyperactivity disorder. *Qualitative Research in Sport, Exercise and Health* 4(1) 62–79.

Haseman, B. and Mafe, D. (2009) Acquiring know-how: research training for practice-led researchers. In Smith, H. and Dean, R. (eds) *Practice-led research, research-led practice in the creative arts*, 211–28. Edinburgh: Edinburgh University Press.

Hay, D. and Kinchin, I. (2008) Using concept mapping to measure learning quality. *Education and Training* 50(2) 167–82.

Hemmings, A., Beckett, G., Kennerly, S. and Yap, T. (2013) Building a community of research practice: intragroup team social dynamics in interdisciplinary mixed methods. *Journal of Mixed Methods Research* 7(3) 261–73.

Henderson, D. and Taimina, D. (2001) Crocheting the hyperbolic plane. *The Mathematical Intelligencer* 23(2) 17–28.

Henderson, S., Holland, J., McGrellis, S., Sharpe, S. and Thomson, R (2007) *Inventing Adulthoods: A Biographical Approach to Youth Transitions*. London: Sage.

Henderson, S., Holland, J., McGrellis, S., Sharpe, S. and Thomson, R (2012) Storying qualitative longitudinal research: sequence, voice and motif. *Qualitative Research* 12(1) 16–34.

Hesmondhaugh, D. and Baker, S. (2011) *Creative labour: media work in three cultural industries*. London: Routledge.

Hesse-Biber, S. (2012) Weaving a multimethodology and mixed methods praxis into randomized control trials to enhance credibility. *Qualitative Inquiry* 18(10) 876–89.

Hesse-Biber, S. (2014) What is feminist research? In Hesse-Biber, S. (ed) *Feminist research practice: a primer*, 3–13. Thousand Oaks, CA: Sage.

Hesse-Biber, S. and Griffin, A. (2013) Internet-mediated technologies and mixed methods research: problems and prospects. *Journal of Mixed Methods Research* 7(1) 43–61.

Hester, M., Donovan, C. and Fahmy, E. (2010) Feminist epistemology and the politics of method: surveying same sex domestic violence. *International Journal of Social Research Methodology* 13(3) 251–63.

Hodgkinson, G. and Sadler-Smith, E. (2014) Self-report assessment of individual differences in preferences for analytic and intuitive processing: a critical review. In Sinclair, M. (ed) *Handbook of Research Methods on Intuition*, 101–15. Cheltenham: Edward Elgar.

Hoffman, A. (2003) *Research for writers* (7th edn). London: A & C Black Publishers Ltd.

Hollway, W. and Jefferson, T. (2000) *Doing qualitative research differently: free association, narrative and the interview method*. London: Sage.

Hong, E. and Milgram, R. (2010) Creative thinking ability: domain generality and specificity. *Creativity Research Journal* 22(3) 272–87.

Howard, P. (2012) How literature works: poetry and the phenomenology of reader response. In Friesen, N., Henriksson, C. and Saevi, T. (eds) *Hermeneutic phenomenology in education: method and practice*, 201–16. Rotterdam: Sense Publishers.

Hughes, C. and Cohen, R. (2010) Feminists really do count: the complexity of feminist methodologies. *International Journal of Social Research Methodology* 13(3) 189–96.

Hughes, J., Kidd, J. and McNamara, C. (2011) The usefulness of mess: artistry, improvisation and decomposition in the practice of research in allied theatre. In Kershaw, B. and Nicholson, H. (eds) *Research methods in theatre and performance*, 186–209. Edinburgh: Edinburgh University Press.

Humphries, J. (2012) I wanted to glimpse: perinatal isolation, women's suffering as motet. *Creative Approaches to Research* 5(2) 141–55.

Hurdley, R. and Dicks, B. (2011) In-between practice: working in the 'thirdspace' of sensory and multimodal methodology. *Qualitative Research* 11(3) 277–92.

Hussain, S. (2011) Toes that look like toes: Cambodian children's perspectives on prosthetic legs. *Qualitative Health Research* 21(10) 1427–40.

Hutchison, A., Johnston, L. and Breckon, J. (2010) Using QSR-NVivo to facilitate the development of a grounded theory project: an account of a worked example. *International Journal of Social Research Methodology* 13(4) 283–302.

Hutton, E. and Sundar, S. (2010) Can video games enhance creativity? Effects of emotion generated by Dance Dance Revolution. *Creativity Research Journal* 22(3) 294–303.

Ignacio, E. (2012) Online methods and analyzing knowledge-production: a cautionary tale. *Qualitative Inquiry* 18(3) 237–46.

Inckle, K. (2010) Telling tales? Using ethnographic fictions to speak embodied 'truth'. *Qualitative Research* 10(1) 27–47.

Iphofen, R. (2011) *Ethical decision-making in social research: a practical guide.* Basingstoke: Palgrave Macmillan.

Ivankova, N. and Kawamura, Y. (2010) Emerging trends in the utilization of integration designs in the social, behavioral and health sciences. In Tashakkori, A. and Teddlie, C. (eds) *The Sage handbook of mixed methods in social and behavioral research* (2nd edn), 581–611. London: Sage.

James, A. (2012) Seeking the analytic imagination: reflections on the process of interpreting qualitative data. *Qualitative Research* 13(5) 562–77.

Jenkins, M. (2010) The Fabulous Ruins of Detroit: selected excerpts. *Qualitative Inquiry* 16(2) 90–103.

Jenkins, N. et al (2010) Putting it in context: the use of vignettes in qualitative interviewing. *Qualitative Research* 10(2) 175–98.

Jewkes, Y. (2012) Autoethnography and emotion as intellectual resources. *Qualitative Inquiry* 18(1) 63–75.

Jochum, V. and Brodie, E. (2013) Understanding people's pathways through participation: putting research into practice. *Voluntary Sector Review* 4(3) 377–84.

Jones, K. (2006) A biographic researcher in pursuit of an aesthetic: the use of arts-based (re)presentations in 'performative' dissemination of life stories. *Qualitative Sociology Review* 2(1) 66–85.

Jones, K. (2012) Connecting research with communities through performative social science. *The Qualitative Report* 17(18) 1–8.

Jones, K. (2013) Infusing biography with the personal: writing Rufus Stone. *Creative Approaches to Research* 6(2) 4–21.

Jones, K. and Leavy, P. (2014) A conversation between Kip Jones and Patricia Leavy: arts-based research, performative social science and working on the margins. *The Qualitative Report* 19(38) 1–7.

Jost, A., Neumann, E. and Himmelmann, K.-H. (2010) Synchronized communication between people with dementia and their volunteer caregivers: a video-based explorative study on temporal aspects of interaction and the transfer to education. *Current Alzheimer Research* 7(5) 439–44.

Kahneman, D. (2011) *Thinking, fast and slow.* London: Allen Lane.

Kahneman, D., Lovallo, D. and Sibony, O. (2011) Before you make that big decision ... *Harvard Business Review* June, 50–60.

Kaniki, A. (2006) Doing an information search. In Terre Blanche, M., Durrheim, K. and Painter, D. (eds) *Research in practice: allied methods for the social sciences*, 18–32. Cape Town: University of Cape Town Press.

Kara, H. (2012) *Research and evaluation for busy practitioners: a time-saving guide.* Bristol: The Policy Press.

Kara, H. (2013) It's hard to tell how research feels: using fiction to enhance academic research and writing. *Qualitative Research in Organizations and Management: An International Journal* 8(1) 70–84.

Katz-Buonincontro, J. (2012) Creativity at the crossroads: pragmatic versus humanist claims in education reform speeches. *Creativity Research Journal* 24(4) 257–65.

Kaufman, C. (2010) Cross-disciplinary theoretical frameworks: adding value to research analysis and dissemination. *International Journal of Arts and Sciences* 3(8) 153–67.

Kelleher, C. and Wagener, T. (2011) Ten guidelines for effective data visualization in scientific publications. *Environmental Modelling & Software* 26(2011) 822–7.

Kenten, C. (2010) Narrating oneself: reflections on the use of solicited diaries with diary interviews. *Forum: Qualitative Social Research* 11(2) Art. 16.

Kershaw, B. and Nicholson, H. (2011) Introduction: doing methods creatively. In Kershaw, B. and Nicholson, H. (eds) *Research methods in theatre and performance*, 1–16. Edinburgh: Edinburgh University Press.

Kershaw, B. with Miller, L./Whalley, J. and Lee, R./Pollard, N. (2011) Practice as research: transdisciplinary innovation in action. In Kershaw, B. and Nicholson, H. (eds) *Research methods in theatre and performance*, 63–85. Edinburgh: Edinburgh University Press.

Kharkhurin, A. (2011) The role of selective attention in bilingual creativity. *Creativity Research Journal* 23(3) 239–54.

Kincheloe, J. (2005) On to the next level: continuing the conceptualization of the bricolage. *Qualitative Inquiry* 11(3) 323–50.

Kiragu, S. and Warrington, M. (2012) How we used moral imagination to address ethical and methodological complexities while conducting research with girls in school against the odds in Kenya. *Qualitative Research* 13(2) 173–89.

Kirk, A. (2012) *Data visualisation: a successful design process*. Birmingham: Packt Publishing.

Klassen, A., Creswell, J., Plano Clark, V., Clegg Smith, K. and Meissner, H. (2012) Best practices in mixed methods for quality of life research. *Quality of Life Research* 21(3) 377–80.

Kluge, M., Grant, B., Friend, L. and Glick, L. (2010) Seeing is believing: telling the 'inside' story of a beginning masters athlete through film. *Qualitative Research in Sport, Exercise and Health* 2(2) 282–92.

Knoblauch, H. (2012) Introduction to the special issue of Qualitative Research: video-analysis and videography. *Qualitative Research* 12(3) 251–4.

Koelsch, L. (2012) The virtual patchwork quilt. *Qualitative Inquiry* 18(10) 823–9.

Kohn, N., Paulus, P. and Korde, R. (2011) Conceptual combinations and subsequent creativity. *Creativity Research Journal* 23(3) 203–10.

Kontos, P. and Naglie, G. (2009) Tacit knowledge of caring and embodied selfhood. *Sociology of Health & Illness* 31(5) 688–704.

Koro-Ljungberg, M., Mazzei, L. and Childers, S. (2012) Against simplicity, against ethics: analytics of disruption as quasi-methodology. *Qualitative Inquiry* 18(9) 752–61.

Kousha, K., Thelwall, M. and Abdoli, M. (2012) The role of online videos in research communication: a content analysis of YouTube videos cited in academic publications. *Journal of the American Society for Information Science and Technology* 63(9) 1710–27.

Kozinets, R. (2010) *Netnography: doing ethnographic research online*. London: Sage.

Kramer, A., Guillory, J. and Hancock, J. (2014) Experimental evidence of massive-scale emotional contagion through social networks. *Psychological and Cognitive Sciences* 111(24) 8788–90.

Krohne K., Torres S., Slettebø A. and Bergland A. (2013) Individualizing standardized tests: physiotherapists' and occupational therapists' test practices in a geriatric setting. *Qualitative Health Research* 23(9) 1168–78.

Lafrenière, D. and Cox, S. (2013) 'If you can call it a poem': toward a framework for the assessment of arts-based works. *Qualitative Research* 13(3) 318–36.

Lal, S., Suto, M. and Ungar, M. (2012) Examining the potential of combining the methods of grounded theory and narrative inquiry: a comparative analysis. *The Qualitative Report* 17(41) 1–22.

Lantsoght, E. (2014) Share your research process via social media. In Daly, I. and Brophy Haney, A. (eds) *53 interesting ways to communicate your research* 25–6. Newmarket: The Professional and Higher Partnership Ltd.

Lapum, J., Ruttonsha, P., Church, K., Yau, T. and David, A. (2011) Employing the arts in research as an analytical tool and dissemination method. *Qualitative Inquiry* 18(1) 100–15.

Lasky, K. (2013) Poetics and creative writing research. In Kroll, J. and Harper, G. (eds) *Research methods in creative writing*, 14–33. Basingstoke: Palgrave Macmillan.

Laux, R. and Barham, C. (2012) Can't see the wood for the trees? Using statistical frameworks to draw the bigger picture. Paper given at International Association of Official Statistics conference, Kiev.

Laux, R. and Pont, M. (2012) Enhancing the impact of assessment. Paper given at the European Conference on Quality in Official Statistics, Athens, 29 May–1 June 2012.

Leavy, P. (2009) *Method meets art: arts-based research practice*. New York: The Guilford Press.

Leavy P. (2010) A/r/t: a poetic montage. *Qualitative Inquiry* 16(4) 240–43.

Leavy, P. (2012) Fiction and the feminist academic novel. *Qualitative Inquiry* 18(6) 516–22.

Lemert, C. (1999) *Social theory: the multicultural and classic readings*. Boulder, CO: Westview Press.

Lenza, M. (2011) Autoethnography and ethnography in criminal justice research and policy development. In Ekunwe, I. and Jones, R. (eds) *Global perspectives on re-entry: exploring the challenges facing ex-prisoners*, 146–72. Finland: Tampere University Press.

Lewis, J. and McNaughton Nicholls, C. (2014) Design issues. In Ritchie, J., Lewis, J., McNaughton Nicholls, C. and Ormston, R. (eds) *Qualitative research practice: a guide for social science students and researchers* (2nd edn), 47–76. London: Sage.

Li P. (2014) Toward the geocentric framework of intuition: the Yin–Yang balancing between the Eastern and Western perspectives on intuition. In Sinclair, M. (ed) *Handbook of research methods on intuition*, 28–41. Cheltenham: Edward Elgar.

Librett, M. and Perrone, D. (2010) Apples and oranges: ethnography and the IRB. *Qualitative Research* 10(6) 729–47.

Liddicoat, A. (2011) *An introduction to conversation analysis* (2nd edn). London: Continuum.

Lillis, T. (2006) Moving towards an 'academic literacies' pedagogy: dialogues of participation. In Ganobcsik–Williams, L. (ed) *Teaching academic writing in UK higher education: theories, practices and models*, 30–48. Basingstoke: Palgrave Macmillan. Cheltenham: Edward Elgar.

Lloyd, K., Rose, D. and Fenton, M. (2006) Identifying uncertainties about the effects of treatments for schizophrenia. *Journal of Mental Health* 15(3) 263–8.

Lockford, L. (2012) Placing words. *Qualitative Inquiry* 18(3) 235–6.

Loffredo, E. and Perteghella, M. (2006) Introduction. In Perteghella, M. and Loffredo, E. *Translation and creativity: perspectives on creative writing and translation studies*, 1–16. London: Continuum.

Löfström, E. (2011) 'Does plagiarism mean anything? LOL.' Students' conceptions of writing and citing. *Journal of Academic Ethics* 9: 257–75.

Lomax, H. (2012) Contested voices? Methodological tensions in creative visual research with children. *International Journal of Social Research Methodology* 15(2) 105–17.

Lomborg, S. (2012) Personal internet archives and ethics. *Research Ethics* 9(1) 20–31.

Luff, P. and Heath, C. (2012) Some 'technical challenges' of video analysis: social actions, objects, material realities and the problems of perspective. *Qualitative Research* 12(3) 255–79.

Lunde, A., Heggen, K. and Strand, R. (2013) Knowledge and power: exploring unproductive interplay between quantitative and qualitative researchers. *Journal of Mixed Methods Research* 7(2) 197–210.

Lyon, F., Möllering, G. and Saunders, M. (2012) Introduction: the variety of methods for the multi-faceted phenomenon of trust. In Lyon, F., Möllering, G. and Saunders, M. (eds) *Handbook of research methods on trust*, 1–15. Cheltenham: Edward Elgar.

McAreavey, R. and Muir, J. (2011) Research ethics committees: values and power in higher education. *International Journal of Social Research Methodology* 14(5) 391–405.

McCarry, M. (2012) Who benefits? A critical reflection of children and young people's participation in sensitive research. *International Journal of Social Research Methodology* 15(1) 55–68.

McCormack, M., Adams, A. and Anderson, E. (2012) Taking to the streets: the benefits of spontaneous methodological innovation in participant recruitment. *Qualitative Research* 13(2) 228–41.

McKee, R. (1998) *Story: substance, structure, style, and the principles of screenwriting.* London: Methuen.

MacKenzie, S. and Wolf, M. (2012) Layering sel(f)ves: finding acceptance, community and praxis through collage. *The Qualitative Report* 17(31) 1–21.

MacKerron, G. and Mourato, S. (2013) Happiness is greater in natural environments. *Global Environmental Change* 23(5) 992–1000.

McKinney, J. and Iball, H. (2011) Researching scenography. In Kershaw, B. and Nicholson, H. (eds) *Research methods in theatre and performance*, 111–36. Edinburgh: Edinburgh University Press.

Macmillan, R. (2011) Seeing things differently? The promise of qualitative longitudinal research on the third sector. *Third Sector Research Centre Working Paper 56.*

Madsen, C. (2000) A personal perspective for research. *Music Educators Journal* 86: 41–54.

Mandlis, L. (2009) Art installation as method: 'fragements' of theory and tape. *Qualitative Inquiry* 15(8) 1352–72.

Mannay, D. (2010) Making the familiar strange: can visual research methods render the familiar setting more perceptible? *Qualitative Research* 10(1) 91–111.

Markham, A. (2012) Fabrication as ethical practice: qualitative inquiry in ambiguous internet contexts. *Information, Communication & Society* 15(3) 334–53.

Markham, A. (2013a) Remix cultures, remix methods: reframing qualitative inquiry for social media contexts. In Denzin, N. and Giardina, M. (eds) *Global dimensions of qualitative inquiry*, 63–81. Walnut Creek, CA: Left Coast Press, Inc.

Markham, A. (2013b) Fieldwork in social media: what would Malinowski do? *Qualitative Communication Research* 2(4) 434–46.

Martin, G., Currie, G. and Lockett, A. (2011) Prospects for knowledge exchange in health policy and management: institutional and epistemic boundaries. *Journal of Health Services Research and Policy* 16(4) 211–17.

Mason, J. (2002) *Qualitative researching* (2nd edn). London: Sage.

Mason, J. and Dale, A. (2011) *Understanding social research: thinking creatively about method.* London: Sage.

Mauthner, M., Birch, M., Miller, T. and Jessop, J. (2012) Conclusion: navigating ethical dilemmas and new digital horizons. In Miller, T., Birch, M., Mauthner, M. and Jessop, J. (eds) *Ethics in qualitative research*, 176–86. London: Sage.

Mayoh, J., Bond, C. and Todres, L. (2012) An innovative mixed methods approach to studying the online health information seeking experiences of adults with chronic health conditions. *Journal of Mixed Methods Research* 6(1) 21–33.

Mellor, R., Slaymaker, E. and Cleland, J. (2013) Recognizing and overcoming challenges of couple interview research. *Qualitative Health Research* 23(10) 1399–407.

Mercer, N. (2010) The analysis of classroom talk: methods and methodologies. *British Journal of Educational Psychology* 80(1) 1–14.

Mertens, D. (2010) Transformative mixed methods research. *Qualitative Inquiry* 16(6) 469–74.

Mewburn, I. (2012) Creative doctoral work. In Evans, T. and Denholm, C. (eds) *Keys to successful doctoral study in Australia and Aotearoa New Zealand* (2nd edn). Camberwell: ACER Press, 126–36.

Mewburn, I. and Thomson, P. (2013) Why do academics blog? An analysis of audiences, purposes and challenges. *Studies in Higher Education* 38(8) 1105–19.

Mitchell, G., Dupuis, S., Jonas-Simpson, C., Whyte, C., Carson, J. and Gillis, J. (2011) The experience of engaging with research-based drama: evaluation and explication of synergy and transformation. *Qualitative Inquiry* 17(4) 379–92.

Monaghan, L., O'Dwyer, M. and Gabe, J. (2013) Seeking university Research Ethics Committee approval: the emotional vicissitudes of a 'rationalised' process. *International Journal of Social Research Methodology* 16(1) 65–80.

Moncur, W. (2013) The emotional wellbeing of researchers: considerations for practice. Conference paper. Session: Ethics in HCI, at CHI 2013: Changing Perspectives, Paris, France.

Mondada, L. (2012) Video analysis and the temporality of inscriptions within social interaction: the case of architects at work. *Qualitative Research* 12(3) 304–33.

Morgan, D., Ataie, J., Carder, P. and Hoffman, K. (2013) Introducing dyadic interviews as a method for collecting qualitative data. *Qualitative Health Research* 23(9) 1276–84.

Morgan, N. (2011) *Write to be published*. Oxford: Snowbooks.

Morris, G., Dahl, S., Brown, P., Scullion, L. and Somerville, P. (2012) *Somewhere nowhere: lives without homes*. Self-published via Lulu at http://www.lulu.com/shop/gareth-morris-and-sam-dahl-and-philip-brown-and-lisa-scullion/somewhere-nowhere-lives-without-homes/paperback/product-20308962.html

Morrow, E., Boaz, A., Brearley, S. and Ross, F. (2012) *Handbook of service user involvement in nursing and healthcare research*. Chichester: Wiley-Blackwell.

Mosher, H. (2013) A question of quality: the art/science of doing collaborative public ethnography. *Qualitative Research* 13(4) 428–41.

Mpofu, E. et al (2006) African perspectives on creativity. In Kaufman, J.C. and Sternberg, R.J. (eds) *The international handbook of creativity*, 465. Cambridge: Cambridge University Press.

Mulder, W. (2011) Improving sequence analysis for the social sciences: a new and more useful method to determine similarity between sociological sequences (master's thesis). Utrecht: Utrecht University.

Mumford, M. et al (2010) Creativity and ethics: the relationship of creative and ethical problem-solving. *Creativity Research Journal* 22(1) 74–89.

Munat, J. (2007) Editor's preface. In *Lexical creativity, texts and contexts*, xii–xvi. Amsterdam/Philadelphia: John Benjamins Publishing Company.

Munté, A., Serradell, O. and Sordé, T. (2011) From research to policy: Roma participation through communicative organization. *Qualitative Inquiry* 17(3) 256–66.

Murray, R. (2009) *Writing for academic journals* (2nd edn). Maidenhead: Open University Press.

Murray, R. (2011) *How to write a thesis* (3rd edn). Maidenhead: Open University Press.

Naples, N. and Gurr, B. (2010) Feminist empiricism and standpoint theory: approaches to understanding the social world. In Ryan-Flood, R. and Gill, R. (eds) *Secrecy and silence in the research process: feminist reflections*, 14–41. Abingdon: Routledge.

Ndimande, B. (2012) Decolonizing research in postapartheid South Africa: the politics of methodology. *Qualitative Inquiry* 18(3) 215–26.

Neale, D. (2009) Voices in fiction. In Neale, D. (ed) 181–95. *A creative writing handbook: developing dramatic technique, individual style and voice*. London: A & C Black Publishers Ltd.

Nęcka, E., Grohman, M. and Słabosz A. (2006) Chapter 10: Creativity studies in Poland. 270–306. In Kaufman, J.C. and Sternberg, R.J. (eds) *The International Handbook of Creativity*, 175. Cambridge: Cambridge University Press.

Nespor, J. (2012) The afterlife of 'teachers' beliefs'. *Qualitative Inquiry* 18(5) 449–60.

Newman, W. (2013) Mapping as allied research. In Jarrett, C., Kim, K.-H. and Senske, N. (eds) *The Visibility of Research: proceedings of the 2013 ARCC spring research conference, 228–36*. University of North Carolina at Charlotte.

Nind, M. (2011) Participatory data analysis: a step too far? *Qualitative Research* 11(4) 349–63.

Niu, W. (2006) Development of creativity research in Chinese societies. In Kaufman, J.C. and Sternberg, R.J. (eds) *The international handbook of creativity*, 386–7. Cambridge: Cambridge University Press.

Notermans, C. and Kommers, H. (2012) Researching religion: the iconographic elicitation method. *Qualitative Research* 13(5) 608–25.

O'Dell, L. et al (2012) The problem of interpretation in vignette methodology in research with young people. *Qualitative Research* 12(6) 702–14.

Odena, O. (2013) Using software to tell a trustworthy, convincing and useful story. *International Journal of Social Research Methodology* 16(5) 355–72.

O'Neill, M. (2008) Transnational refugees: the transformative role of art? *Forum: Qualitative Social Research* 9(2) Art. 59.

O'Reilly, M. and Parker, N. (2013) 'Unsatisfactory saturation': a critical exploration of the notion of saturated sample sizes in qualitative research. *Qualitative Research* 13(2) 190–7.

O'Reilly, M., Karim, K., Taylor, H. and Dogra, N. (2012) Parent and child views on anonymity: 'I've got nothing to hide'. *International Journal of Social Research Methodology* 15(3) 211–23.

Ostrer, C. and Morris, B. (2009) First-hand experiences of different approaches to collaborative research. In Sweeney, A., Beresford, P., Faulkner, A., Nettle, M. and Rose, D. (eds) *Survivor research*, 71–81. Ross on Wye: PCCS Books.

Owen, H. (2008) *Open space technology: a user's guide.* San Francisco, CA: Berrett-Koehler Publishers.

Owton, H. (2013) Integrating multiple representations: fighting asthma. *Qualitative Inquiry* 19(8) 600–3.

Pahl, K., Steadman-Jones, R. and Pool, S. (2013) Dividing the drawers. *Creative Approaches to Research* 6(1) 71–88.

Paletz, S., Peng, K. and Li, S. (2011) In the world or in the head: external and internal implicit theories of creativity. *Creativity Research Journal* 23(2) 83–98.

Papathomas, A. and Lavallee, D. (2010) Athlete experiences of disordered eating in sport. *Qualitative Research in Sport, Exercise and Health* 2(3) 354–70.

Parker, D. (2004) Life writing as narrative of the good: *Father and Son* and the ethics of authenticity. In Eakin, P. (ed) *The ethics of life writing*, 53–72. Ithaca, NY: Cornell University Press.

Patten, U. (2007) Stories of aboriginal heritage through a multi media exploration of gumleaf music. MA thesis, Royal Melbourne Institute of Technology.

Paulus, T., Lester, J. and Britt, V. (2013) Constructing hopes and fears around technology: a discourse analysis of introductory qualitative research texts. *Qualitative Inquiry* 19(9) 639–51.

Perrin, H. (2014) Writing press releases. In Daly, I. and Brophy Haney, A. (eds) *53 interesting ways to communicate your research*, 43–4. Newmarket: The Professional and Higher Partnership Ltd.

Perry, K. (2011) Ethics, vulnerability, and speakers of other languages: how university IRBs (do not) speak to research involving refugee participants. *Qualitative Inquiry* 17(10) 899–912.

Petersen, I., Mason, A., Bhana, A., Bell, C. and McKay, M. (2006) Mediating social representations using a cartoon narrative in the context of HIV/AIDS: the AmaQhawe Family Project in South Africa. *Journal of Health Psychology* 11(2) 197–208.

Petray, T. (2012) A walk in the park: political emotions and ethnographic vacillation in activist research. *Qualitative Research* 12(5) 554–64.

Petros, S. (2012) Use of a mixed methods approach to investigate the support needs of older caregivers to family members affected by HIV and AIDS in South Africa. *Journal of Mixed Methods Research* 6(4) 275–93.

Petticrew, M. and Roberts, H. (2005) *Systematic reviews in the social sciences: a practical guide.* Oxford: Blackwell.

Pickering, L. (2009) Dancing my true dance: reflections on learning to express myself through ecstatic dance in Hawai'i. *Anthropology Matters Journal* 11(1) 1–12.

Piirto, J. (2009) The question of quality and qualifications: writing inferior poems as qualitative research. In Prendergast, M., Leggo, C. and Sameshima, P. (eds) *Poetic inquiry: vibrant voices in the social sciences*, 83–100. Rotterdam: Sense Publishers.

Piper, H. and Sikes, P. (2010) All teachers are vulnerable but especially gay teachers: using composite fictions to protect research participants in pupil–teacher sex-related research. *Qualitative Inquiry* 16(7) 566–74.

Plano Clark, V. et al (2013) Practices for embedding an interpretive qualitative approach within a randomized clinical trial. *Journal of Mixed Methods Research* 7(3) 219–42.

Poon, J. and Ainuddin, R. (2011) Selected ethical issues in the analysis and reporting of research: survey of business school faculty in Malaysia. *Journal of Academic Ethics* 9: 307–22.

Pope, C. (2010) Talking T-shirts: a visual exploration of youth material culture. *Qualitative Research in Sport, Exercise and Health* 2(2) 133–52.

Powell, K. (2010) Making sense of place: mapping as a multisensory research method. *Qualitative Inquiry* 16(7) 539–55.

Prager, P. (2012) Making an art of creativity: the cognitive science of Duchamp and Dada. *Creativity Research Journal* 24(4) 266–77.

Preiser, S. (2006) Creativity research in German-speaking countries. In Kaufman, J.C. and Sternberg, R.J. (eds) *The International Handbook of Creativity*, 175. Cambridge: Cambridge University Press.

Prendergast M., Leggo C. and Sameshima P. (2009) *Poetic Inquiry: Vibrant Voices in the Social Sciences*. Rotterdam: Sense Publishers.

Prendergast, M. (2009a) Introduction. In Prendergast, M., Leggo, C. and Sameshima, P. (eds) *Poetic inquiry: vibrant voices in the social sciences*, xix–xlii. Rotterdam: Sense Publishers.

Prendergast, M. (2009b) The scholar dances. *Qualitative Inquiry* 15(8) 1373–5.

Priem, R. and Weibel, A. (2012) Measuring the decision to trust using metric conjoint analysis. In Lyon, F., Möllering, G. and Saunders, M. (eds) *Handbook of research methods on trust*, 212–25. Cheltenham: Edward Elgar.

Procter, R., Vis, F. and Voss, A. (2013) Reading the riots on Twitter: methodological innovation for the analysis of big data. *International Journal of Social Research Methodology* 16(3) 197–214.

Raingruber, B. (2009) Asilomar. In Prendergast, M., Leggo, C. and Sameshima, P. (eds) *Poetic inquiry: vibrant voices in the social sciences*, 259–72. Rotterdam: Sense Publishers.

Rapley, T. (2011) Some Pragmatics of Data Analysis. In Silverman D (ed) *Qualitative Research: Issues of Theory, Method and Practice*, pp 274–90. London: Sage.

Rapport, F. (2004) Introduction: shifting sands in qualitative methodology. In Rapport, F. (ed) *New qualitative methodologies in health and social care research*, 1–17. London: Routledge.

Rapport, N. (2004) From the porter's point of view: participant observation by the interpretive anthropologist in the hospital. In Rapport, F. (ed) *New qualitative methodologies in health and social care research*, 99–122. New York: Routledge.

Redondo, G., Santa Cruz, I. and Rotger, J. (2011) Why Mondragon? Analyzing what works in overcoming inequalities. *Qualitative Inquiry* 17(3) 277–83.

Reeves, C. (2010) A difficult negotiation: fieldwork relations with gatekeepers. *Qualitative Research* 10(3) 315–31.

Reilly, R. (2011) 'We knew her ...'. Murder in a small town: A hybrid work in three voices. *Qualitative Inquiry* 17(7) 599–601.

Reis, A. (2011) Bringing my creative self to the fore: accounts of a reflexive research endeavour. *Creative Approaches to Research* 4(1) 2–18.

Rhodes, C. and Brown, A. (2005) Writing responsibly: narrative fiction and organization studies. *Organization* 12(4) 467–91.

Richardson, L. (2014) Audience matters. In Denzin, N. and Giardina, M. (eds) *Qualitative inquiry outside the academy*, 61–70. Walnut Creek, CA: Left Coast Press.

Ridley-Ellis, D. (2014) Stand-up comedy for researchers. In Daly, I. and Brophy Haney, A. (eds) *53 interesting ways to communicate your research*, 57–8. Newmarket: The Professional and Higher Partnership Ltd.

Robinson, A. et al (2011) Mixed methods data collection in dementia research: a 'progressive engagement' approach. *Journal of Mixed Methods Research* 5(4) 330–44.

Robinson, S. and Mendelson, A. (2012) A qualitative experiment: research on mediated meaning construction using a hybrid approach. *Journal of Mixed Methods Research* 6(4) 332–47.

Robson, C. (2011) *Real world research* (3rd edn). Chichester: John Wiley & Sons.

Rodriguez, K. and Lahman, M. (2011) Las Comadres: rendering research as performative. *Qualitative Inquiry* 17(7) 602–12.

Romanyshyn, R. (2013) *The wounded researcher: research with soul in mind*. New Orleans, LA: Spring Journal, Inc.

Rooke, B. (2013) Four pillars of internet research ethics with Web 2.0. *Journal of Academic Ethics* 11: 265–8.

Rose, D., Fleischmann, P., Wykes, T. and Bindman, J. (2002) *Review of consumers' perspectives on electro convulsive therapy*. London: SURE.

Rose, G. (2012) *Visual methodologies: an introduction to researching with visual materials*. London: Sage.

Roulston, K. (2010) Considering quality in qualitative interviewing. *Qualitative Research* 10(2) 199–228.

Rowsell, J. (2011) Carrying my family with me: artifacts as emic perspectives. *Qualitative Research* 11(3) 331–46.

Runco, M. and Acar, S. (2012) Divergent thinking as an indicator of creative potential. *Creativity Research Journal* 24(1) 66–75.

Runco, M. and Jaeger, G. (2012) The standard definition of creativity. *Creativity Research Journal* 24(1) 92–6.

Ryan-Flood, R. and Gill, R. (2010) Introduction. In Ryan-Flood, R. and Gill, R. (eds) *Secrecy and silence in the research process: feminist reflections*, 1–11. Abingdon: Routledge.

Sakellariou, D., Boniface, G. and Brown, P. (2013) Using joint interviews in a narrative-based study on illness experiences. *Qualitative Health Research* 23(11) 1563–70.

Salanti, G. (2012) Indirect and mixed-treatment comparison, network, or multiple-treatments meta-analysis: many names, many benefits, many concerns for the next generation evidence synthesis tool. *Research Synthesis Methods* 3: 80–97.

Sameshima, P. and Vandermause, R. (2009) Methamphetamine addiction and recovery: poetic inquiry to feel. In Prendergast, M., Leggo, C. and Sameshima, P. (eds) *Poetic inquiry: vibrant voices in the social sciences*, 275–86. Rotterdam: Sense Publishers.

Sangha, J., Slade, B., Mirchandani, K., Maitra, S. and Shan, H. (2012) An ethnodrama on work-related learning in precarious jobs: racialization and resistance. *Qualitative Inquiry* 18(3) 286–96.

Schoneboom, A. (2010) Project Skive: can a multimedia art exhibit function as an ethnography of workplace resistance? *Creative Approaches to Research* 3(1) 3–15.

Schwebel, M. (2009) Jack London: a case study of moral creativity. *Creativity Research Journal* 21(4) 319–25.

SCIE (2007) *Collection of examples of service user and carer participation in systematic reviews.* London: SCIE.

Scott, S. et al (2012) The reluctant researcher: shyness in the field. *Qualitative Research* 12(6) 702–14.

Seal, L. (2012) Emotion and allegiance in researching four mid-20th-century cases of women accused of murder. *Qualitative Research* 12(6) 686–701.

Selby, E., Shaw, E. and Houtz, J. (2005) The creative personality. *Gifted Child Quarterly* 49(1) 300–14.

Shanahan, M.-C. (2011) Science blogs as boundary layers: creating and understanding new writer and reader interactions through science blogging. *Journalism* 12(7) 903–19.

Sheridan, J., Chamberlain, K. and Dupuis, A. (2011) Timelining: visualizing experience. *Qualitative Research* 11(5) 552–69.

Shields, S. (2002) *Speaking from the heart: gender and the social meaning of emotion.* Cambridge: Cambridge University Press.

Shimp, C. (2007) Quantitative behavior analysis and human values. *Behavioural Processes* 75: 146–55.

Shordike, A. et al (2010) Respecting regional culture in an international multi-site study: a derived etic method. *Qualitative Research* 10(3) 333–55.

Sieber, J. and Tolich, M. (2013) *Planning ethically responsible research.* Thousand Oaks, CA: Sage.

Sliep, Y. (2012) We compose our own requiem: an autoethnographic study of mourning. *Creative Approaches to Research* 5(2) 61–85.

Slotnick, R. and Janesick, V. (2011) Conversations on method: deconstructing policy through the researcher reflective journal. *The Qualitative Report* 16(5) 1352–60.

Smerek, R. (2014) Why people think deeply: meta-cognitive cues, task characteristics and thinking dispositions. In Sinclair, M. (ed) *Handbook of research methods on intuition*, 3–14. Cheltenham: Edward Elgar.

Smith, E., Gidlow, B. and Steel, G. (2012) Engaging adolescent participants in academic research: the use of photo-elicitation interviews to evaluate school-based outdoor education programmes. *Qualitative Research* 12(4) 367–87.

Smith, G.J.W. and Carlsson, I. (2006) Creativity under the Northern Lights. In Kaufman, J.C. and Sternberg, R.J. (eds) *The international handbook of creativity*, 202. Cambridge: Cambridge University Press.

Smith, H. and Dean, R. (2009) Introduction: practice-led research, research-led practice – towards the iterative cyclic web. In Smith, H. and Dean, R. (eds) *Practice-led research, research-led practice in the creative arts*, 1–38. Edinburgh: Edinburgh University Press.

Smith, J. (2009) Judging research quality: from certainty to contingency. *Qualitative Research in Sport, Exercise and Health* 1(2) 91–100.

Smith, J. (2012) Reflections on using life history to investigate women teachers' aspirations and career decisions. *Qualitative Research* 12(4) 486–503.

Smith, S., Fisher, S. and Heath, A. (2011) Opportunities and challenges in the expansion of cross-national survey research. *International Journal of Social Research Methodology* 14(6) 485–502.

Sorin, R., Brooks, T. and Haring, U. (2012) Exploring children's environmental understandings through the arts. *Creative Approaches to Research* 5(1) 15–31.

Souza, K. (2014) Presenting – know your audience. In Daly, I. and Brophy Haney, A. (eds) *53 interesting ways to communicate your research*, 83–4. Newmarket: The Professional and Higher Partnership Ltd.

Sparkes, A. (2009) Ethnography and the senses: challenges and possibilities. *Qualitative Research in Sport, Exercise and Health* 1(1) 21–35.

Spencer, K. (2013) New modes of creative writing research. In Kroll, J. and Harper, G. (eds) *Research methods in creative writing*, 78–101. Basingstoke: Palgrave Macmillan.

Stacey, K. and Vincent, J. (2011) Evaluation of an electronic interview with multimedia stimulus materials for gaining in-depth responses from professionals. *Qualitative Research* 11(5) 605–24.

Stack, C. (1974) *All our kin: strategies for survival in a Black community.* New York: Harper & Row.

Stark, L. (2012) *Behind closed doors: IRBs and the making of ethical research.* Chicago: University of Chicago Press.

Stein, S. (1998) *Solutions for writers: practical craft techniques for fiction and non-fiction.* London: Souvenir Press.

Stenvoll, D. and Svensson, P. (2011) Contestable contexts: the transparent anchoring of contextualization in text-as-data. *Qualitative Research* 11(5) 570–86.

Sternberg, R.J. (2006) Introduction. In Kaufman, J.C. and Sternberg, R.J. (eds) *The international handbook of creativity*, 1–9. Cambridge: Cambridge University Press.

Stewart, S. (2012) Poetry: the edge of knowing. *Creative Approaches to Research* 5(2) 105–18.

Stierand, M. and Dörfler, V. (2014) Researching intuition in personal creativity. In Sinclair, M. (ed) *Handbook of research methods on intuition*, 176–87. Cheltenham: Edward Elgar.

Stone, B. (2009) Running man. *Qualitative Research in Sport, Exercise and Health* 1(1) 67–71.

Straus, S., Tetroe, J. and Graham, I. (2011) Knowledge translation is the use of knowledge in health care decision making. *Journal of Clinical Epidemiology* 64(1) 6–10.

Strauss, A. and Corbin, J. (1998) *Basics of qualitative research: techniques and procedures for developing grounded theory.* Thousand Oaks, CA: Sage.

Sullivan, A. (2009) On poetic occasion in inquiry: concreteness, voice, ambiguity, tension, and associative logic. In Prendergast, M., Leggo, C. and Sameshima, P. (eds) *Poetic inquiry: vibrant voices in the social sciences*, 111–26. Rotterdam: Sense Publishers.

Sullivan, G. (2009) Making space: the purpose and place of practice-led research. In Smith, H. and Dean, R. (eds) *Practice-led research, research-led practice in the creative arts*, 41–65. Edinburgh: Edinburgh University Press.

Sutton, B. (2011) Playful cards, serious talk: a qualitative research technique to elicit women's embodied experiences. *Qualitative Research* 11(2) 177–96.

Swann, J. (2006) The art of the everyday. In Maybin, J. and Swann, J. (eds) *The art of English: everyday creativity*, 3–53. Basingstoke: Palgrave Macmillan.

Swann, J., Pope, R. and Carter, R. (eds) (2011) *Creativity in Language and Literature: The State of the Art.* Basingstoke: Palgrave Macmillan.

Swartz, S. (2011) 'Going deep' and 'giving back': strategies for exceeding ethical expectations when researching amongst vulnerable youth. *Qualitative Research* 11(1) 47–68.

Sweetman, D., Badiee, M. and Creswell, J. (2010) Use of the transformative framework in mixed methods studies. *Qualitative Inquiry* 16(6) 441–54.

Taber, N. (2010) Institutional ethnography, autoethnography, and narrative: an argument for incorporating multiple methodologies. *Qualitative Research* 10(1) 5–25.

Takeda, A. (2012) Reflexivity: unmarried Japanese male interviewing married Japanese women about international marriage. *Qualitative Research* 13(3) 285–98.

Tamas, S. (2009) Sketchy rendering: seeing an other. *Qualitative Inquiry* 15(3) 607–17.

Tamas, S. (2010) Walking the lines: art, research, and unknowing. *Creative Approaches to Research* 3(2) 5–20.

Tankana, K. (2007) The roots of the social model: a life history of Paul Hunt (translated by Yuki Kosuge) www.disability-studies.leeds.ac.uk/files/library/Tankana-Life-history-of-Paul-Hunt1.pdf (viewed 20 October 2014).

Taylor, C. and White, S. (2000) *Practising reflexivity in health and welfare: making knowledge.* Buckingham: Open University Press.

Taylor, S. (2012) 'One participant said ...': the implications of quotations from biographical talk. *Qualitative Research* 12(4) 388–401.

Teddlie, C. and Tashakkori, A. (2008) *Foundations of mixed methods research: integrating quantitative and qualitative approaches in the social and behavioural sciences.* London: Sage.

Telford, R. and Faulkner, A. (2004) Learning about service user involvement in mental health research. *Journal of Mental Health* 13(6) 549–59.

Tenenbaum, G., Razon, S., Thompson, B., Filho, E. and Basevitch, I. (2009) The judgement of research quality: a response to John Smith. *Qualitative Research in Sport, Exercise and Health* 1(2) 116–24.

Teo, L. and Waugh, R. (2010) A Rasch measure of fostering creativity. *Creativity Research Journal* 22(2) 206–18.

Terre Blanche, M. and Durrheim, K. (2006) Histories of the present: social science research in context. In Terre Blanche, M., Durrheim, K. and Painter, D. (eds) *Research in practice: allied methods for the social sciences*, 1–17. Cape Town: University of Cape Town Press.

Teye, J. (2012) Benefits, challenges, and dynamism of positionalities associated with mixed methods research in developing countries: evidence from Ghana. *Journal of Mixed Methods Research* 6(4) 379–91.

Thomson, R. et al (2012) Acting up and acting out: encountering children in a longitudinal study of mothering. *Qualitative Research* 12(2) 186–201.

Thornicroft, G. and Tansella, M. (2005) Growing recognition of the importance of service user involvement in mental health service planning and evaluation. *Epidemiologia e Psichiatria Sociale* 14(1) 1–3.

Tierney, W. and Hallett, R. (2010) In treatment: writing beneath the surface. *Qualitative Inquiry* 16(8) 674–84.

Tolich, M. (2012) My eye-opening midnight swim: An outward bound autoethnography. *New Zealand Journal of Outdoor Education: Ko Tane Mahuta Pupuke* 3(1) 9–23.

Tonkin, E., Pfeiffer, H. and Tourte, G. (2012) Twitter, information sharing and the London riots? *Bulletin of the American Society for Information Science and Technology* 38(2) 49–57.

Tonnaer, A. (2012) Fifteen minutes in limbo: on the intricacies of rapport in multi-sited fieldwork on tourism. *Qualitative Research* 12(5) 565–74.

Toolan, M. (2012) Poems: wonderfully repetitive. In Jones, R. (ed) *Discourse and Creativity*, 17–34. Harlow: Pearson Education Limited.

Tracy, S. (2010) Qualitative quality: eight 'Big-Tent' criteria for excellent qualitative research. *Qualitative Inquiry* 16(10) 837–51.

Trigger, D., Forsey, M. and Meurk, C. (2012) Revelatory moments in fieldwork. *Qualitative Research* 12(5) 513–27.

Tugwell, P., Knottnerus, J. and Idzerda, L. (2011) Editorial: definitions and framework for knowledge translation to continue to evolve. *Journal of Clinical Epidemiology* 64(1) 1–2.

Tuhiwai Smith, L. (2012) *Decolonizing methodologies* (2nd edn). London: Zed Books.

Turner, D. (2014) Telling the story: what can be learned from parents' experience of the professional response following the sudden, unexpected death of a child. PhD thesis, University of Sussex.

van Doorn, N. (2013) Assembling the affective field: how smartphone technology impacts ethnographic research practice. *Qualitative Inquiry* 19(5) 385–96.

Vallack, J. (2012) News from Dodoma: a play about research in Tanzania. *Creative Approaches to Research* 5(1) 32–49.

Vannini, P. (2013) Popularizing ethnography: reflections on writing for popular audiences in magazines and blogs. *Qualitative Research* 13(4) 442–51.

Vannini, P., Ahluwalia-Lopez, G., Waskul, D. and Gottschalk, S. (2010) Performing taste at wine festivals: a somatic layered account of material culture. *Qualitative Inquiry* 16(5) 378–96.

Vaughn, N., Jacoby, S., Williams, T., Guerra, T., Thomas, N. and Richmond, T. (2012) Digital animation as a method to disseminate research findings to the community using a community-based participatory approach. *American Journal of Community Psychology* 51(1–2) 30–42.

Verran, H. (2014) Number. In Lury, C. and Wakeford, N. (eds) *Inventive methods: the happening of the social*, 110–24. Abingdon: Routledge.

Vickers, M. (2010) The creation of fiction to share other truths and different viewpoints: a creative journey and an interpretive process. *Qualitative Inquiry* 16(7) 556–65.

Villalba, E. (2012) Searching for the holy grail of measuring creativity. *Creativity Research Journal* 24(1) 1–2.

Vincent, J. and Crossman, J. (2009) 'Alicia in Wonderland' at the 'Little Lleyton Open': selected Australian newspapers' narratives about Alicia Molik and Lleyton Hewitt at the centennial Australian Open. *Qualitative Research in Sport, Exercise and Health* 1(3) 258–78.

Walsh, E., Anders, K. and Hancock, S. (2013) Understanding, attitude and environment: the essentials for developing creativity in STEM researchers. *International Journal for Researcher Development* 4(1) 19–38.

Wang, S., Zhang, X. and Martocchio, J. (2011) Thinking outside of the box when the box is missing: role ambiguity and its linkage to creativity. *Creativity Research Journal* 23(3) 211–21.

Ward, V., Smith, S., House, A. and Hamer, S. (2011) Exploring knowledge exchange: a useful framework for practice and policy. *Social Science and Medicine* 74: 297–304.

Warne, T. and McAndrew, S. (2009) Constructing a bricolage of nursing research, education and practice. *Nurse Education Today* 29: 855–8.

Wassenaar, D. (2006) Ethical issues in social science research. In Terre Blanche, M., Durrheim, K. and Painter, D. (eds) *Research in practice: allied methods for the social sciences*, 60–79. Cape Town: University of Cape Town Press.

Watson, C. (2009) Picturing validity: autoethnography and the representation of self? *Qualitative Inquiry* 15(3) 526–44.

Watson, C. (2011) Staking a small claim for fictional narratives in social and educational research. *Qualitative Research* 11(4) 395–408.

Webster, H. (2014) Blogging. In Daly, I. and Brophy Haney, A. (eds) *53 interesting ways to communicate your research*, 75–6. Newmarket: The Professional and Higher Partnership Ltd.

Weiner-Levy, N. and Popper-Giveon, A. (2012) When horizons do not merge. *Qualitative Inquiry* 18(1) 20–30.

Weller, S. (2012) Evolving creativity in qualitative longitudinal research with children and teenagers. *International Journal of Social Research Methodology* 15(2) 119–33.

Westbury, M. (2014) Digital curation – collecting and sharing online resources. In Daly, I. and Brophy Haney, A. (eds) *53 interesting ways to communicate your research*, 105–6. Newmarket: The Professional and Higher Partnership Ltd.

Wetton, N. and McWhirter, J. (1998) Images and curriculum development in health education. In Prosser, J. (ed) *Image-based research: a sourcebook for qualitative researchers*, 263–83. London: RoutledgeFalmer.

White, C., Woodfield, K., Ritchie, J. and Ormston, R. (2014) Writing up qualitative research. In Ritchie, J., Lewis, J., McNaughton Nicholls, C. and Ormston, R. (eds) *Qualitative research practice: a guide for social science students and researchers* (2nd edn), 367–400. London: Sage.

White, A. et al (2010) Using visual methodologies to explore contemporary Irish childhoods. *Qualitative Research* 10(2) 143–58.

Whittemore, R. and Knafl, K. (2005) The integrative review: updated methodology. *Methodological Issues in Nursing Research* 52(5) 546–53.

Wibberley, C. (2012) Getting to grips with bricolage: a personal account. *The Qualitative Report* 17 Art. 50.

Wiles, R., Crow, G. and Pain, H. (2011) Innovation in qualitative research methods: a narrative review. *Qualitative Research* 11(5) 587–604.

Wiles, R., Coffey, A., Robinson, J. and Heath, S. (2012) Anonymisation and visual images: issues of respect, 'voice' and protection. *International Journal of Social Research Methodology* 15(1) 41–53.

Williams, S. and Keady, J. (2012) Centre stage diagrams: a new method to develop constructivist grounded theory – late-stage Parkinson's disease as a case exemplar. *Qualitative Research* 12(2) 218–38.

Windsor, L. (2013) Using concept mapping in community-based participatory research: a mixed methods approach. *Journal of Mixed Methods Research* 7(3) 274–93.

Woodthorpe, K. (2011) Researching death: methodological reflections on the management of critical distance. *International Journal of Social Research Methodology* 14(2) 99–109.

Wright Mills, C. (1959) *The Sociological Imagination*. New York: Oxford University Press.

Yamamoto, K. (2010) Out of the box: the origination and form in creativity. *Creativity Research Journal* 22(3) 345–6.

Young, T. and Avery, S. (2006) Teaching writing within a discipline: the speak–write project. In Ganobcsik-Williams, L. (ed) *Teaching academic writing in UK higher education: theories, practices and models*, 85–97. Basingstoke: Palgrave Macmillan.

Zabelina, D. and Robinson, M. (2010) Don't be so hard on yourself: self-compassion facilitates creative originality among self-judgmental individuals. *Creativity Research Journal* 22(3) 288–93.

Index

Note: Page numbers in *italics* refer to tables.